AF559993

ENV BOOKS SERIES

SOIL CHARACTERISTICS AND AGRO-ECOLOGY

Editors

Dr. Avnish Chauhan

Associate Professor
Department of Applied Sciences
Phonics Group of Institutions
Roorkee (Uttarakhand) (India)

Dr. Pawan Kumar 'Bharti'

Vice President (Executive)
Society for Environment, Health, Awareness of Nutrition & Toxicology (SEHAT)
1775, Sohan Ganj, Near Clock Tower, Delhi-7, (India)
E-mail: *gurupawanbharti@rediffmail.com*

Associate Editor

Dr. Abhishek Swami

Sr. Scientist
Department of Applied Science
Droancharya Group of Insitituions
Greater Noida-201 308 (India)

DISCOVERY PUBLISHING HOUSE PVT. LTD.
NEW DELHI-110 002

Published by:
Tilak Wasan

DISCOVERY PUBLISHING HOUSE PVT. LTD.
4383/4B, Ansari Road, Darya Ganj
New Delhi-110 002 (India)
Phone : +91-11-23279245, 43596064-65
Fax : +91-11-23253475
E-mail : discoverypublishinghouse@gmail.com
sales@discoverypublishinggroup.com
web : www.discoverypublishinggroup.com

First Edition: **2015**

ISBN: 978-93-5056-758-6

Soil Characteristics and Agro-ecology

Printed at:
Infinity Imaging Systems
Delhi

ENV Books Series, India

Calls lengthy and error free chapters for further volumes of books on various environmental issues. (Send your manuscripts to envbooks@gmail.com)

Founding Editor (Editor-in-Chief)

Dr. Pawan Kumar 'Bharti'
Society for Environment, Health, Awareness of
Nutrition & Toxicology (SEHAT-India)
1775, Sohanganj, Near Clock Tower, Delhi-7, India
E-mail:*gurupawanbharti@rediffmail.com*

Other Titles by Editor-in-Chief:

1. **Advances in Biotechnology and Ecological Sciences (2013)**
   Bharti, P.K., Chauhan, A. and Ray, J. (eds.)
   (ISBN: 978-93-5056-358-8).
2. **Advances in Agriculture and Ecology (2013)**
   Bharti, P.K.; Chauhan, A. and Ezeaku Peter Ikemefuna (eds.)
   (ISBN: 978-93-5056-362-5).
3. **Agriculture and Environmental Biotechnology (2014)**
   Bharti, P.K. and Chauhan, A. (eds.)
   (ISBN: 978-93-5056-479-0).
4. **Agriculture Ecology and Environment (2014)**
   Bharti, P.K. and Olubukola O. Babalola (eds.)
   (ISBN: 978-93-5056-480-6).
5. **Agro-forestry and Climate Change (2014)**
   Bharti, Pawan K. and Singh, Narayan (eds.)
   (ISBN: 978-93-5056-514-8).
6. **Aquaculture and Fisheries Environment (2014)**
   Gupta, S.K. and Pawan K. Bharti (eds.)
   (ISBN: 978-93-5056-408-0).
7. **Aquatic Biodiversity and Pollution (2013)**
   Bharti, P.K.; Chauhan, A. and Kaoud, H.A.H. (eds.)
   (ISBN: 978-93-5056-359-5).
8. **Aquatic Ecology and Biotechnology (2014)**
   Bharti, P.K. and Zaki, M.S.A. (eds.)
   (ISBN: 978-93-5056-451-6).

9. **Aquatic Environment and Toxicology (2013)**
Bharti, Pawan K. (ed.)
(ISBN: 978-93-5056-236-9).

10. **Biodiversity, Biotechnology and Environmental Conservation (2015)**
Bharti, P.K. and Bhandari, G. (eds.)
(ISBN: 978-93-5056-750-0).

11. **Biodiversity of Aquatic Ecosystem: *Significance, Threat and Conservation* (2013)**
Bharti, P.K. and Kaoud, H.A.H. (eds.)
(ISBN: 978-93-5056-297-0).

12. **Biotechnology, Agro-ecology and Environment (2015)**
Chauhan, Avnish and Bharti, P.K. (eds.)
(ISBN: 978-93-5056-757-9).

13. **Clean Technologies and Environmental Protection (2015)**
Chauhan, A.; Sharma, S. and Bharti, P.K. (eds.)
(ISBN: 978-93-5056-731-9).

14. **Climate Change and Agriculture (2012)**
Bharti, P.K. and Chauhan, Avnish (eds.)
(ISBN: 978-93-5056-148-5).

15. **Climate Change and Biodiversity (2013)**
Bharti, P.K. and Chauhan, Avnish (eds.)
(ISBN: 978-93-5056-360-1).

16. **Conservation and Cultivation of Medicinal Plants (2015)**
Bharti, P.K. and Singh Narayan (eds.)
(ISBN: 978-93-5056-740-1).

17. **Eco-toxicology and Eco-technology (2013)**
Bharti, P.K. and Zaki, M. (eds.)
(ISBN: 978-93-5056-313-7).

18. **Environmental Biotechnology and Application (2013)**
Bharti, P.K. and Chauhan, Avnish (eds.)
(ISBN: 978-93-5056-262-8).

19. **Environmental Conservation and Biotechnology (2014)**
Chauhan, A. and P.K. Bharti (eds.)
(ISBN: 978-93-5056-512-4).

20. **Environmental Health and Problems (2013)**
Bharti, P.K. and Gajananda, Kh. (eds.)
(ISBN: 978-93-5056-263-5).

21. **Environmental Pollution and Biodiversity (2012)**
Bharti, P.K.; Chauhan, Avnish and Kumar, P. (eds.)
(ISBN: 978-93-5056-149-2).

22. **Fisheries and Toxicology (2014)**
Zaki, M.S.A.; Bharti, P.K. and Chauhan, A. (eds.)
(ISBN: 978-93-5056-452-3).

23. **Fish Habitat and Aquaculture (2015)**
Bharti, P.K.; Gupta Kr. Sanjay (eds.)
(ISBN: 978-93-5056-744-9).

24. **Freshwater Ecosystem and Xenobiotics (2013)**
Bharti, P.K.; Zaki, M. and Chauhan, A. (eds.)
(ISBN: 978-93-5056-299-4).

25. **Limnology and Aquatic Science (2015)**
Sharma, S. and Bharti, P.K. (eds.)
(ISBN: 978-93-5056-735-7).

26. **Medicinal Plants: *Distribution, Utilization and Significance* (2015)**
Sharma, P.; Bharti, P.K. and Narayan Singh (eds.)
(ISBN: 978-93-5056-734-0).

27. **Microbial Applications and Environment (2014)**
Bharti, Pawan K. (ed.)
(ISBN: 978-93-5056-515-5).

28. **Microbial Ecology and Habitat (2014)**
Bharti, Pawan K. (ed.)
(ISBN: 978-93-5056-514-8).

29. **Natural Ecosystem and Climate Change (2015)**
Bharti, P.K., and Kh. Gajananda (ed.)
(ISBN: 978-93-5056-745-6).

30. **Prakriti me Aushadhi (*in Hindi*) (2012)**
Singh, J.R.; Bharti, P.K. and Bharti, B.
(ISBN: 978-93-5056-200-0).

31. **Seed Technology, Plant Growth and Cropping System (2015)**
Tyagi, P.K. and Bharti, P.K. (eds.)
(ISBN: 978-93-5056-738-8).

32. **Soil Contamination and Conservation (2015)**
Ezeaku, P.I. and Bharti, P.K. (eds.)
(ISBN: 978-93-5056-737-1).

33. **Soil Quality and Contamination (2013)**
Bharti, P.K. and Chauhan, Avnish (eds.)
(ISBN: 978-93-5056-361-8).

34. **Waste Disposal and Management (2015)**
Bharti, P.K.; Tabassum, B. and Bajaj, P. (eds.)
(ISBN: 978-93-5056-729-6).

35. **Water Resources and Agriculture (2014)**
Bharti, P.K. and Ezeaku Peter Ikemefuna (eds.)
(ISBN: 978-93-5056-481-3).

Preface

The main reason of soil pollution or contamination is the presence of man-made waste. The waste produced from nature itself such as dead plants, carcasses of animals and rotten fruits and vegetables only adds to the fertility of the soil. However, our waste products are full of chemicals that are not originally found in nature and lead to soil pollution and changes in soil characteristics.

Soil characteristics can be influenced by Accidental Spills, Acid rain, Intensive farming, Deforestation, Genetically modified plants, Nuclear wastes, Industrial Accidents, Landfill and illegal dumping, Agricultural practices, such as application of pesticides, herbicides and fertilizers, Mining and other industries, Oil and fuel dumping, Buried wastes, Disposal of coal ash, Drainage of contaminated surface water into the soil, Electronic waste, etc. The most common chemicals, which can alter the soil characteristics, are petroleum hydrocarbons, solvents, pesticides, lead, and other heavy metals.

The plants that feed us grow in soil and keeping it healthy is essential to maintaining a beautiful planet. However, like all other forms of nature, soil also suffers from pollution. The pollution of soil is a common thing these days, and it happens due to the presence of man-made elements. Effects occur to agricultural lands, which have certain types of soil contamination. Contaminants typically alter plant metabolism, often causing a reduction in crop yields. This has a secondary effect upon soil characteristics and conservation, since the languishing crops cannot shield the Earth's soil from erosion.

Soil characteristics and agricultural ecology has a reversible relationship in between. Soil quality can be improved with the help of agriculture or plants, whereas plant growth or agriculture productivity can be enhanced due to fertile soils. Soils and plants both are important for each other.

This book updates the subject matter, illustrations and problems to incorporate new concepts and issues related to soil pollution, alteration in soil characteristics, soil contamination and agricultural ecology.

Thanks are due to contributors from different institutions and publisher for their interest in this book. We hope this book will provide a multi-disciplinary forum to explore emerging areas in the field of soil pollution, alteration in soil characteristics, soil contamination and agricultural ecology.

There is no doubt that this book will be one of inspiration for all professionals in the field. It is a very good framework to understand the complex nature of processes and technology, and as such it will be useful for researchers, practitioners and other parties who need a working knowledge of this fascinating subject.

–Editors

(envbooks@gmail.com)

Contents

Pages: 1-28

SOIL CHARACTERISTICS AND AGRO-ECOLOGY

Edited by: Dr. Avnish Chauhan; Dr. Pawan Kumar 'Bharti'

ISBN: 978-93-5056-758-6

Edition: 2015

Published by: Discovery Publishing House Pvt. Ltd., New Delhi (India)

1

Physico-Chemical Characteristics of Soil Affected by Automobile Exhaust Pollution

Abhishek Swami[1] and Deepika Chauhan[2]

ABSTRACT

Top soil is more productive and rich in nutrients and organic matter. Top soil is always in exposure of air pollutants specially pollutants nearby road side. The main source of road side air pollutats are automobiles. Automobile exhaust emits hamrmfull gases which are condensed on top soil and make soil environment unfavourable for plants and other organism. Present study has been carried out around the haridwar city at different study sites, it has been obsereved that soil samles collected from road side has less nutrients than soil samples collected from 100 m apart from road side.

INTRODUCTION

Soil serves as an efficient medium for sink of several gaseous air pollutants. The absorption of the gases by soil can be brought about purely by chemical means or through biochemical reactions. Most of the scavenging of atmospheric pollutants takes place through precipitation and dry

1 Department of Applied Science, Droancharya Group of Insitituions, Greater Noida - 201 308, (India)

2 Department of Life Sciences, S.P.R. Chauhan Degree College, Haridwar (UK), (India)

deposition. Soil possesses a number of organic and inorganic chemicals compounds together with sufficient moisture that can directly react with the atmospheric pollutants. For example, SO_2 and NO_2 can be chemically converted into sulphates and nitrates in the soil, which get incorporated later into the bodies of plants and microorganisms. Several hydrocarbons can get metabolized directly by microorganisms in the soil. Soil acts as a major sink for atmospheric carbon monoxide through soil bacteria.

MATERIAL METHODS

The study is envisaged to be conducted around Haridwar city, along a stratch of about 30 Km. This area has very high diversity of vegetational physiography. Soil samples were collected from five locations and analyzed for various physico-chemical parameters.

Soil samples were collected on monthly basis. All soil samples were collected by digging upto 5 m.detpth of soil profile; and collected in poly bagas for further analysis in the laboratory. Physico-chemical parameters of soil samples were alnalyzed as per the method proposed by Goel and Trivedi (1983).

RESULTS AND DISCUSSION

Monthly data on various physico–chemical properties of soil samples collected from polluted and control areas are given in the Tables 1.1 (A&B), 1.2 (A&B), 1.3 (A&B) and 1.4 (A&B).

TEMPERATURE

Soil temperature is one of the deciding factors in the process of litter decomposition, thereby in ultimate release of organically bound energy to the soil micro-organisms and releasing the inorganic elements to the soil nutrient pool, in the whole process of energy cycle. Temperature of soil from polluted areas of site 1, 2, 3 and 4 ranged between 13.0 ± 0.11 °C (Jan.) to 28.2 ± 0.26 °C (May), 13.5 ± 0.32 °C (Jan.) to 30.0 ± 0.18 °C (June), 13.0 ± 0.21 °C (Jan.) to 28.0 ± 0.27 °C (June) and 12.5 ± 0.09 °C (Jan.) to 32.4 ± 0.19 °C (June), respectively during 2003-04. Temperature of soil from control area ranged between 12.4 ± 0.27 °C (Jan.) to 27.5 ± 0.16 °C (May), 13.0 ± 0.66 °C (Jan.) to 29.7 ± 0.22 °C (June), 12.0 ± 0.20 °C (Jan.) to 27.0 ± 0.17 °C (June) and 11.0 ± 0.11 °C (Jan.) to 31.5 ± 0.16 °C (June) at site 1, 2, 3 and 4, respectively during of 2004-05.

Thus the temperature of soil at polluted area was always higher in comparison to control area. This increase in temperature varied from 2.04% (June) to 7.14% (Dec.), 1.00% (June) to 8.10% (Nov.), 1.17% (Feb.) to 7.69% (Jan. and May) and 2.38% (July) to 12.00% (Jan.) at the site of 1, 2, 3 and 4, respectively, during 2003-04.

Table 1.1 (A): Monthly Mean Values of Some Physico-chemical Parameters of Soil Collected from Site- 1 during 2003-05

Months	Parameters											
	Temperature (°C)			Moisture Content (%)			pH			Organic Matter (%)		
	P	C	D%	P	C	D%	P	C	D%	P	C	D%
2003-04												
December	14.0 ± 0.26	13.0 ± 0.28	7.14	6.60 ± 0.20	7.12 ± 0.17	7.30	5.50 ± 0.11	6.10 ± 0.10	9.38	1.11 ± 0.11	1.27 ± 0.13	12.59
January	13.0 ± 0 .11	12.4 ± 0.27	4.61	7.50 ± 0.22	8.00 ± 0.50	6.25	6.00 ± 0.12	6.15 ± 0.07	2.43	1.15 ± 0.08	1.26 ± 0.22	8.73
February	16.0 ± 0.15	15.0 ± 0.22	6.25	10.12 ± 0.31	11.00 ± 0.37	8.00	6.10 ± 0.07	6.24 ± 0.09	2.24	1.16 ± 0.06	1.30 ± 0.19	14.00
March	17.0 ± 0.20	16.5 ± 0.29	2.49	8.87 ± 0.50	9.70 ± 0.80	8.55	6.10 ± 0.08	6.32 ± 0.13	3.48	1.14 ± 0.07	1.32 ± 0.11	18.00
April	23.0 ± 0.10	22.1 ± 0.19	3.91	6.61 ± 0.60	7.06 ± 0.23	6.37	6.10 ± 0.10	6.20 ± 0.10	1.61	1.20 ± 0.09	1.40 ± 0.17	14.28
May	28.2 ± 0.26	27.5 ± 0.16	2.48	3.89 ± 0.30	4.21 ± 0.12	7.60	6.10 ± 0.12	6.37 ± 0.13	4.23	1.17 ± 0.09	1.33 ± 0.11	12.03
June	24.5 ± 0.22	24.0 ± 0.17	2.04	2.43 ± 0.40	2.90 ± 0.71	16.20	6.15 ± 0.07	6.40 ± 0.12	3.90	1.15 ± 0.08	1.27 ± 0.08	9.44
July	26.0 ± 0.17	24.9 ± 0.20	4.23	6.06 ± 0.37	6.70 ± 0.67	9.55	5.90 ± 0.09	6.30 ± 0.20	6.34	1.20 ± 0.05	1.29 ± 0.13	6.97
August	25.0 ± 0.16	24 ± 0.22	4.00	6.63 ± 0.29	7.09 ± 0.66	6.48	5.50 ± 0.10	6.10 ± 0.05	9.83	1.15 ± 0.11	1.27 ± 0.14	9.44
September	21.0 ± 0.19	20.3 ± 0.29	3.33	4.21 ± 0.25	4.89 ± 0.79	13.90	5.87 ± 0.11	6.50 ± 0.09	9.69	1.11 ± 0.07	1.25 ± 0.11	11.20
October	20.0 ± 0.13	19.1 ± 0.22	4.50	3.67 ± 0.37	4.00 ± 0.66	8.25	5.80 ± 0.12	6.34 ± 0.05	8.51	1.15 ± 0.09	1.28 ± 0.13	10.40
November	19.0 ± 0.11	18.1 ± 0.26	4.73	7.19 ± 0.22	7.85 ± 0.72	9.42	6.00 ± 0.12	6.40 ± 0.11	6.25	1.11 ± 0.05	1.29 ± 0.19	13.95

(Table Contd...)

Months	Parameters											
	Temperature (°C)			Moisture Content (%)			pH			Organic Matter (%)		
	P	C	I%	P	C	D%	P	C	D%	P	C	D%
2004-05												
December	14.0 ± 0.15	13.0 ± 0.27	4.97	7.11 ± 0.29	7.80 ± 0.19	8.84	6.08 ± 0.11	6.35 ± 10	4.25	1.13 ± 0.08	1.30 ± 0.11	13.07
January	13.5 ± 0.19	13.0 ± 0.20	3.70	10.11 ± 0.25	10.50 ± 0.27	3.71	6.10 ± 0.11	6.47 ± 0.19	5.71	1.18 ± 0.16	1.29 ± 0.13	8.57
February	16.5 ± 0.11	16.0 ± 0.15	3.03	8.42 ± 0.22	9.12 ± 0.22	7.67	5.95 ± 0.09	6.40 ± 0.09	7.03	1.12 ± 0.11	1.27 ± 0.11	11.81
March	17.2 ± 0.10	16.0 ± 0.15	6.97	6.67 ± 0.31	7.00 ± 0.34	4.71	5.92 ± 0.10	6.35 ± 0.06	6.77	1.12 ± 0.11	1.22 ± 0.13	8.19
April	22.0 ± 0.10	21.1 ± 0.11	4.09	4.50 ± 0.41	5.00 ± 0.37	10.00	6.20 ± 0.08	6.50 ± 0.30	4.61	1.17 ± 0.06	1.27 ± 0.10	7.87
May	29.9 ± 0.22	29.1 ± 0.17	2.67	2.00 ± 0.11	2.60 ± 0.59	23.07	6.10 ± 0.11	6.53 ± 0.50	6.58	1.16 ± 0.09	1.26 ± 0.13	7.93
June	23.0 ± 0.25	22.0 ± 0.22	4.34	2.90 ± 0.17	3.33 ± 0.55	12.91	5.90 ± 0.12	6.60 ± 0.13	10.60	1.15 ± 0.11	1.29 ± 0.15	10.58
July	25.0 ± 0.20	24.0 ± 0.22	4.00	4.93 ± 0.98	5.00 ± 0.37	11.40	6.00 ± 0.12	6.35 ± 0.15	5.51	1.13 ± 0.10	1.22 ± 0.09	7.37
August	23.7 ± 0.19	22.2 ± 0.21	6.32	4.80 ± 0.50	4.95 ± 0.49	3.03	5.92 ± 0.13	6.29 ± 0.11	5.88	1.17 ± 0.09	1.32 ± 0.12	11.36
September	21.0 ± 0.19	20.0 ± 0.26	4.76	3.22 ± 0.22	3.70 ± 0.11	12.97	5.53 ± 0.09	6.21 ± 0.13	10.95	1.16 ± 0.08	1.29 ± 0.10	10.07
October	19.7 ± 0.26	18.6 ± 0.27	5.58	3.68 ± 0.89	4.00 ± 0.19	8.00	5.80 ± 0.12	6.07 ± 0.10	4.48	1.14 ± 0.12	1.25 ± 0.09	8.08
November	19.0 ± 0.24	18.0 ± 0.28	5.26	3.11 ± 0.17	3.60 ± 0.20	13.61	5.67 ± 0.11	6.27 ± 0.11	9.56	1.12 ± 0.07	1.25 ± 0.09	10.40

Where: P = Polluted area, C = Control area, D =% Decrease, I =% Increase

Table 1.1 (B): Monthly Mean Values of Some Physico-chemical Parameters of Soil Collected from Site- 1 during 2003-05

Months	Parameters								
	Calcium mg/100 gm			Nitrogen (%)			Potassium mg/100 gm		
	P	C	D%	P	C	D%	P	C	D%
2003-04									
December	119.02 ± 1.47	123.11 ± 1.01	3.32	0.130 ± 0.01	0.157 ± 0.02	17.19	13.37 ± 1.00	15.10 ± 1.11	11.45
January	120.11 ± 1.33	122.25 ± 1.19	1.75	0.132 ± 0.02	0.144 ± 0.09	8.33	15.50 ± 1.19	17.30 ± 0.12	10.40
February	119.57 ± 1.92	123.00 ± 2.20	2.78	0.140 ± 0.01	0.157 ± 0.02	10.80	12.50 ± 1.02	15.50 ± 0.95	19.35
March	113.50 ± 1.74	120.00 ± 1.18	5.41	0.129 ± 0.04	0.143 ± 0.02	9.79	11.50 ± 0.92	14.37 ± 1.11	19.97
April	112.55 ± 1.58	119.19 ± 1.10	5.57	0.135 ± 0.03	0.141 ± 0.03	4.25	10.50 ± 0.87	12.60 ± 1.02	16.66
May	118.11 ± 1.60	121.17 ± 2.00	2.52	0.139 ± 0.03	0.145 ± 0.03	4.13	11.50 ± 0.95	13.80 ± 1.12	16.66
June	119.00 ± 1.39	124.50 ± 2.11	4.41	0.136 ± 0.04	0.150 ± 0.05	9.33	10.50 ± 0.20	13.30 ± 1.97	21.05
July	115.45 ± 1.40	125.11 ± 2.11	7.72	0.133 ± 0.03	0.141 ± 0.03	5.67	12.55 ± 1.17	15.22 ± 1.02	17.54
August	112.00 ± 1.88	121.00 ± 1.92	7.43	0.144 ± 0.04	0.157 ± 0.02	8.28	13.12 ± 1.00	15.00 ± 0.95	12.53
September	117.51 ± 1.72	124.00 ± 1.72	5.23	0.133 ± 0.02	0.140 ± 0.02	5.00	14.00 ± 1.29	16.11 ± 0.99	13.09
October	119.20 ± 1.92	124.19 ± 1.92	4.01	0.132 ± 0.02	0.151 ± 0.04	12.52	11.15 ± 1.22	13.12 ± 1.11	15.01
November	118.50 ± 2.01	125.37 ± 1.11	5.47	0.137 ± 0.02	0.146 ± 0.02	6.16	11.12 ± 1.06	13.44 ± 1.27	17.26

(Table Contd...)

Months	Parameters								
	Calcium mg/100 gm			Nitrogen (%)			Potassium mg/100 gm		
	P	C	D%	P	C	D%	P	C	D%
2004-05									
December	114.11 ± 1.70	127.11 ± 1.98	10.22	0.130 ± 0.04	0.140 ± 0.04	7.14	13.12 ± 1.09	15.00 ± 1.17	12.53
January	111.51 ± 1.11	119.30 ± 2.00	6.57	0.139 ± 0.05	0.143 ± 0.02	2.79	13.20 ± 1.02	14.55 ± 1.10	9.27
February	114.25 ± 2.20	121.12 ± 1.81	5.67	0.141 ± 0.04	0.152 ± 0.02	7.23	12.10 ± 1.11	14.50 ± 0.97	16.50
March	117.12 ± 1.52	122.00 ± 1.70	4.00	0.130 ± 0.01	0.145 ± 0.02	10.34	11.11 ± 0.77	14.00 ± 0.99	20.64
April	117.00 ± 1.75	123.15 ± 1.92	4.99	0.141 ± 0.02	0.165 ± 0.01	9.61	10.00 ± 0.11	12.00 ± 1.00	16.66
May	120.21 ± 1.80	125.67 ± 1.25	4.34	0.129 ± 0.04	0.140 ± 0.03	7.85	10.00 ± 1.10	12.90 ± 0.12	22.48
June	111.90 ± 1.70	117.17 ± 1.17	4.49	0.135 ± 0.05	0.150 ± 0.02	10.00	10.10 ± 1.08	11.12 ± 0.97	9.17
July	112.11 ± 2.12	122.50 ± 1.24	8.48	0.131 ± 0.04	0.145 ± 0.03	9.33	12.92 ± 1.12	16.82 ± 1.10	23.18
August	115.47 ± 1.97	123.34 ± 1.01	6.38	0.140 ± 0.03	0.159 ± 0.02	11.94	12.00 ± 1.19	15.11 ± 1.11	20.58
September	113.63 ± 1.90	125.00 ± 1.77	9.09	0.131 ± 0.03	0.141 ± 0.04	7.09	10.12 ± 1.03	12.21 ± 0.98	17.11
October	115.11 ± 1.77	121.47 ± 1.29	5.23	0.141 ± 0.03	0.155 ± 0.04	9.03	10.50 ± 1.00	12.00 ± 1.15	12.50
November	115.00 ± 1.20	121.42 ± 1.22	5.28	0.166 ± 0.05	0.177 ± 0.03	6.21	10.00 ± 0.78	13.12 ± 1.11	23.78

Where: P = Polluted site C = Control Site, D =% Decrease

Table 1.2 (A): Monthly Mean Values of Some Physico-chemical Parameters of Soil Collected from Site- 2 during 2003-05

Months	Parameters											
	Temperature (°C)			Moisture Content (%)			pH			Organic Matter (%)		
	P	C	D%	P	C	D%	P	C	D%	P	C	D%
2003-04												
December	16.9 ± 0.21	16.0 ± 0.16	5.32	6.00 ± 0.39	6.24 ± 0.29	3.84	6.57 ± 0.10	7.93 ± 0.12	17.15	1.81 ± 0.11	2.00 ± 0.17	9.50
January	13.5 ± 0.32	13.0 ± 0.66	3.84	5.82 ± 0.69	6.11 ± 0.19	4.74	6.55 ± 0.07	8.01 ± 0.12	18.22	1.82 ± 0.17	1.98 ± 0.28	9.59
February	16.0 ± 0.26	15.0 ± 0.22	6.25	6.52 ± 0.66	7.00 ± 1.00	6.85	6.27 ± 0.08	7.77 ± 0.13	19.30	1.90 ± 0.13	1.98 ± 0.33	4.04
March	20.8 ± 0.28	20.0 ± 0.34	3.84	3.50 ± 0.72	4.00 ± 0.80	12.50	6.33 ± 0.11	7.65 ± 0.18	17.25	1.59 ± 0.15	1.72 ± 0.32	7.55
April	23.5 ± 0.40	23.0 ± 0.17	2.12	3.11 ± 0.82	3.69 ± 0.60	15.71	6.25 ± 0.13	7.88 ± 0.11	20.68	1.65 ± 0.20	1.81 ± 0.31	8.83
May	28.5 ± 0.32	28.0 ± 0.20	1.75	2.00 ± 0.19	2.91 ± 0.97	31.27	6.55 ± 0.10	7.73 ± 0.10	15.26	1.32 ± 0.10	1.57 ± 0.23	10.14
June	30.0 ± 0.18	29.7 ± 0.22	1.00	2.00 ± 0.11	3.00 ± 0.92	33.33	6.45 ± 0.10	7.54 ± 0.07	14.45	1.48 ± 0.17	1.60 ± 0.21	7.50
July	28.3 ± 0.29	28.0 ± 0.29	1.06	6.19 ± 0.66	7.18 ± 0.80	13.78	6.33 ± 0.09	7.95 ± 0.12	20.37	1.66 ± 0.13	1.77 ± 0.19	6.21
August	24.5 ± 0.35	24.0 ± 0.32	2.04	10.11 ± 0.92	11.00 ± 0.55	8.09	6.43 ± 0.06	7.91 ± 0.12	18.71	1.11 ± 0.12	1.22 ± 0.11	9.01
September	21.5 ± 0.32	21.0 ± 0.19	2.32	9.50 ± 0.17	10.19 ± 0.87	6.77	6.48 ± 0.12	8.11 ± 0.18	20.09	1.70 ± 0.12	1.90 ± 0.15	10.52
October	21.7 ± 0.22	21.0 ± 0.40	3.33	6.63 ± 0.82	7.11 ± 0.89	6.75	6.48 ± 0.12	8.11 ± 0.18	20.09	1.39 ± 0.13	1.55 ± 0.17	10.32
November	18.5 ± 0.17	17.0 ± 0.18	8.10	3.66 ± 0.55	4.25 ± 0.37	13.88	6.39 ± 0.11	7.83 ± 0.12	18.39	1.38 ± 0.15	1.55 ± 0.26	10.96

(Table Contd…)

Months	Parameters											
	Temperature (°C)			Moisture Content (%)			pH			Organic Matter (%)		
	P	C	I%	P	C	D%	P	C	D%	P	C	D%
2004-05												
December	17.0 ± 0.22	16.0 ± 0.15	5.88	5.25 ± 0.66	6.61 ± 0.89	20.57	6.42 ± 0.12	7.66 ± 0.19	16.18	1.80 ± 0.21	1.95 ± 0.19	7.69
January	13.9 ± 0.22	13.0 ± 0.16	6.47	5.40 ± 0.55	6.92 ± 0.55	21.96	6.35 ± 0.10	7.71 ± 0.17	17.63	1.69 ± 0.21	1.80 ± 0.20	6.11
February	15.5 ± 0.55	15.0 ± 0.12	3.22	6.70 ± 0.69	7.55 ± 0.66	11.25	6.45 ± 0.08	7.77 ± 0.13	16.98	1.76 ± 0.22	1.91 ± 0.26	7.85
March	21.5 ± 0.58	21.0 ± 0.20	2.32	2.95 ± 0.61	3.92 ± 0.72	24.74	6.44 ± 0.06	7.97 ± 0.15	19.19	1.51 ± 0.22	1.69 ± 0.27	10.65
April	22.5 ± 0.48	22.0 ± 0.12	2.22	2.57 ± 0.81	3.11 ± 0.65	17.36	6.25 ± 0.07	7.50 ± 0.18	16.66	1.56 ± 0.20	1.65 ± 0.28	5.45
May	29.7 ± 0.78	29.0 ± 0.16	2.35	1.99 ± 0.12	2.90 ± 0.44	31.37	6.25 ± 0.10	7.90 ± 0.11	21.51	1.40 ± 0.26	1.55 ± 0.23	9.67
June	31.5 ± 0.19	31.0 ± 0.20	1.58	1.31 ± 0.18	2.00 ± 0.53	34.50	6.40 ± 0.12	8.11 ± 0.11	21.08	1.72 ± 0.21	1.92 ± 0.26	10.41
July	28.0 ± 0.26	27.0 ± 0.39	3.57	4.55 ± 0.59	5.00 ± 0.89	9.00	6.44 ± 0.12	8.25 ± 0.19	21.93	1.22 ± 0.22	1.39 ± 0.30	12.23
August	24.0 ± 0.41	23.5 ± 0.25	2.08	11.30 ± 1.00	12.00 ± 0.55	5.83	6.37 ± 0.16	8.22 ± 0.19	22.50	1.61 ± 0.19	1.72 ± 0.19	6.39
September	24.0 ± 0.41	23.0 ± 0.24	6.12	9.55 ± 0.87	10.00 ± 0.95	4.50	6.50 ± 0.10	7.61 ± 0.10	14.58	1.71 ± 0.13	1.88 ± 0.22	9.04
October	21.0 ± 0.29	20.6 ± 0.32	1.90	7.12 ± 0.98	8.00 ± 0.98	11.00	6.60 ± 0.09	7.90 ± 0.10	16.45	1.42 ± 0.16	1.59 ± 0.27	10.69
November	19.0 ± 0.66	18.0 ± 0.41	5.26	6.00 ± 0.66	7.00 ± 0.78	14.28	6.40 ± 0.07	8.10 ± 0.09	20.98	1.60 ± 0.25	1.72 ± 0.25	6.97

Where: P = Polluted area, C = Control area, D =% Decrease, I =% Increase

Table 1.2 (B): Monthly Mean Values of Some Physico-chemical Parameters of Soil Collected from Site- 2 during 2003-05

Months	Parameters								
	Calcium mg/100 gm			Nitrogen (%)			Potassium mg/100 gm		
	P	C	D%	P	C	D%	P	C	D%
2003-04									
December	81.23 ± 1.17	86.90 ± 1.10	6.52	0.082 ± 0.003	0.092 ± 0.003	16.32	15.00 ± 1.11	19.18 ± 1.00	21.54
January	82.11 ± 1.22	87.11 ± 1.05	5.69	0.082 ± 0.002	0.089 ± 0.004	7.86	15.15 ± 1.11	18.80 ± 1.02	16.11
February	82.15 ± 1.34	86.12 ± 1.22	4.60	0.080 ± 0.009	0.084 ± 0.003	4.76	14.92 ± 0.89	17.12 ± 0.89	12.85
March	84.11 ± 1.29	91.13 ± 1.86	7.70	0.082 ± 0.005	0.086 ± 0.003	5.81	14.87 ± 0.92	18.80 ± 0.92	20.90
April	84.00 ± 1.22	89.12 ± 2.00	5.74	0.081 ± 0.006	0.086 ± 0.004	5.81	15.19 ± 0.99	17.15 ± 0.99	11.42
May	83.56 ± 1.30	86.00 ± 1.19	2.83	0.080 ± 0.002	0.088 ± 0.003	9.09	15.00 ± 1.07	18.56 ± 0.92	19.18
June	83.00 ± 1.18	87.12 ± 1.80	4.72	0.084 ± 0.005	0.091 ± 0.006	7.69	14.80 ± 1.11	18.11 ± 1.11	18.27
July	82.92 ± 1.11	88.80 ± 1.11	6.62	0.083 ± 0.004	0.092 ± 0.006	9.78	14.57 ± 1.02	18.56 ± 1.07	21.49
August	83.00 ± 1.11	85.80 ± 1.17	3.26	0.084 ± 0.002	0.093 ± 0.007	9.67	14.66 ± 1.17	17.23 ± 1.05	14.91
September	84.11 ± 1.12	89.12 ± 1.20	5.62	0.084 ± 0.003	0.092 ± 0.007	8.69	15.00 ± 1.11	18.00 ± 1.02	16.66
October	83.81 ± 1.12	90.00 ± 1.39	6.87	0.085 ± 0.007	0.095 ± 0.002	10.52	15.77 ± 1.08	18.50 ± 1.01	14.75
November	82.15 ± 1.25	86.00 ± 1.20	4.47	0.084 ± 0.003	0.089 ± 0.001	5.61	16.11 ± 1.08	19.11 ± 0.92	15.69

(Table Contd...)

Months	Parameters								
	Calcium mg/100 gm			Nitrogen (%)			Potassium mg/100 gm		
	P	C	D%	P	C	D%	P	C	D%
2004-05									
December	81.13 ± 1.29	85.00 ± 2.11	4.55	0.081 ± 0.001	0.087 ± 0.009	6.89	14.12 ± 1.11	19.20 ± 0.91	26.45
January	82.66 ± 1.19	85.15 ± 1.17	2.92	0.082 ± 0.007	0.088 ± 0.006	6.81	15.43 ± 1.27	18.11 ± 0.92	14.79
February	82.90 ± 1.23	89.12 ± 2.02	6.97	0.085 ± 0.006	0.092 ± 0.002	7.60	14.50 ± 1.55	18.00 ± 1.00	19.44
March	83.33 ± 1.20	89.12 ± 1.80	6.49	0.081 ± 0.003	0.089 ± 0.001	8.98	14.40 ± 1.12	18.23 ± 1.02	21.00
April	85.11 ± 1.15	87.15 ± 1.87	2.34	0.080 ± 0.002	0.087 ± 0.006	8.04	15.50 ± 1.12	18.05 ± 1.07	14.12
May	81.11 ± 1.20	85.25 ± 1.11	4.85	0.082 ± 0.001	0.087 ± 0.005	5.74	15.50 ± 1.01	17.80 ± 1.10	12.92
June	83.70 ± 1.11	87.15 ± 1.92	3.95	0.083 ± 0.002	0.085 ± 0.003	2.35	15.00 ± 1.11	18.60 ± 0.98	19.35
July	83.00 ± 1.13	87.00 ± 1.20	4.59	0.083 ± 0.002	0.089 ± 0.002	6.74	14.00 ± 1.03	18.70 ± 1.11	25.13
August	82.44 ± 1.22	86.80 ± 1.87	5.03	0.081 ± 0.003	0.091 ± 0.002	10.98	15.00 ± 1.02	19.20 ± 1.07	20.41
September	83.55 ± 1.29	88.50 ± 1.02	5.59	0.084 ± 0.002	0.093 ± 0.003	9.67	15.17 ± 1.12	19.09 ± 1.01	20.53
October	82.00 ± 1.30	89.12 ± 1.11	7.89	0.082 ± 0.002	0.097 ± 0.001	15.46	16.00 ± 0.93	18.50 ± 0.89	13.51
November	82.74 ± 1.33	87.00 ± 1.87	4.89	0.084 ± 0.004	0.096 ± 0.001	12.5	16.00 ± 1.00	19.19 ± 1.00	16.62

Where: P = Polluted site C = Control Site, D =% Decrease

Table 1.3 (A): Monthly Mean Values of Some Physico-chemical Parameters of Soil Collected from site- 3 during 2003-05

Months	Parameters											
	Temperature (°C)			Moisture Content (%)			pH			Organic Matter (%)		
	P	C	I%	P	C	D%	P	C	D%	P	C	D%
2003-04												
December	13.5 ± 0.26	13.0 ± 0.22	3.70	4.00 ± 0.29	4.50 ± 0.30	11.11	5.67 ± 0.08	6.20 ± 0.09	8.54	2.95 ± 0.17	3.52 ± 0.20	16.19
January	13.0 ± 0.21	12.0 ± 0.20	7.69	5.10 ± 0.32	5.60 ± 0.30	8.92	5.60 ± 0.09	6.25 ± 0.09	10.4	3.02 ± 0.17	3.40 ± 0.22	11.17
February	17.0 ± 0.22	16.8 ± 0.19	1.17	7.72 ± 0.39	8.30 ± 0.25	6.98	5.50 ± 0.10	6.12 ± 0.11	10.13	3.09 ± 0.22	3.60 ± 0.21	14.16
March	19.5 ± 0.29	18.0 ± 0.16	7.69	6.46 ± 0.40	7.11 ± 0.22	9.14	5.66 ± 0.11	6.37 ± 0.13	11.14	3.05 ± 0.20	3.52 ± 0.22	13.35
April	23.5 ± 0.32	22.7 ± 0.12	3.40	3.67 ± 0.30	4.29 ± 0.26	14.45	5.55 ± 0.17	6.12 ± 0.15	9.31	3.11 ± 0.17	3.82 ± 0.19	18.58
May	26.1 ± 0.21	26.0 ± 0.16	3.83	2.99 ± 0.20	3.50 ± 0.25	14.57	5.63 ± 0.10	6.19 ± 0.11	9.04	2.85 ± 0.22	3.19 ± 0.25	10.65
June	28.0 ± 0.27	27.0 ± 0.17	3.57	4.46 ± 0.27	5.00 ± 0.20	10.58	5.60 ± 0.07	6.22 ± 0.14	9.96	2.80 ± 0.11	3.44 ± 0.30	18.60
July	27.0 ± 0.21	26.3 ± 0.26	2.59	6.50 ± 0.26	7.00 ± 0.27	7.14	5.68 ± 0.12	6.25 ± 0.11	9.12	2.89 ± 0.25	3.50 ± 0.19	17.42
August	26.8 ± 0.30	25.0 ± 0.19	3.10	9.97 ± 0.42	10.70 ± 0.29	6.82	5.59 ± 0.14	6.15 ± 0.15	9.10	2.91 ± 0.25	3.22 ± 0.23	9.62
September	23.9 ± 0.31	23.0 ± 0.21	3.76	8.11 ± 0.40	8.89 ± 0.20	8.77	5.60 ± 0.11	6.15 ± 0.16	8.94	2.73 ± 0.22	3.20 ± 0.23	14.06
October	22.0 ± 0.27	21.0 ± 0.27	4.76	5.89 ± 0.29	6.12 ± 0.20	3.75	5.55 ± 0.18	6.30 ± 0.19	11.90	2.95 ± 0.22	3.40 ± 0.27	13.23
November	18.0 ± 0.25	17.0 ± 0.28	5.55	2.90 ± 0.35	3.12 ± 0.29	7.05	5.60 ± 0.16	6.23 ± 0.20	10.40	2.85 ± 0.19	3.35 ± 0.22	14.92

(Tablc Contd...)

Months	Parameters											
	Temperature (°C)			Moisture Content (%)			pH			Organic Matter (%)		
	P	C	I%	P	C	D%	P	C	D%	P	C	D%
2004-05												
December	14.0 ± 0.22	13.0 ± 0.28	7.14	3.50 ± 0.29	4.11 ± 0.20	14.84	5.50 ± 0.11	6.21 ± 0.12	11.43	3.00 ± 0.18	3.47 ± 0.20	13.54
January	14.5 ± 0.28	13.8 ± 0.17	4.82	5.90 ± 0.30	6.49 ± 0.27	9.09	5.64 ± 0.10	6.19 ± 0.09	8.85	3.02 ± 0.19	3.50 ± 0.15	13.71
February	16.0 ± 0.20	15.4 ± 0.20	3.75	6.68 ± 0.22	7.05 ± 0.35	5.24	5.61 ± 0.09	6.17 ± 0.11	9.07	2.89 ± 0.22	3.45 ± 0.19	16.23
March	20.0 ± 0.20	19.5 ± 0.21	2.50	5.80 ± 0.21	6.70 ± 0.38	13.43	5.54 ± 0.07	6.20 ± 0.17	10.64	3.00 ± 0.21	3.60 ± 0.19	16.66
April	23.0 ± 0.21	21.5 ± 0.17	6.52	4.70 ± 0.30	5.15 ± 0.32	8.73	5.55 ± 0.11	6.15 ± 0.19	9.75	2.88 ± 0.22	3.11 ± 0.20	7.39
May	26.9 ± 0.22	25.0 ± 0.16	7.06	3.00 ± 0.33	3.47 ± 0.40	13.54	5.60 ± 0.11	6.20 ± 0.21	9.67	2.81 ± 0.19	3.17 ± 0.30	11.35
June	29.0 ± 0.25	28.7 ± 0.19	1.03	4.12 ± 0.26	4.50 ± 0.30	8.44	5.69 ± 0.14	6.27 ± 0.17	9.25	2.80 ± 0.27	3.19 ± 0.29	12.22
July	27.8 ± 0.30	26.1 ± 0.15	6.11	5.30 ± 0.25	5.92 ± 0.29	10.47	5.70 ± 0.19	6.30 ± 0.12	9.52	2.90 ± 0.22	3.40 ± 0.28	14.70
August	26.5 ± 0.31	25.1 ± 0.20	5.28	8.35 ± 0.25	9.00 ± 0.29	7.22	5.80 ± 0.20	6.09 ± 0.11	4.76	2.88 ± 0.19	3.20 ± 0.26	10.00
September	23.0 ± 0.29	22.0 ± 0.21	4.34	7.90 ± 0.40	8.50 ± 0.20	7.05	5.60 ± 0.12	6.10 ± 0.10	8.19	3.15 ± 0.20	3.79 ± 0.20	16.88
October	22.0 ± 0.22	21.0 ± 0.17	4.54	5.50 ± 0.35	6.00 ± 0.29	8.33	5.60 ± 0.17	6.28 ± 0.07	10.82	3.30 ± 0.22	3.90 ± 0.22	15.38
November	19.0 ± 0.25	18.0 ± 0.13	5.26	2.50 ± 0.36	2.80 ± 0.37	10.71	5.55 ± 0.13	6.18 ± 0.10	10.19	3.00 ± 0.20	3.40 ± 0.26	11.76

Where: P = Polluted area, C = Control area, D =% Decrease, I =% Increase

Table 1.3 (B): Monthly Mean Values of Some Physico-chemical Parameters of Soil Collected from site- 3 during 2003-05

Months	Parameters								
	Calcium mg/100 gm			Nitrogen (%)			Potassium mg/100 gm		
	P	C	D%	P	C	D%	P	C	D%
2003-04									
December	58.66 ± 1.50	59.12 ± 1.68	0.77	0.498 ± 0.03	0.504 ± 0.07	1.19	12.00 ± 1.19	14.50 ± 0.82	17.24
January	54.60 ± 1.66	55.11 ± 1.11	0.92	0.488 ± 0.05	0.509 ± 0.07	4.12	12.50 ± 1.11	14.50 ± 0.88	13.79
February	54.00 ± 1.50	55.00 ± 1.66	1.81	0.472 ± 0.04	0.513 ± 0.04	7.99	12.37 ± 1.09	15.00 ± 1.11	17.53
March	53.09 ± 1.53	54.80 ± 1.92	3.12	0.492 ± 0.02	0.525 ± 0.06	6.28	12.48 ± 1.11	16.12 ± 1.12	22.58
April	54.25 ± 1.51	55.70 ± 1.72	2.60	0.491 ± 0.04	0.520 ± 0.06	5.57	13.97 ± 1.07	15.12 ± 1.07	7.60
May	55.50 ± 1.55	56.17 ± 1.54	1.19	0.477 ± 0.07	0.525 ± 0.03	9.14	13.22 ± 1.03	14.67 ± 1.01	10.96
June	57.50 ± 1.50	58.15 ± 1.59	1.11	0.479 ± 0.05	0.517 ± 0.02	7.35	13.11 ± 1.11	15.00 ± 1.11	12.6
July	56.00 ± 1.60	57.11 ± 1.66	1.94	0.489 ± 0.05	0.515 ± 0.02	5.04	12.77 ± 1.29	14.11 ± 1.05	9.49
August	55.40 ± 1.54	56.00 ± 1.22	1.07	0.495 ± 0.02	0.508 ± 0.03	2.55	12.00 ± 1.07	15.37 ± 1.01	21.92
September	58.39 ± 1.50	59.50 ± 1.34	1.86	0.490 ± 0.04	0.510 ± 0.05	3.92	13.11 ± 1.11	15.40 ± 1.00	14.87
October	56.50 ± 1.59	57.00 ± 1.11	0.87	0.477 ± 0.04	0.517 ± 0.02	7.36	12.40 ± 1.01	15.44 ± 1.02	19.68
November	56.50 ± 1.52	57.11 ± 1.32	0.89	0.486 ± 0.02	0.543 ± 0.06	10.49	13.50 ± 1.05	16.00 ± 1.09	15.62

(Table Contd...)

Months	Parameters								
	Calcium mg/100 gm			Nitrogen (%)			Potassium mg/100 gm		
	P	C	D%	P	C	D%	P	C	D%
2004-05									
December	57.60 ± 1.62	58.11 ± 1.68	0.87	0.485 ± 0.08	0.529 ± 0.05	8.31	12.90 ± 1.02	14.11 ± 1.17	8.57
January	53.40 ± 1.78	54.80 ± 2.07	2.55	0.492 ± 0.02	0.509 ± 0.04	3.33	12.30 ± 1.04	14.20 ± 1.22	13.38
February	54.50 ± 1.92	55.00 ± 2.00	0.90	0.482 ± 0.04	0.510 ± 0.03	5.49	12.00 ± 1.22	14.20 ± 1.20	15.49
March	53.12 ± 2.00	54.70 ± 1.98	2.88	0.483 ± 0.06	0.513 ± 0.04	5.84	12.00 ± 1.09	15.29 ± 1.15	21.51
April	57.71 ± 2.22	58.28 ± 1.72	1.67	0.480 ± 0.02	0.520 ± 0.03	7.69	13.05 ± 0.92	16.00 ± 1.02	18.43
May	55.60 ± 2.11	56.11 ± 1.62	0.90	0.487 ± 0.04	0.517 ± 0.02	5.80	13.00 ± 0.88	15.00 ± 1.15	13.33
June	55.89 ± 2.11	56.50 ± 1.66	1.07	0.477 ± 0.03	0.516 ± 0.05	7.55	12.44 ± 1.12	14.40 ± 1.22	13.61
July	55.00 ± 1.98	56.59 ± 1.72	2.80	0.492 ± 0.06	0.529 ± 0.04	6.99	12.00 ± 1.11	14.60 ± 1.10	17.80
August	54.89 ± 1.80	55.44 ± 1.89	0.99	0.497 ± 0.04	0.515 ± 0.06	3.49	12.37 ± 1.01	14.80 ± 1.06	16.41
September	57.80 ± 1.77	58.60 ± 1.32	1.36	0.482 ± 0.04	0.528 ± 0.05	8.71	12.71 ± 1.05	16.00 ± 1.00	20.56
October	55.72 ± 1.69	56.12 ± 1.44	0.71	0.488 ± 0.03	0.527 ± 0.08	7.40	12.50 ± 0.95	16.87 ± 0.98	25.90
November	56.81 ± 1.89	57.10 ± 1.54	0.50	0.483 ± 0.02	0.510 ± 0.05	5.29	12.12 ± 0.82	16.11 ± 0.85	24.76

Where: P = Polluted site C = Control site, D =% Decrease

Table 1.4 (A): Monthly Mean Values of Some Physico-chemical Parameters of Soil Collected from Site- 4 during 2003-05

Months	Parameters											
	Temperature (°C)			Moisture Content (%)			pH			Organic Matter (%)		
	P	C	I%	P	C	D%	P	C	D%	P	C	D%
2003-04												
December	14.0 ± 0.10	13.5 ± 0.16	3.57	4.00 ± 0.12	4.50 ± 0.19	11.11	5.90 ± 0.07	6.37 ± 0.10	7.37	1.67 ± 0.17	2.29 ± 0.11	27.07
January	12.5 ± 0.09	11.0 ± 0.11	12.0	4.60 ± 0.16	5.00 ± 0.09	8.00	5.87 ± 0.10	6.31 ± 0.10	6.90	1.65 ± 0.22	2.35 ± 0.22	29.78
February	18.7 ± 0.10	17.0 ± 0.13	9.09	5.47 ± 0.22	6.12 ± 0.16	10.62	5.97 ± 0.11	6.30 ± 0.12	5.23	1.80 ± 0.32	2.21 ± 0.19	18.55
March	23.5 ± 0.11	22.6 ± 0.13	3.82	2.40 ± 0.29	3.33 ± 0.17	27.92	6.00 ± 0.08	6.25 ± 0.17	4.00	1.80 ± 0.30	2.25 ± 0.12	20.00
April	25.6 ± 0.12	24.6 ± 0.08	3.90	1.80 ± 0.22	2.50 ± 0.11	28.0	6.10 ± 0.19	6.39 ± 0.13	4.53	1.75 ± 0.11	2.30 ± 0.16	23.91
May	28.9 ± 0.19	27.9 ± 0.12	3.46	1.59 ± 0.25	2.07 ± 0.19	23.18	5.91 ± 0.11	6.30 ± 0.14	6.19	1.59 ± 0.17	2.15 ± 0.19	26.04
June	32.4 ± 0.19	31.5 ± 0.16	2.77	1.61 ± 0.20	2.11 ± 0.12	23.69	5.87 ± 0.10	6.28 ± 0.16	6.52	1.66 ± 0.18	2.20 ± 0.11	24.54
July	29.4 ± 0.20	28.7 ± 0.16	2.38	7.59 ± 0.19	8.11 ± 0.15	6.41	5.80 ± 0.11	6.25 ± 0.11	7.20	1.89 ± 0.11	2.66 ± 0.12	28.94
August	28.3 ± 0.10	27.1 ± 0.14	4.24	11.50 ± 0.16	12.11 ± 0.15	5.03	5.95 ± 0.08	6.29 ± 0.19	5.40	1.77 ± 0.13	2.09 ± 0.13	15.31
September	25.2 ± 0.12	24.4 ± 0.12	3.17	9.99 ± 0.16	10.70 ± 0.18	6.63	5.80 ± 0.07	6.22 ± 0.12	6.75	1.89 ± 0.16	2.56 ± 0.12	26.17
October	23.2 ± 0.12	22.0 ± 0.16	5.17	4.50 ± 0.12	5.00 ± 0.14	10.00	5.86 ± 0.10	6.32 ± 0.11	7.27	1.72 ± 0.19	2.35 ± 0.15	17.50
November	21.5 ± 0.15	20.0 ± 0.19	6.97	2.47 ± 0.10	3.00 ± 0.11	17.66	5.95 ± 0.13	6.30 ± 0.09	5.55	1.76 ± 0.20	2.20 ± 0.16	20.00

(Table Contd…)

Months	Parameters											
	Temperature (°C)			Moisture Content (%)			pH			Organic Matter (%)		
	P	C	I%	P	C	D%	P	C	D%	P	C	D%
2004-05												
December	15.1 ± 0.16	14.7 ± 0.11	2.64	3.70 ± 0.11	4.30 ± 0.12	13.95	5.83 ± 0.19	6.35 ± 0.16	8.18	1.65 ± 0.20	2.29 ± 0.12	27.94
January	12.1 ± 0.17	11.7 ± 0.10	3.30	3.65 ± 0.15	4.00 ± 0.11	8.75	5.84 ± 0.11	6.38 ± 0.11	8.46	1.60 ± 0.22	2.10 ± 0.16	23.80
February	17.5 ± 0.19	16.9 ± 0.10	3.42	5.11 ± 0.19	5.90 ± 0.10	13.38	5.95 ± 0.12	6.22 ± 0.10	4.34	1.77 ± 0.16	2.11 ± 0.11	16.11
March	23.7 ± 0.13	23.0 ± 0.10	2.95	3.12 ± 0.22	3.80 ± 0.15	17.89	6.00 ± 0.11	6.27 ± 0.09	4.30	1.80 ± 0.20	2.30 ± 0.13	21.73
April	24.1 ± 0.14	23.0 ± 0.07	4.56	2.43 ± 0.29	3.00 ± 0.11	19.00	5.90 ± 0.09	6.35 ± 0.10	7.08	1.82 ± 0.27	2.28 ± 0.16	20.17
May	27.7 ± 0.16	27.0 ± 0.08	2.52	2.00 ± 0.11	2.50 ± 0.11	20.00	5.84 ± 0.12	6.33 ± 0.11	7.74	1.77 ± 0.20	2.47 ± 0.19	28.34
June	30.7 ± 0.12	29.7 ± 0.10	3.25	1.69 ± 0.15	2.17 ± 0.10	22.11	5.80 ± 0.15	6.33 ± 0.10	8.37	1.88 ± 0.20	2.39 ± 0.17	21.33
July	29.8 ± 0.10	29.0 ± 0.15	2.68	6.36 ± 0.18	7.10 ± 0.09	10.42	5.87 ± 0.16	6.30 ± 0.11	6.82	1.89 ± 0.11	2.51 ± 0.15	24.70
August	27.7 ± 0.09	26.5 ± 0.16	4.33	12.71 ± 0.17	13.51 ± 0.15	5.92	5.96 ± 0.10	6.20 ± 0.12	3.87	1.75 ± 0.15	2.42 ± 0.11	27.68
September	25.9 ± 0.11	24.5 ± 0.15	5.40	9.60 ± 0.13	10.10 ± 0.17	4.90	5.78 ± 0.15	6.31 ± 0.13	9.66	1.79 ± 0.19	2.22 ± 0.10	19.36
October	24.1 ± 0.12	23.5 ± 0.20	2.48	5.85 ± 0.11	6.44 ± 0.20	9.16	5.88 ± 0.19	6.27 ± 0.10	6.22	1.69 ± 0.20	2.37 ± 0.10	28.69
November	19.9 ± 0.15	19.1 ± 0.22	4.02	3.12 ± 0.10	3.87 ± 0.17	19.37	5.92 ± 0.17	6.20 ± 0.08	4.51	1.90 ± 0.17	2.42 ± 0.22	2.48

Where: P = Polluted area, C = Control area, D =% Decrease, I =% Increase

Table 1.4 (B): Monthly Mean Values of Some Physico-chemical Parameters of Soil Collected from Site- 4 during 2003-05

Months	Parameters								
	Calcium mg/100 gm			Nitrogen (%)			Potassium mg/100 gm		
	P	C	D%	P	C	D%	P	C	D%
2003-04									
December	63.50 ± 1.912	69.10 ± 1.21	8.10	0.279 ± 0.03	0.368 ± 0.02	24.18	16.10 ± 1.01	18.00 ± 0.92	10.55
January	65.11 ± 1.92	70.00 ± 1.29	6.98	0.277 ± 0.04	0.660 ± 0.02	24.31	17.11 ± 1.00	18.50 ± 1.10	7.51
February	62.12 ± 1.54	75.55 ± 1.22	17.77	0.275 ± 0.02	0.356 ± 0.01	22.75	17.00 ± 1.06	17.70 ± 1.10	3.95
March	67.17 ± 1.62	72.00 ± 1.20	6.70	0.282 ± 0.03	0.372 ± 0.03	24.19	16.50 ± 1.07	18.57 ± 0.97	11.14
April	65.20 ± 1.72	75.00 ± 1.54	13.06	0.289 ± 0.03	0.361 ± 0.02	19.94	17.12 ± 1.09	18.20 ± 0.92	5.93
May	66.66 ± 1.80	72.12 ± 1.63	7.57	0.280 ± 0.05	0.368 ± 0.01	23.91	17.20 ± 1.07	19.11 ± 0.99	9.99
June	66.12 ± 1.70	73.92 ± 1.92	10.55	0.283 ± 0.05	0.370 ± 0.02	23.51	17.39 ± 1.11	19.50 ± 1.02	10.82
July	65.52 ± 1.62	68.00 ± 1.80	3.64	0.281 ± 0.02	0.371 ± 0.04	24.25	16.50 ± 0.92	18.37 ± 1.02	10.17
August	62.50 ± 1.12	70.50 ± 1.22	11.34	0.279 ± 0.07	0.370 ± 0.02	24.59	18.00 ± 1.11	19.00 ± 1.16	5.26
September	61.12 ± 1.91	70.00 ± 1.17	12.68	0.285 ± 0.02	0.369 ± 0.04	22.76	17.12 ± 1.12	18.00 ± 1.07	4.88
October	62.30 ± 1.92	68.50 ± 1.11	9.05	0.283 ± 0.04	0.367 ± 0.04	22.88	17.29 ± 1.17	18.17 ± 1.02	4.84
November	63.55 ± 1.22	69.10 ± 1.12	8.32	0.277 ± 0.05	0.365 ± 0.03	24.10	17.50 ± 1.22	18.39 ± 1.04	4.83

(Table Contd...)

Months	Parameters								
	Calcium mg/100 gm			Nitrogen (%)			Potassium mg/100 gm		
	P	C	D%	P	C	D%	P	C	D%
				2004-05					
December	64.00 ± 1.87	72.75 ± 1.10	12.02	0.269 ± 0.06	0.363 ± 0.02	25.89	18.00 ± 1.12	19.50 ± 1.02	7.69
January	62.11 ± 1.82	68.20 ± 1.22	8.92	0.266 ± 0.06	0.362 ± 0.05	26.51	18.15 ± 1.16	20.00 ± 1.11	9.25
February	64.44 ± 1.92	69.50 ± 1.15	7.28	0.274 ± 0.02	0.359 ± 0.02	23.67	17.17 ± 1.12	18.82 ± 1.05	8.76
March	65.00 ± 1.68	73.11 ± 1.13	11.09	0.269 ± 0.04	0.369 ± 0.01	27.10	16.17 ± 1.01	18.20 ± 1.08	11.15
April	65.00 ± 1.68	72.77 ± 1.20	10.67	0.266 ± 0.04	0.360 ± 0.04	26.11	17.11 ± 1.07	18.50 ± 1.11	7.51
May	67.20 ± 1.77	74.42 ± 1.33	9.70	0.272 ± 0.07	0.372 ± 0.05	26.88	17.50 ± 1.00	19.00 ± 1.03	7.89
June	66.55 ± 1.52	69.90 ± 1.39	4.79	0.288 ± 0.03	0.366 ± 0.03	21.31	18.01 ± 1.06	19.57 ± 1.02	7.97
July	63.14 ± 1.96	68.50 ± 1.50	7.82	0.270 ± 0.04	0.362 ± 0.03	25.41	18.17 ± 1.02	19.50 ± 1.01	6.28
August	63.30 ± 2.01	67.11 ± 1.12	5.67	0.259 ± 0.04	0.357 ± 0.02	27.45	18.30 ± 1.04	19.65 ± 1.07	6.87
September	62.35 ± 2.01	69.12 ± 1.30	9.79	0.271 ± 0.01	0.362 ± 0.02	25.13	18.60 ± 1.11	20.00 ± 1.01	7.00
October	64.11 ± 2.09	68.11 ± 1.60	5.87	0.284 ± 0.05	0.366 ± 0.05	22.40	16.30 ± 1.22	18.00 ± 1.01	9.44
November	62.55 ± 1.87	67.50 ± 1.11	7.33	0.285 ± 0.02	0.367 ± 0.04	22.34	17.75 ± 1.29	18.92 ± 1.09	6.18

Where: P = Polluted site C = Control site, D =% Decrease

Temperature of soil at polluted area during 2004-05 ranged between 13.5 ± 0.19 °C (Jan.) to 29.9 ± 0.22 °C (May), 13.9 ± 0.22 °C (Jan.) to 31.5 ± 0.19 °C (June), 14.0 ± 0.22 °C (Dec.) to 29.0 ± 0.25 °C (June) and 12.1 ± 0.17 °C (Jan.) to 30.7 ± 0.12 °C (June) at site 1, 2, 3 and 4, respectively. At control area, it was ranged between 13.0 ± 0.27 °C (Dec.) to 29.1 ± 0.17 °C (May), 13.0 ± 0.16 °C (Jan.) to 31.0 ± 0.20 °C (June), 13.0 ± 0.28 °C (Dec.) to 28.7 ± 0.19 °C (June) and 11.7 ± 0.10 °C (Jan.) to 29.7 ± 0.10 °C (June) at site 1, 2, 3 and 4, respectively. In second year of study, higher temperature of soil was also recorded at polluted area.

MOISTURE CONTENT

Soil moisture is the amount of water in a given amount of soil, present in the form of capillary water, which is used by green plants during the process of photosynthesis. Moisture content of soil sampled from polluted area during 2003-04, ranged between 2.43 ± 0.40% (June) to 10.12 ± 0.31% (Feb.), 2.00 ± 0.19% (May) to 10.11 ± 0.92% (Aug.), 2.90 ± 0.35% (Nov.) to 9.97 ± 0.42% (Aug.) and 1.59 ± 0.25% (May) to 9.99 ± 0.16% (Sept.) at site 1, 2, 3 and 4, respectively. Moisture content of soil sampled from control areas ranged between 2.90 ± 0.71% (June) to 11.00 ± 0.37% (Feb.), 2.91 ± 0.91% (May) to 11.00 ± 0.55% (Aug.), 3.12 ± 0.29% (Nov.) to 10.70 ± 0.29% (Aug.) and 2.07 ± 0.19% (May) to 12.11 ± 0.15% (Aug.) at site 1, 2, 3 and 4, respectively.

During second year of study, moisture content of soil of the polluted area ranged between 2.00 ± 0.11% (May) to 10.11 ± 0.25% (Jan.), 1.31 ± 0.18% (June) to 11.30 ± 1.00% (Aug.), 2.50 ± 0.36% (Nov.) to 8.35 ± 0.25% (Aug.) and 1.69 ± 0.15% (June) to 9.60 ± 0.13% (Sept.) at site 1, 2, 3 and 4, respectively. Moisture content of soil of control area ranged between 2.60 ± 0.59% (May) to 10.50 ± 0.27% (Jan.), 2.00 ± 0.53% (June) to 12.00 ± 0.55% (Aug.), 2.80 ± 0.37% (Nov) to 9.00 ± 0.29% (Aug.) and 2.17 ± 0.10% (June) to 13.51 ± 0.15% (Aug.) at site 1, 2, 3 and 4, respectively.

Reduction in moisture content of soil from polluted area in comparison to soil from control area was thus recorded in both the years, which ranged from 3.03% (Aug.) to 23.07% (May), 4.50% (Sept.) to 34.50% (June), 5.24% (Feb.) to 14.84% (Dec.) and 4.90% (Sept.) to 22.11% (June) at the site of 1, 2, 3 and 4, during the 2004– 05.

pH: pH of the soil is the measure of H^+ ion activity of the soil water system. It indicates wheather soil is acidic, neutral or alkaline in nature. pH of soil samples collected from polluted area during 2003-04 ranged between 5.50 ± 0.11 (Dec.) to 6.15 ± 0.07 (June), 6.25 ± 0.13 (April) to 6.57 ± 0.10 (Dec.), 5.50 ± 0.10 (Feb.) to 5.68 ± 0.12 (July) and 5.80 ± 0.11 (July) to 6.10 ± 0.19 (April) at site 1, 2, 3 and 4, respectively. Whereas in control area it ranged between 6.10 ± 0.10 (Dec.) to 6.50 ± 0.09 (Sept.), 7.54 ± 0.07 (June) to 8.11 ± 0.18 (Sept. and Oct.), 6.12 ± 0.15 (April) to 6.37 ± 0.13 (March) and 6.22 ± 0.12 (Sept.) to 6.39 ± 0.13 (April) at the site 1, 2, 3 and 4, respectively.

During the second year of the study, pH of soil samples collected from polluted area ranged between 5.53 ± 0.09 (Sept.) to 6.20 ± 0.08 (April), 6.25 ± 0.10 (May) to 6.60 ± 0.09 (Oct.), 5.54 ± 0.07 (March) to 5.80 ± 0.20 (Aug.) and 5.78 ± 0.15 (Sept.) to 6.00 ± 0.11 (March) at the site 1, 2, 3 and 4, respectively and in control area it varied from 6.07 ± 0.10 (Oct.) to 6.60 ± 0.13 (June), 7.50 ± 0.18 (April) to 8.25 ± 0.19 (July), 6.09 ± 0.11 (Aug.) to 6.30 ± 0.12 (July) and 6.20 ± 0.12 (Aug.) to 6.38 ± 0.11 at sites 1, 2, 3, and 4, respectively.

Thus there was a reduction in soil pH at polluted area towards the acidic side in comparison to soil samples of control area, which ranged between 1.61% (April) to 9.83% (Aug.), 14.45% (June) to 20.68% (April), 8.54% (Dec.) to 11.90% (Oct.) and 4.00% (Mach) to 7.37% (Dec.) at the site of 1, 2, 3 and 4, during 2003–04 and 4.25% (Dec.) to 10.95% (Sept.), 14.58% (Sept.) to 22.50% (Aug.), 4.76% (Aug.) to 11.43% (Dec.) and 3.87% (Aug.) to 9.66% (Sept.) at sites 1, 2, 3, and 4, respectively, during 2004-05.

Organic matter: The top layer of soil consists of organic matter such as plant litter, decaying excreta and remains of variety of organisms such as bacteria, algae, fungi, protozoa, nematodes, worms, molluscs, arthopods etc. Organic matter is the carbonaceous part of forest litter. Organic matter in the soil samples collected from polluted area during 2003-04 ranged between 1.11 ± 0.11% (Dec.) to 1.20 ± 0.09% (April), 1.11 ± 0.12% (Aug.) to 1.90 ± 0.13% (Feb.), 2.73 ± 0.22% (Sept.) to 3.11 ± 0.17% (April) and 1.59 ± 0.17% (May) to 1.89 ± 0.16% (Sept.) at site 1, 2, 3, and 4, respectively, whereas at control area it ranged between 1.25 ± 0.11% (Sept.) to 1.40 ± 0.17% (April), 1.22 ± 0.11% (Aug.) to 2.00 ± 0.17% (Dec.), 3.19 ± 0.25% (May) to 3.82 ± 0.19% (April) and 2.09 ± 0.13% (Aug.) to 2.66 ± 0.12% (July) at sites 1, 2, 3, and 4, respectively.

During 2004-05, organic matter in the soil samples of polluted area ranged between 1.12 ± 0.11% (Feb. and March) to 1.18 ± 0.16% (Jan.), 1.22 ± 0.22% (July) to 1.80 ± 0.21% (Dec.), 2.80 ± 0.27% (June) to 3.30 ± 0.22% (Oct.) and 1.60 ± 0.22% (Jan.) to 1.90 ± 0.17% (Nov.) at sites 1, 2, 3, and 4, respectively and at control area it ranged between 1.22 ± 0.13% (March) to 1.32 ± 0.12% (Aug.), 1.39 ± 0.30% (July) to 1.95 ± 0.19% (Dec.), 3.11 ± 0.20% (April) to 3.90 ± 0.22% (April) and 2.10 ± 0.16% (Jan.) to 2.51 ± 0.15% (July) at sites 1, 2, 3, and 4, respectively.

Thus there was a reduction in organic matter of the soil samples collected from polluted area in comparison to control area during both the year of study. In the first year the reduction ranged between 6.97% (July) to 18.00% (March), 4.04% (Feb.) to 10.96% (Nov.), 9.62% (Aug.) to 18.60% (June) and 15.31% (Aug.) to 29.78% (Jan.) at sites 1, 2, 3, and 4, respectively. In the second year, it varied from 7.37% (July) to 13.07% (Dec.), 5.45% (April) to 12.23% (July), 7.39% (April) to 16.88% (Sept.) and 2.48% (Nov.) to 28.69% (Oct.) at sites 1, 2, 3, and 4, respectively.

Calcium: The calcium is an essential nutrient to plants and widely distributed and generally one of the abundant elements in soil. Calcium is absorbed by plants as Ca^{+2} from soil solution. Calcium content of soil sampled from polluted area varied from 112.00 ± 1.88 mg/100g (Aug.) to 120.11 ± 1.33 mg/100g (Jan.), 81.23 ± 1.17 mg/100g (Dec.) to 84.11 ± 1.29 mg/100g (March), 53.09 ± 1.53 mg/100g (March) to 58.66 ± 1.50 mg/100g (Dec.) and 61.12 ± 1.91 mg/100g (Sept.) to 67.17 ± 1.62 mg/100g (March) at the sites 1, 2, 3, and 4, respectively, whereas at control area, calcium content was ranged between 119.19 ± 1.10 mg/100g (April) to 125.37 ± 1.11 mg/100g (Nov.), 85.80 ± 1.17 mg/100g (Aug.) to 91.13 ± 1.86 mg/100g (March), 54.80 ± 1.92 mg/100g (March) to 59.50 ± 1.34 mg/100g (Sept.) and 68.00 ± 1.80 mg/100g (July) to 75.55 ± 1.22 mg/100g (Feb.) at sites 1, 2, 3 and 4, respectively during 2003-04.

During the 2004-05, calcium content of soil sampled from polluted area ranged between 111.51 ± 1.11 mg/100g (Jan.) to 120.21 ± 1.80 mg/100g (May), 81.11 ± 1.20 mg/100g (May) to 85.11 ± 1.15 mg/100g (April), 53.12 ± 2.00 mg/100g (March) to 57.80 ± 1.77 mg/100g (Sept.) and 62.11 ± 1.82 mg/100g (Jan.) to 67.20 ± 1.77 mg/100g (May) at sites 1, 2, 3 and 4, respectively. Whereas at control area, calcium content varied form 117.17 ± 1.17 mg/100g (June) to 127.11 ± 1.98 mg/100g (Dec.), 85.00 ± 2.11 mg/100g (Dec.) to 89.12 ± 2.02 mg/100g (Feb.), 54.70 ± 1.98 mg/100g (March) to 58.60 ± 1.32 mg/100g (Sept.) and 67.11 ± 1.12 mg/100g (Aug.) to 74.42 ± 1.33 mg/100g (May) at sites 1, 2, 3 and 4, respectively. Thus there was a reduction in calcium content at polluted area during both the years of study.

Nitrogen: Soil nitrogen is present as organic nitrogen, ammonical nitrogen, and nitrate and nitrite nitrogen. Major portion of soil nitrogen exists in combination with organic matter. Nitrogen contents in the soil samples collected from polluted area during the 2003-04 varied form 0.129 ± 0.04% (March) to 0.144 ± 0.04% (Aug.), 0.080 ± 0.009% (Feb.) to 0.085 ± 0.007% (Oct.), 0.472 ± 0.04% (Feb.) to 0.498 ± 0.03% (Dec.) and 0.275 ± 0.02% (Feb.) to 0.285 ± 0.02% (Sept.) at sites 1, 2, 3 and 4, respectivley and at control area it varied from 0.140 ± 0.02% (Sept.) to 0.157 ± 0.02% (Dec., Feb. and Aug.), 0.084 ± 0.003% (Feb.) to 0.095 ± 0.002% (Oct.), 0.504 ± 0.07% (Dec.) to 0.543 ± 0.06% (Nov.) and 0.356 ± 0.01% (Feb.) to 0.372 ± 0.03% (March) at site 1, 2, 3 and 4, respectively.

During 2004-05, nitrogen content of soil sampled from polluted area varied from 0.129 ± 0.04% (May) to 0.141 ± 0.04% (Feb.), 0.080 ± 0.002% (April) to 0.085 ± 0.006% (Feb.), 0.477 ± 0.03% (June) to 0.497 ± 0.04% (Aug.) and 0.259 ± 0.04% (Aug.) to 0.288 ± 0.03% (June) at sites 1, 2, 3 and 4, respectively, while at control area it was ranged between 0.140 ± 0.04% (Dec.) to 0.177 ± 0.03% (Nov.), 0.085 ± 0.03% (June) to 0.097 ± 0.001% (Oct.), 0.509 ± 0.04% (Jan.) to 0.529 ± 0.05% (Dec.) and 0.357 ± 0.02% (Aug.) to 0.372 ± 0.05% (May) at sites 1, 2, 3 and 4, respectively during 2004-05. The higher amount of nitrogen was thus recorded from the soil sampled from control area during both the years of the study.

Potassium: Exchangeable potassium is the major source of potassium of plants. It is present in relatively large quantities in most of soils. During 2003-04, potassium content of soil sampled from polluted area ranged between 10.50 ± 0.87 mg/100g (April) to 15.50 ± 1.19 mg/100g (Jan.), 14.57 ± 1.02 mg/100g (July) to 16.11 ± 1.08 mg/100g (Nov.), 12.00 ± 1.19 mg/100g (Dec.) to 13.97 ± 1.03 mg/100g (April) and 16.10 ± 1.01 mg/100g (Dec.) to 18.00 ± 1.11 mg/100g (Aug.) at sites 1, 2, 3 and 4, respectively. Whereas potassium content in the soil sampled from control area ranged between 12.60 ± 1.02 mg/100g (April) to 17.30 ± 0.12 mg/100g (Jan.), 17.12 ± 0.89 mg/100g (Feb.) to 19.18 ± 1.00 mg/100g (Dec.), 14.11 ± 1.05 mg/100g (July) to 16.12 ± 1.12 mg/100g (March) and 17.70 ± 1.10 mg/100g (Feb.) to 19.50 ± 1.02 mg/100g (June) at sites 1, 2, 3 and 4, respectively during 2003-04.

During the second year of the study, potassium content of the soil samples collected from polluted area ranged between 10.00 ± 0.78 mg/100g (Nov.) to 13.20 ± 1.02 mg/100g (Jan.), 14.00 ± 1.03 mg/100g (July) to 16.00 ± 1.00 mg/100g (Nov.), 12.00 ± 1.22 mg/100g (Feb.) to 13.05 ± 0.92 mg/100g (April) and 16.17 ± 1.01 mg/100g (March) to 18.60 ± 1.11 mg/100g (Sept.) at sites 1, 2, 3 and 4, respectively. Whereas potassium content of soil sampled from control area was ranged between 11.12 ± 0.97 mg/100g (June) to 16.82 ± 1.10 mg/100g (July), 17.80 ± 1.10 mg/100g (May) to 19.20 ± 1.07 mg/100g (Aug.), 14.11 ± 1.17 mg/100g (Dec.) to 16.87 ± 0.98 mg/100g (Oct.) and 18.00 ± 1.11 mg/100g (Oct.) to 20.00 ± 1.01 mg/100g (Jan. and Sept.) at sites 1, 2, 3 and 4, respectively. There was observed a reduction in potassium content of soil samples of polluted area in comprison to control area in both years of study. The soil show marked response due to vehicular pollution. Pollutants emitted from vehicles changed the physico-chemical properties of soil.

The effects of environmental pollution on vegetation have been studied by *Sceffer and Hedgcock(1955), Pyatt (1970)* and *Feder (1970)*, and reported microscopic effects as foliar injury, appearance of chlorotic spots on leaves, flower and fruits, distortion, twisting or curling and wilting of younger leaves, stunted growth due to shortening of internodes etc.Nikfield (1967) revealed that species diversity of the plant community increases with decrease in pollutant concentration. *Davison and Blakemore (1976)* found that gaseous form is absorbed through the leaves, while the particulate form is generally absorbed on the outer surface of the plant and thus less injurious to the plant. *Shetty and Chaperkar (1978)* used plants for monitoring of dust fall in some localities of Bombay. They found that leaves of *Mirabilis* captured dust in higher quantities as compared to some other plants, because of the presence of epidermal hairs. Leaves of trees like *Erythrina, Mangifera indica, Polyathia* and *Thespesia* collected from Bombay environment showed that they could be used as reliable indicator of dust fall.

Das (1980) made a comparative study of the dust collecting potential of some common Indian ornamentals and Avenue trees. He noted *Ficus,*

Mangifera, Tectona and *Polathia* as better dust collectors than *Cassia, Poinciana* and *Sesbania*. *Das et al., (1981)* found that upper surface of leaf collected more dust particles than lower surface. *Vora and Bhatnagar* (1986) have done comprative study of dust fall on the leaves in high pollution and low pollution area of Ahmedabad to find out sensitive and resistant tree species to industrial dust pollution and *Ficus religiosa, Cordiamina, Calotropis procera, Ficus drupacae* were selected in both low pollution and high pollution area. They observed very high accumulation of dust in high pollution area from automobile exhaust and residential commercial activities in comparison to low pollution areas similarly *Rawat (2001)* studied impacts of automobile pollution on some roadside plant species on Mussoorie Road. *Bhatti and Iqbal* (1988) investigated the automobile exhaust on the phenology, periodicity and productivity of some roadside trees .In the study of leaf strength, area and dry weight of four species on four sites at Karachi in 1985 to 1986, all species showed some reduction in foliage productivity on the more heavily polluted site. *Guaiacum officinale* was the worst affected followed by *Ficus bengalensis, Eucalyptus* and *Azardirachta indica* appeared to be least affected and are recommended for road side planting.

Hussain et al. (1994) studied some road side wild trees of Peshawar city. They collected the leaves of *Ficus, Zizyphus mauritiand, Prosopis glandulosa, Dalbergia sissoo* and *Acacia nilotica* from highly polluted road side and less polluted road side and control. They found that leaf area of all the polluted plants were severally reduced in comparison with control and also the chlorophyll content decreased in all the polluted plant species. Studies on the impact of air pollution on plant response have attracted much interest among plant photosynthesis and ecology. It has been shown that absorption of sulphur-dioxide depends on atmospheric humidity. The presence of sulphur dioxide in the air stimulates stomatal opening or closing, both of which are regulated by relative humidity and the concentration of sulphur dioxide and CO_2 in the air. It has also been suggested that SO_2 injury depends on the rate of SO_2 absorption. (Thomas and Hill 1935; Majernik and Mansfield, 1970, 1971; Thomas, 1951; Bressan et al., 1978).

A decrease in chlorophyll content has often been suggested as an indicator of air pollution mainly because of SO_2 injury. In sensitive lichens, chronic exposure to even a low concentration (0.01ppm) of SO_2 resulted in a loss of chlorophyll in *Evernia mesomopha* control fumigation with a low level of SO_2 caused a gradual decline in the chlorophyll content, which was accompanied by a decrease in photosynthesis. *Furukawa et al., (1980)* found highly significant correlation between injury and the amount of SO_2 absorbed. Plants that are sensitive to SO_2, absorbed greater amounts of gas than those which are resistant to it. Because of greater absorption of labeled nitrogen dioxide by plants during the day than at night, it was suggested that the gaseous uptake was dependent on stomatal aperture *Kaji et al., (1980)*. *Singh (1983)* found that chlorophyll concentration and biomass of the plants at affected sites (due to SO_2) were reduced as compared to that of controlled site.

Viz. et al., (1983) found the greater loss of photosynthesis pigment in leaves of *B. retuse, M. indica, Tectona grandis, Cassia fistula* and *Dalbergia sissoo* from healthy and polluted environment and studied foliar pigment and phenol concentration. He found that in the leaves from polluted environment chlorophyll a,b and carotenoids decreased significantly whereas the phenol content increased. *Treshow (1984)* found that the interference by pollutants or varied combinations of different pollutants often lead to loss of the normal green colour of the foliage and killing of tissue or some other clearly visible expressions.

Saxena (1985) reported that air pollution induced changes in foliar pigment and ascorbic acid content in *Bougainvillea* species. He observed significant increase in stomatal frequency and leaf area index in polluted area, but concentration of chlorophyll a and b, carotenoids and ascorbic acid were reduced. *Ram (1989)* studied the factors associated with black tip and internal necrosis in mango and their control and observed that black tip and girdle necrosis disorders of mango fruit occurring in northern but not in southern India are caused by gases mainly SO_2, ethylene and CO emitted from nearby brick kilns. Incidence of black tip could be reduced by fruits with NaOH (0.6-0.8%) or Na_2CO_3 solution to neutralize acidic gases, or by planting less susceptible cultivars such as langra, internal fruit necrosis, taper tip and tip pulp are disorders caused not only by brick kilns gases, but by boron deficiency and could be remedied with 0.8% borax sprays.

Shrivastava and Rajvanshi et al., (1991) did work on the evaluation of particulate pollution around the limestone, kilns and its impact on plants. It is suggested that particulate lime deposition alters the quality and quantity of light incident on the leaf surface and thus affects chlorophyll synthesis, photosynthesis and growth.

Tiwari and Bansal (1994) studied air pollution tolerance indices (APTI) of some planted trees in urban areas of Bhopal. APTI values of twenty five species growing in various localities in Bhopal were collected. They found that air pollution tolerance level of each plant was different and plants sharing more APTI value are more tolerant to air pollution than those having lower APTI value. Species having low APTI value may act as a bio- indicator of pollution.

Eiler (1997) studied the influence of road dust on the energy balance of leaves, absorption of radiation by clean and dusty leaves. Dusty leaves of *Hedera helix* growing near sheet with asphalt pavement absorbed 30% more radiation than cleaned leaves. In *Rhododendrom catawbinse* dusty leaves absorbed 16% more covered with whitish road dust showed only 4% increase in total absorption. *Madan* (*1998*) studied the effect of air pollution on certain tree species in Mussoorie in order to find out the air pollution tolerance index of some species. She found that higher the level of ascorbic acid in the leaves, the greater the tolerance. Out of eight species she found that *Aesuolous indica* has the highest level of ascorbic acid and thus the more tolerant species.

REFERENCES

Abbas, A., Malibari, Z., Ahmad and Saquid, M. (1991). Effect of Air Pollution on *Ganaphalium pensylvanicum* Wild-A Crop Land Weed. *Geobios.,* 18: 7-10.

Aberg, B. (1958). *Air Pollution Ecology*, Himanshu Publications, Udaipur.

Aslam, M., Minocha, A.K., Kalra, P.D., and Srivastava, R.S. (1992). Fugitive Dust Emission from Stone Crushers. *Indian J. Environ. Hlth.,* 34 (3): 187-191.

Annonymous (2003). Effect of Cement Dust on Soyabean, *Glycine max* (L.) merr. and Maize, zea Mays Linn: In Fluorescence Studies. *Geobios.*, 30 (4): 209-212.

Azad, A.K. and T. Kitada (1988): Characteristics of Air Pollution in the City of Dhaka Bangladesh in Winter. *Atmos. Env.*, 32: 7-12.

Beerling, D.J., and Chaloner, W.G., (1992). Stomatal Density Responses of Egyptian *Olea europaea L.* Leaves to CO_2 Change Since 1327 BC. *Annals of Botans.,* 71: 431-435.

Garg, S.S., Kumar, N. and Das, G. (2000). Effect of the Bansal Ramraj Mill Dust on Vegetation and Health Jaitwara, District Santna. *IJEP.*, 20 (5): 326-328.

Gurtu, D., Vaidya, M. and Gajghate, D.G. (2001). World Scenario of Particulate Matter, NO_2, and SO_2: A review. *IJEP.*, 21 (8): 683-695.

Heck, W.W., Taylor, O.C. and Tingey, D.T. (1988). Asessement of Crop Loss from Air Pollutants. Elsevier Applied Sciences, London.

Hussain, N., Farrukh, A., Zahir, T., Zaman, S. and Saijque, A.R. (1994). Air Borne Particultae and Their Effect on Some Road Side Trees of Peshawar City. *Sarhad Journal of Agriculture.,* 10 (1): 85-91.

Hutchinson, G.L., Millington, R.J. and Peters, D.B. (1972). *Science.*, 175: 771-779.

Ignacimuthu, S. and Muralaytharan, V. (1994). Effect of Cement Kiln on Dust on Root Tip Cells of *Allium cepa. J. Ecotoxico. Environ. Monit.*, 4 (3 & 4): 263-265.

Jain, R., Dwivedi, D.K. and Gupta, A.B. (2004). Status of Air Quality at Selected Traffic Junctions of Jaipur City. *Nature Environment and Pollution Technology.,* 3(4): 435-442.

Jaysree, J. (2000). Automobile Pollution in Thiruvananthapuram City. *J. Poll. Res.,* 19 (13): 55-61.

Jha, R.K. (1999). Effect of Coal Dust Pollution on the Vegetation Around Dhanbad Coalfield. *Biojournal.*, 11 (1&2): 59-61.

Jonathan, C. and Ojha, K.G. (2004). Ambient Air Quality of I.T.O. Residential Area, New Delhi With Reference to Sulphur Dioxide. *Poll. Res.,* 23 (1): 93-96.

Joshi, G. and Jain, C. (2000). Suspended Particulate in the Ambient Air at the Road Sides of Indore City. *Poll. Res.*, 19 (3): 365-367.

Joshi, O.P., Pawar, K. and Wagela, D.K. (1993). Air Quality Monitoring at Indore City With Special Reference to SO_2 and Tree Bark pH. *J. Environ. Biol.,* 14 (2): 157-162.

Joshi, P.C., Swami, A. and Gangwar, K.K. (2006). Air Quality Monitoring at Two Selected Traffic Intersections in the City of Haridwar. *Him. J. Env. Zool.,* 20 (2): 219-221.

Kaji, M., Yoneyana, T., Tostuka, T. and Iwaki, H., (1980). Absorption of Atmostpheric NO_2 by Plants and Soils, VI: Transformation of NO_2 Through the Plant. In: Studies on the Effects of Pollutants on Plant and Mechanism of Phytotoxicity: *Res. Rep Notl. Envin. Stud., Japan*, 11: 1-8.

Kalpanan, V., Palaniappan, S.P. and Balasubramanian, S. (1995). A Survey of Lead Pollution in Coimbatore - Pollachi Highway of Tamil Nadu. *IJEP.* 15 (9): 661-664.

Kalyani, Y. and Charya, M.A.S. (1995). Biomonitoring of Air Pollution in Warangal City, Andhra Pradesh. *Acta. Botanica Indica.,* 23 (1): 21-24.

Karpate, R.R and Choudhary, A.D. (1997). Effect of Thermal Power Station's Waste on Wheat., *J. Environ. Biol.,* 18 (1): 1-10.

Karthiyanyini, R., Ponnammal, N.M., and Joseph R. (2005). Air Pollution Tolerance of Certain Plants of Coimbatore-Ooty Highways, Near I.T.I. Area, Coimbatore, Tamilnadu, *Poll. Res.*, 24 (2): 363-365.

Kashyap, M.K., Jain, A. and Banerjee, S.K. (2001). Foliar Biochemical Composition of Some Plant Species Growing Near Thermal Power Plant. *Indian J. Environ. Sci.*, 5 (1): 11-17.

Madan, S. (1998). Consequence of Tourist Activities on Environment of Mussorie Hills in the Garhwal Himalaya of U.P India. Thesis. I.C.F.R.E, F.R.I, New Forest, Dehradun, India.

Mahendra, S.P. and Krishanmurthy. (2004). Air Quality Deterioration due to Pollution from Road Traffic in Bangalor City., *J. Exotoxicol. Environ.Monit.* 14 (1): 9-14.

Mahendra, S.P. and Krishnamurthy (2003). Assessment of Carbon Monoxide Levels at Selected Traffic Intersections in Urban Area of Bangalore. *J. Ecotoxicol. Environ. Monit.,* 14 (2): 101-104.

Majernik, O. and Mansfield, T.A. (1970-71). Direct Effect of SO_2 Pollution on the Degree of Opening of Stomata. *Nature.,* 227: 377-8.

Malhotra, S.S. and Hocking, D. (1976). Biochemical and Cytological Effects of SO_2 on Plant Metabolism. *New Phytol.,* 76: 229-237.

Mandal, M. and Mukherji, S. (2000). Changes in Chlorophyll Content, Chlorophllase Activity, Hill Reaction, Photosynthetic CO_2 Uptake, Sugar and Starch Content in Five Dicotyledonous Plants Exposed to Automobile Exhaust Pollution. *J. Environ. Biol.,* 21 (1): 37-41.

Mandloi, B.L. and Dubey, P.S. (1988). The Industrial Emission and Plant Response at Pithanpur (M.P). *Int. J. Ecol. Environ. Sci.,* 14: 75-99.

Manninen, S., Huttunen, S., Rautio, P. and Paramaki, P. (1996). Assessing the Critical Level of SO_2 for Scots Pine. *Environ. Pollut.* 93: 27-38.

Mansfield, T.A. (1986). The Physiology of Stomata: New Insights into Old Problems. In: Steward, F.C. (Ed.). *Plant Physiology,* a Treatise, Vol. IX. Academic Press, Orlando., 155-224.

Mapson, L.W. (1958). Metabolism of Ascorbic Acid in Plants, *Ann. Rev. Plant physiol.,* 119-150.

Meenakshi, T. and Mahadevan. A.V. (1991). Ambient Air Quality in Madhurai. *Environmedia.,* 10 (3): 161-164.

Meenambal, T. and Akli, K. (2000). Ambient Air Quality at Selected Sites in Coimbatore City. *IJEP.,* 20(1): 49-53.

Mehrotra, G.K. (2001). Study of Air Pollution by Lime and Cement Industries. *IJEP.*, 21 (3): 203-205.

Meikap, B.S., Satyanarayana, A., Nag, A., and Biswas, M.N. (1999). Scrubbing of SO_2 from Waste Gas Stream by Horizontal CO-current Flow Ejector System. *IJEP.,* 19 (7): 523-529.

Mishra, R.M and Gupta, A.K. (1993). Pollution Oriented Occupational Health Problems of Limestone Crusher Workers. *Conx. and Ecol.,* 11(3): 634-637.

Monaci, F. and Bargagli, R. (1997). Barium and Other Trace Elements as Indicators of Vehicle Emissions. *Water, Air and Soil Pollution.,* 100: 89-98.

Monaci, F., Moni, F., Lanciotti, E., Grechi, D. and Bargagli, .R. (2000). Biomonitoring of Air Borne Metals in Urban Environments: New Trace of Vehicle Emission, in Place of Lead. *Environmental Pollution.,* 107: 321-327.

Nikfield, H. (1961). Phytotoxicity of Acidic Gases and its Significance in Air Pollution Control. In: Air Pollution Springer Verlag, Berlin.

Nowak, D.J., McHale P.J., Ibarra, M., Crane, D., Stevens, J., and Luley, C. (1998). Modeling the Effect of Urban Vegetation on Air Pollution, In: Air Pollution Modeling and its Application XII. (S. Gryning and N Chaumerliac, eds.) Plenum Press, New York., 399-407.

Pacyana, J.M., Larssen, S. and Semb, A. (1991). Europian Survey for No_x Emission with Emphasis on Western Europe. *Atmos. Env.,* 25 A: 425-439.

Pajenkomp, H. (1961). Zem –Zalk- Gips, 14: 88-95.

Palaniswamy, M., Gunamani, T. and Swaminathan, K. (1995). Effect of Air Pollution Caused by Automobile Exhaust Gases on Crop Plants. *Proc. Acad. Environ. Bio.*, 4 (2): 255-260.

Pandey, D.D. and Satya, N. (1995). Effect of Stone Crusher Dust Pollution on Grain Characteristics of Maize. *Env. Eco.,* 13 (4): 901-903.

Pandey, D.D., Nirala, A.K. and Gautam, R.R. (1999). Impact of Stone Crusher Dust Pollution on Maize Crops. *Indian J. Env. Eco. Plan.* 2 (2): 43-46.

Pawar, K. and P.S. Dubey (1985). Effects of Air Pollution on the Photosynthetic Pigments of *Ipomea fistulosa* and *Phoenix sylvestris.* All India Seminar on Air Pollution Control, Abs. 19-21, 4 (1985).

Pearce, D and Crowards, T. (1996). Particulate Matter and Human Health in the United Kingdom. *Energy Policy.,* 7: 609-619.

Pearson, M., and Mansfield, T.A. (1993) Interacting Effects of Ozone and Water Stress on Stomata Resistance of Beech (*Fagus sylvatica* L.). *New Phytologist* 123: 351-358.

Perkauskas, D. and Milkelinskiene, A. (1998). Evalution of SO_2 and NO_2 Concentration Levels in Vilnius (Lithuania) Using Passive Diffusion Samplers. *Environmental Pollution.,* 102: 249-252.

Prasad, K.S.S. and Reddy, Y.J. (1988). Lands of Air Pollution in the Indian Cities. *Env. Eco.*, 6 (4): 933-937.

Pyatt, B.F. (1970). Lichens as Indicator of Air Pollution in a Steel Producing Town in South Wales. *Environ. Pollut.*, 14: 19-25.

Raina, A.K and Sharma, A. (2003). Effect of Vehicular Pollution on the Leaf Micro Morphology, Anatomy and Chlorophyll Contents of *Syzgium cumini* L. *IJEP.*, 23 (8): 897-902.

Raina, A.K. and Agarawal, B. (2004). Effect of Vehicular Exhaust on Some Tree in Jammu – II. *J. Indust. poll. cont.*, 20 (2): 229-232.

Raina, A.K., Singh, C.D., Deepika, R. and Kumar, A. (2004). Effect of Vehicular Exhaust on Some Trees in Jammu-I. *Indian J. Environ. and Ecolplan.,* 8 (1): 149-152.

Rajasekhar, R.V.J., Samy, I.K., Sridhar, M. and Muthusubramanian, P. (2001). Estimation of Suspended Particulate Matter in the Ambient Air of Madurai City by Sedimentation and Filtration Methods. *IJEP.*, 21 (8): 673-676.

Ram, S. (1989). Factors Associated with Black Tip and Internal Necrosis in Mango and Their Control. Second International Symposium on Mango, Banglore, India No. 231: 797-884.

Ramakrishnaiah, H., and Somasekhar, R.K. (2003). Higher Plants as Biomonitors of Automobile Pollution. *Eco. Env Conserv.*, 9 (3): 337-343.

Rampal, R.K. and Manhas, K. (2004). Assessment of Indoor SPM Levels in Suburban Residential Area of Jammu (J & K), India. *Indian J. Environ. & Ecoplan.* 8 (1): 91-96.

Rani, M., Pal, N., and Sharma R.K. (2006). Effect of Railway Engines Emission on the Some Micromorphology of Some Field Plants. *J. Environ. Biol.*, 21 (2): 373-376.

Rao, D.N. and Leblance, F. (1966). Effect of Sulphur Dioxide on lichen algae With Special Reference to Chloroplast. *Bryologist.,* 69: 69-72.

Rao, Koteswara., Nabar, R.D. and Sabnia, C.M.(1988). Ambient Air Quality at Vishakhapatnam. India. *J. Env. Prot.,* 8: 821-826.

Rao, M.V. and Dubey, P.S. (1985). Plant Response Against SO_2 in Field Conditions. *Asian Environ.,* 10: 1-9.

Rao, M.V. and Dubey, P.S. (1988). Plant Response Against SO_2 in Field Conditions. *Asian Environ.,* 10: 1-9.

Rao, S. (1991) Effect of Cement Dust Pollution on Plants. *J. Swamy Botl. Club.*, 8 (1& 2): 35-39.

Rawat, R. (2001). Effects of Air Pollution on Some Road Side Plants of Mussorie Hills. M.Sc. Dissertation, Gurukula Kangri University, Haridwar.

Reddy, M.K. and Suneeta, M. (2001). Status of Ambient Air Quality at Hazira With Reference to Modified Air Quality Index. *IJEP.,* 21 (18): 707-712.

Sinha, R.K. (1993). Automobile Pollution in India and its Human Impact. *Environmentalist.,* 13 (2): 111-115.

Swami, A., Bhatt, D., and Joshi, P.C. (2004). Effects of Automobile Pollution on Sal (*Shorea robusta*) and Rohini (*Mallotus phillipinensis*) at Asarori Dehradun. *Him. J. Env. Zool.,* 18 (1): 57-61.

Thomas, M.D. (1951). Gas Damage to Plants., *Annual Report on Plnat Physiology.,* 2: 293.

Thomas, M.D. (1961) Effect of Air Pollution on Plants; in *Air Pollution* WHO Monograph, Series No. 46, (Geneva: WHO)., 233-278.

Thomas, M.D. and Hill, G.R. (1967). Absorption of SO_2 by *alfalfa* and its Relation to Leaf Injury. *Plant Physiology.,* 35: 291-296.

Tiwari, S. and Bansal, S. (1994). Air Pollution Tolerance Indices of Some Planted Trees in Urban Areas of Bhopal. *Acta Ecol.*, 16 (1): 1-8.

Tiwari, S. and Bansal. S. (1993). Effect of NO_2 Pollution on *Mimusops elengi* Linn. *Asian J. Plant Sci.,* 5 (1): 83-87.

Tiwari, S., Rani, A. and Agarwal, S.K. (1995). A Systematic Study of Meteorological and Ambient Air Quality Assessment at the Industrial City, Kota. *IJEP.,* 15 (10).

Trivedi, P.K. and Goel, R.K.(1983). Chemical and Biological Method for Water and Soil Pollution, Environmental Publication, Karad, India.

Pages: 29-48

SOIL CHARACTERISTICS AND AGRO-ECOLOGY

Edited by: **Dr. Avnish Chauhan; Dr. Pawan Kumar 'Bharti'**

ISBN: 978-93-5056-758-6

Edition: **2015**

Published by: **Discovery Publishing House Pvt. Ltd., New Delhi (India)**

2

Soil Pollution
An Overview

Ravish Kumar Chauhan

ABSTRACT

Among the various resources available for human-life, the earth is most important. In actual practice all resources like wind, water, trees, vegetation, food, wood, minerals are dependent on earth in one way or the other. For the existence of life, it is essential to protect these resources. The protection of earth becomes most important because any deterioration in the quality of earth affects all other resources. However in modern world maximum pressure is on the earth due to which the soil quality is deteriorating. There was no major evidence of human influence on soil and environment prior to 20th century. Up to this period environmental degradation was mainly due to natural phenomenon like flood, cyclone, earthquake, forest-fire etc.

Up to this period, natural resources were within the reach of regenerative capacities. Therefore what was degraded was repaired in a limited span of time. But after population explosion in the world and due to rapid urbanization, uncontrolled industrialization, unplanned constructions etc. the situation started changing and become unmanageable. Gradually with the passage of time, the

Department of Chemistry, Indira Gandhi National College, Ladwa - 136 132 (Kurukshetra), Haryana (India).

need and greed of mankind has led to serious degradation in the quality of soil. The pollution and contamination in soil has major consequences on human health. Plants and crops grown on polluted soil absorb pollutants and then pass on to us. This can lead to sudden surge in small illness. Long term exposure to contaminated soil can cause congenital illness and chronic health problems which cannot be cured easily.

The growth of plants and microorganisms like fungi, bacteria, microbes etc. present in soil is retarded due to the presence of toxic substances in polluted soil. The toxic chemicals present in polluted soil can decrease its fertility which leads to decrease in yield of the crops. The soil structure is altered to large extent due to the presence of hazardous chemicals in it. In this article, I have described various factors responsible for soil pollution, their effects on the quality of soil and some preventive measures to minimize the harmful effects of soil pollution. Some suggestions also have been made which can be adopted by coming generations to protect the soil in particular and our planet earth in general from the menace of pollution.

INTRODUCTION

Any alternation in the nature of soil is called soil pollution. It is caused mainly due to human activities, though some natural processes are also responsible for soil pollution. The natural processes responsible for soil pollution include volcanic eruptions, heavy rains, floods, drought, earth quakes, landslides, hurricanes etc. In most of the natural processes the wastes produced from nature itself such as dead plants, rotten fruits and vegetables, carcasses of animals are useful as they increase the fertility of the soil. The main reason why the soil becomes contaminated is due to unethical manmade developments (Barrow, 1995) which are responsible for large quantity of undesirable waste. The presence of man-made chemicals in soil is due industrial activities, agricultural chemicals, improper disposal of waste, use of contaminated water for irrigation.

The most common chemicals involved are petroleum hydrocarbons, polynuclear aromatic hydrocarbons, industrial solvents, pesticides and herbicides, salts present in untreated water, lead, and other heavy metals. Contamination is correlated directly to the degree of industrialization and urbanization, and intensity of chemicals used. With rapid rise of huge concrete buildings, construction of bridges and roads, encroachment in natural paths of rivers, canals etc. the remaining one part of the earth which we rarely see is the soil. The plants which feed the humans as well as animals grow in soil and keeping it pollution free is essential to live a healthy and peaceful life. However, the man made products are full of chemicals which not are not originally found in nature and lead to soil pollution.

The health risks due to soil pollution or contamination are primarily from direct contact with the contaminated soil, vapours containing contaminants and contamination of water supplies within or underlying the soil (Murthy, 2004). Mapping of contaminated land is very well done in North America and Western Europe with many of these countries having a well defined legal framework to deal with this environmental problem. Developing countries tend to be less tightly regulated because of time consuming and expensive tasks, requiring extensive amounts of geology, hydrology, chemistry, computer modeling skills despite some of them having undergone significant industrialization.

CAUSES OF SOIL POLLUTION

There are many factors responsible for soil pollution. Some of them are listed below:

- Acid rain
- Intensive farming
- Deforestation
- Genetically modified plants
- Nuclear wastes
- Agricultural practices, such as application of pesticides, herbicides and fertilizers
- Mining
- Oil and fuel dumping
- Buried wastes
- Sewage sludge
- Electronic waste

MATERIAL AND METHODS

Acid rain, as the name indicates is a rain or any other form of precipitation which is acidic, meaning thereby that it possesses elevated concentration of hydrogen ions i. e. low pH. Distilled water has a neutral pH of 7.Solutions or liquids with a pH less than 7 are acidic, and those with a pH greater than 7 are alkaline. Pure or unpolluted rain has an acidic pH, but usually not lowers than 5.7, because carbon dioxide and water in the air react together to form carbonic acid, a weak acid according to the following reaction:

$$H_2O\ (l) + CO_2\ (g) \rightleftharpoons H_2CO_3\ (aq)$$

Carbonic acid then can ionize in water forming low concentrations of hydronium and bicarbonate ions:

$$H_2O\ (l) + H_2CO_3\ (aq) \rightleftharpoons HCO_3^-\ (aq) + H_3O^+\ (aq)$$

However, unpolluted rain can also contain other chemicals which affect its acidity level (low pH). For example, nitric acid produced by electric discharge in the atmosphere such as lightning (Likens et al., 1987) increase the acidity level of rain. Similarly gases like sulfur dioxide, nitrogen oxides etc., present in atmosphere react with water molecules to produce acids which are also responsible for acid rain. Nitrogen oxides can also be produced naturally by lightning strikes and sulfur dioxide is produced by volcanic eruptions.

Soil biology and chemistry can be seriously damaged by acid rain. The polluted water could dissolve away some of the important nutrients found in soil and change the structure of the soil. Some microbes are unable to tolerate even small changes in pH and are killed (Rodhe et al. 2002). The enzymes of these microbes are denatured by the acid. Therefore they are killed or are unable to perform their normal activities. The increased concentration of hydronium ions of acid rain also mobilizes toxic metals such as aluminium, and leach away essential nutrients and minerals such as magnesium (US EPA).

$$2\ H^{+}\ (aq) + Mg^{2+}\ (clay) \rightleftharpoons 2\ H^{+}\ (clay) + Mg^{2+}\ (aq)$$

Due to leaching of base cations such as calcium and magnesium by acid rain soil chemistry can be dramatically changed, thereby affecting sensitive species, such as sugar maple (Acer saccharum) (Likens et al. 1969, 2002).Therefore efforts should be made to reduce the emission of gases like sulfur dioxide, nitrogen oxides etc. in the atmosphere.

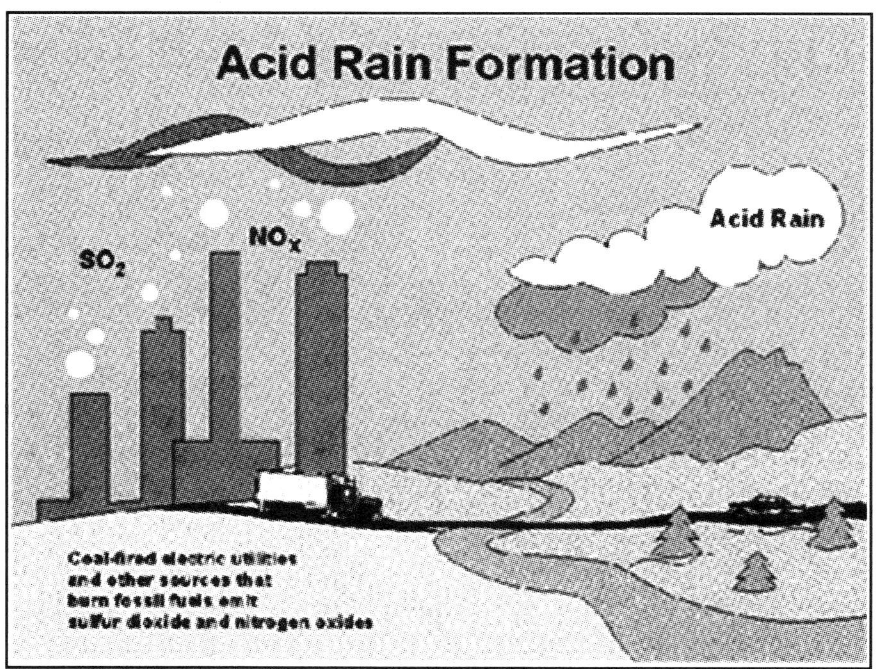

Fig. 2.1: Formation of Acid Rain
Source: www.rpi.edu

PREVENTIVE MEASURES FROM ACID RAIN

Acid rain, also called as acid deposition can be reduced by awareness among the people including individual as well as the whole society. It is a world phenomenon and has to be considered world-wide to preserve the integrity of natural habitat as well the soil. Acid rain is caused by the release of sulfur dioxide (SO_2) and nitrogen oxides (NO_x) which are added to atmosphere when fossil fuels are burnt. Coal contains sulfur as impurity. When coal is burned the sulfur is oxidized to form SO_2. NO_x are formed when any fossil fuel is burned. To meet the heavy need of electricity in today's world large amount of fossil fuels such as coal, natural gas oils etc. has to be burnt.

The emissions of SO_2 can be reduced using coal containing less sulfur or washing the coal. The smoke obtained after burning the coal can be treated using devices called "scrubbers" to remove SO_2. Similarly the Power plants which use natural gas as fuel produce much less SO_2 than burning coal. The NO_x emissions from automobiles can be reduced using catalytic converters. The reduction in the amounts of these gases in atmosphere will make less acidic rain (high pH) which will be less harmful to the soil.

Intensive farming or intensive agriculture is an increased agricultural production characterized by high use of inputs such as capital, labour, or heavy use of pesticides and chemical fertilizers. This is in contrast to traditional farming in which the inputs per unit land are lower.

However the traditional farming is almost pollution free. With intensification besides the use of manpower the use of animals and machines (Reid et al. 2011) become important. Ultimately machines have overpowered all the traditional methods in developed and some of the developing countries.

Intensive animal farming involves large number of animal which require large amounts of food, water and medical facilities. The large or confined indoor intensive livestock operations cause pollution and health issues.

In agricultural mechanization the use of mechanical ploughing, plastic mulches, chemical fertilizers has enabled a substantial increase in production, yet it has also dramatically increased environmental pollution by soil erosion and poisoning water with chemicals.

PREVENTIVE MEASURES FROM INTENSIVE FARMING

Due to intensive farming arable land is turning to desert and becoming non-arable. For the ever increasing population food production will have to increase every year most of that will have to be grown on the fertile soils that cover just 11% of the global land surface. However, there is little new land that can be made fertile and existing land is being lost and degraded. We can make a difference to help purify soils and restore balance to once fertile grounds, including our own backyard or farm. At the same time we can maintain the soil fertility by crop rotation. The most important factor here is the population control so that food production is sufficient for the people.

Fig. 2.2: Intensive Farming by Using Heavy Machinery
Source: www.euractive.com

Deforestation is the removal of a forest or stand of trees where the land is thereafter converted to a non-forest use (SAF net Dictionary, 2008). This land is then converted into farms, ranches or it is used for urbanization or industrialization. Deforestation occurs due to cutting down of trees which are used as fuel or timber. Sometimes deforestation takes place as a result of natural calamities such as landslides, heavy rains, floods, high-speed wind flow, forest-fire etc. Deforestation is occurring on large scale due to lack of moral values, lack of knowledge, inadequate forest management and deficient environmental laws.

Deforested regions typically incur significant adverse soil erosion and frequently degrade into wasteland. Undisturbed forests have a very low rate of soil loss, approximately 2 metric tons per square kilometer. Deforestation results in soil erosion – a cause of land pollution. The increased rates of soil erosion, increases the amount of runoff and reduces the protection of the soil from tree litter and waste. Forestry operations themselves also increase erosion through the development of roads and the use of machinery. The trees also decrease the rate of landslides. The roots of trees bind the soil together and keep the soil intact. Without the roots of plants and trees to hold the soil particles, the particles become more prone to being dislodged by wind and water. The eroded soil loses its nutrients and organic matter, as well as its ability to hold water.

As such, soil erosion can render fertile land as no longer suited for agriculture, or even turn originally fertile land into barren deserts.

Fig. 2.3 (a) & (b): Deforestation due to Chopped or Fallen Trees
Sources: http://nimbuseco.com and www. worldwildlife.org

PREVENTIVE MEASURES FROM DEFORESTATION

The soil pollution by deforestation can be prevented to ban the cutting of trees. If cutting of trees is necessary for one reason or the other new plantation must be done immediately to replace the cut trees. There should be proper monitoring of trees planted every year under various scheme and efforts must be done for their survival. This will help maintain structure of the soil

Genetically Modified Plants are also known as genetically modified or GM crops or biotech crops. By using genetic techniques their DNA are modified to introduce new trait in the plants so that the crops develop resistance to pests, diseases, chemical treatments and adverse environmental conditions. Due to the advocacy of scientific community for the GM crops that they provide better yield and poses no health risk (Ronald, 2011), the farmers have largely adopted GM technology. The increase in total surface area of land in recent years cultivated with GM crops support the fact.

GM crops also provide a number of ecological benefits (Andrew Pollack, 2010). However, objections are also there on various grounds, including environmental concerns, whether food produced from GM crops is safe or not.

Fig. 2.4: Genetically Modified Vegetables
Source: www.worldvision.com

PREVENTIVE MEASURES FROM GENETICALLY MODIFIED PLANTS

The chemicals used to grow genetically modified plants are a major source of environmental pollution. The studies show that these chemicals degrade and deplete soils of vitals minerals and beneficial bacteria, both of which protect crops from pests, viruses etc. The presence of Roundup herbicide, Bt bacteria and other GM byproducts in soil also support these observations. To protect soil the amount of chemicals used for GM crops should be decreased.

Nuclear wastes or radioactive wastes are wastes which contain radioactive materials. The nuclear wastes are obtained as by-product in nuclear power plants, fission reactions in research, natural fission processes and medicines. The radioactive waste is harmful to all forms of life due to emission of radiations from it (Attix, 1986 and Anderson et al., 1992).The natural radioactive wastes are more hazardous due to their long half life periods.

One or more highly radioactive substances present in radioactive nuclear wastes pollute the earth to a dangerous level of toxicity. The harmful radiations emitted by nuclear waste affect the living beings by damaging tissues, cells and red blood corpuscles. The nuclear wastes radiations can cause the diseases like cancer, leukemia, etc. The soil fertility also decreases due to the presence of nuclear waste in soil.

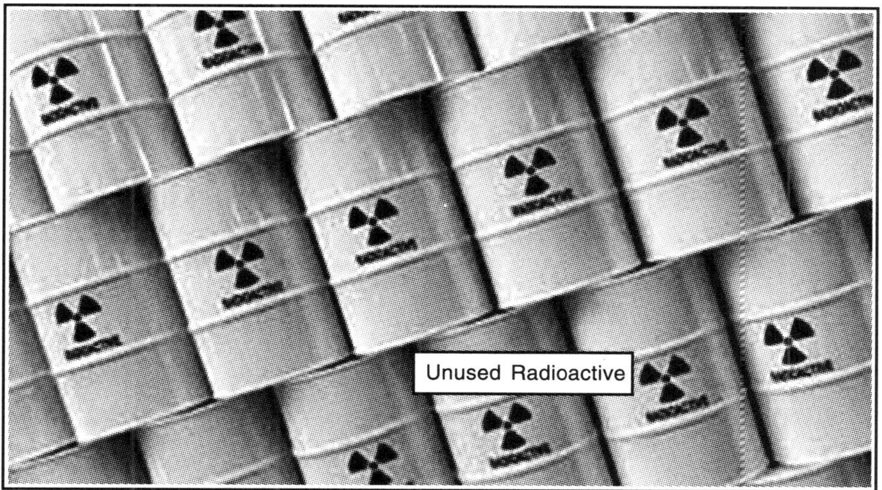

Fig. 2.5: Nuclear Waste
Source: www. Pollutionparticles.blogspot.com

PREVENTIVE MEASURES FROM NUCLEAR WASTES

The radioactive waste decays very slowly. It remains active and dangerous for hundreds of years. It can be seen as the ultimate non-biodegradable waste. Thus it is extremely dangerous to all forms of life and to all ecosystems. Therefore, the disposal of this waste is of prime importance. Originally the radioactive waste was stored in sealed containers and buried underground. The waste was sealed in used fuel containers and tanks. It was then buried. However this is not proper way to protect the environment and soil from the effect of this hazardous waste because after sometimes the material, from which the containers and tanks are made decays or corrodes, allowing the radioactive waste to seep into the ground.

Due to this effects of radiation poisoning were seen in some communities and ecosystems. Now countries have identified certain areas in so-called 'wastelands' or unoccupied ground, such as deserts to built underground storage bunkers. The nuclear waste has now been stored in these storage bunkers. One such nuclear waste storage facility is the Yucca Mountain site in Nevada, in the United States of America. Now there is pressure on the governments world-wide to adopt stricter forms of radioactive waste treatment. Proposals have been made to break down nuclear waste into harmless substances. This breaking down of nuclear waste is a far more expensive option, but in the end, it promises to be a safer process for humans and for the environment.

Modern Agricultural practices in which large amount of pesticides, herbicides (Gullan et al., 2010) and fertilizers are used. A pesticide is a substance or mixture of substances which is used to kill a pest. It may be a chemical, a virus or bacteria, antimicrobial, disinfectant or device used against any pest. The pesticides are used to kill insects, plant pathogens, weeds, mollusks, birds, mammals, fish, and microbes etc. which spoil foods, destroy property or spread diseases.

Herbicides are the chemicals which are used to kill weeds. They are similar to auxins and most are biodegradable by soil bacteria. However, the herbicides derived from trinitrotoluene contain impurity dioxin, which is very toxic and fatal even in low concentrations.

Insecticides are chemical substances which are used to control pests which damage crops. In tropics it is known that one third of the total production is lost during food storage because the insects damage not only standing crops but also stored ones. Examples of some insecticides are DDT, Aldrin, Dieldrin, BHC etc.

The use of chemicals has gone up tremendously since we use modern pesticides, herbicides and fertilizers .The chemicals presents in them are not produced in nature and cannot be broken by nature. Therefore, they seep into the ground after they mix with water and slowly reduce the fertility of the soil. They can damage the composition of the soil and make it easier to be eroded by water and air. These chemicals are also absorbed by plants and when the plants decompose after their death, they cause soil pollution since they become a part of the land.

PREVENTIVE MEASURES FROM THE EFFECT OF MODERN AGRICULTURAL PRACTICES

A good management plan can help to avoid the excessive use of pesticides, herbicides, fertilizers and to maintain the fertility of soil without wasting nutrients. By measuring the level of nutrients already present in the soil a balanced amount of fertilizers, organic manure and lime can be added.

Fig. 2.6 (a) & (b): Soil Pollution by Agriculture Practices
Sources: en.wikipedia.org and http://projects.nsapps.net

Mining results in soil erosion, formation of sinkholes, loss of biodiversity, and contamination of soil, ground water, surface water by chemicals from mining processes. Erosion of exposed hillsides, mine dumps, tailings dams and resultant siltation of drainages, creeks and rivers can significantly impact the surrounding areas (Mileusnic et al., 2014). Modern mining is an industry that involves the exploration and removal of minerals from the earth, easily, economically and with minimum damage to the environment. Mining is important because minerals are major sources of energy as well as materials. For a nation mining is necessary to have adequate supplies of minerals and materials to meet the needs of its people at economic costs.

(A)

(B)

Fig. 2.7 (a) & (b): Soil Pollution by Mining

Sources: en.wikipedia.org and www. Imgarcade.com

Mining can cause physical disturbances to the landscape, creating eyesores such as waste-rock piles and open pits. Such disturbances may contribute to the decline of wildlife and plant species in an area. It is also possible that many of the premining surface features cannot be replaced after mining ceases. Mine subsidence i. e.ground movements of the earth's surface due to the collapse of overlying strata into voids created by underground mining can cause damage to buildings and roads.

Preventive Measures from the effect of Mining: Mining can be made environmentally sustainable by developing methods (Rankin, 2014) which reduce the impact of mining operations. The mining operations should be conducted in such a manner so that their impacts are minimized and mining sites are left in an acceptable state for reuse by people or ecosystems. Mining activities use land at every stage, including exploration, operation, closure and post closure. Even vegetation is cleared at the mining site. To reduce land use mining area should be reduced the amount of waste produced should be minimized; biodiversity should be maintained by transplanting plants. In some cases, additional forest logging is done in the vicinity of mines to increase the available room for the storage of the created debris and soil.

Oil and fuel dumping is a procedure used by aircraft to lower its weight in certain emergency situations before a return to the airport shortly after takeoff, or before landing short of its intended destination. It is done to reduce risk of fire. There are two types of weight limits for an Aircraft: the maximum takeoff weight and the maximum structural landing weight. The maximum structural landing weight should be lower than the maximum takeoff weight. An aircraft on a normal, routine flight take off at the higher weight, consume fuel en route, and arrive at a lower weight for safe landing. In case of emergency if an aircraft lands at more than its maximum allowable weight it might suffer structural damage, or even break apart on landing. To avoid this situation the fuel is either jettisoned unburned (Carls et al., 2001) into the atmosphere or burned directly (dump and burn). The unburned fuel is still oxidized to water vapours and CO_2, even though at a slower reaction rate. In A dump and burn process the fuel is ignited, intentionally, using the plane's afterburner. A spectacular flame combined with high speed makes this a popular display for air shows or as a finale to fireworks. The chemicals evolved after oil and fuel dumping deteriorates the quality of soil and makes them unsuitable for cultivation.

PREVENTIVE MEASURES FROM OIL AND FUEL DUMPING

The soil pollution occurring due to oil and fuel dumping is difficult to prevent because oil and fuel dumping is not a regular phenomenon; it is carried out when the landing of aircraft is done in emergency situations. It is not a wasteful phenomenon as it seems because the airlines find that oil and fuel dumping can be cheaper than not dumping in certain circumstances.

Fig. 2.8: Air-craft performing Oil and Fuel Dump and Burn
Source: en. wikipedia.org

The best way to prevent soil pollution by oil and fuel dumping is to dump or burn the fuel far away from the fertile land; however the site of dumping has to be decided by the control room.

Fig. 2.9: Soil Pollution by Oil and Fuel Dumping
Source: southern studies.org

Buried wastes: Most rubbish which contains unsafe material is buried in landfill sites. Even common household items (Chauhan, 2013) can contain toxic material including poisonous metals. The dumped waste damages microbial population and other fauna by releasing various poisonous substances & disturbing their natural habitats. Garbage dumping, specially polymers, plastics etc. reduce the soil fertility because they are non biodegradable. Due to the presence of these wastes the soil texture is altered and an artificial environment is created inside the soil. These waste change the soil texture and prepare artificial environment inside the soil. This disturbs root movement of trees and habitats of the soil fauna.

(A)

(B)

Fig. 2.10 (a) & (b): Soil Pollution by Buried Waste

Sources: www.education.nationalgeographic.com and tangledjourneys.com

PREVENTIVE MEASURES FROM BURIED WASTE

The waste has to be first treated to reduce its volume or toxicity. Untreated waste contaminates the soil therefore proper methods should be adopted for management of solid waste disposal. The waste can be treated physically, chemically and biologically until its volume is reduced and it become less hazardous. Acidic and alkaline wastes should be first neutralized; the insoluble material should be allowed to degrade before being disposed. Anaerobic and aerobic decomposition of biodegradable municipal and domestic waste is to be done before disposal .The other methods include incineration and pyrolysis of solid waste. The incineration of wastes is expensive and leaves a huge residue and adds to air pollution. The pyrolysis is the process of combustion in absence or limited supply of oxygen or air. The gas or liquid thus obtained after pyrolysis can be used as fuel. Pyrolysis of carbonaceous wastes like firewood, coconut waste, palm waste, corn combs, cashew shells, rice husk, paddy straw, saw dust give charcoal along with other products like tar, methyl alcohol, acetone, acetic acid and fuel gas. Last resort is that new areas of storage of hazardous waste should be investigated which are situated away from residential areas.

Sewage Sludge is another factor responsible for soil pollution. It is obtained by treatment of waste water (Chauhan et al. 2012). The treated sewage sludge can be used as a fertilizer to the land. In the European Union, the the sewage sludge from urban Waste Water Treatment Plants is allowed to be sprayed onto land because it has good agricultural properties due to high nitrogen and phosphate content and valuable organic matter.

However now its use as fertilizer has become controversial because it is a byproduct of sewage treatment and it generally contains more contaminants such as poorly biodegradable trace organic compounds, pathogenic organisms (virus, bacteria etc.), pesticides and heavy metals than other soil. Effect on health, serious illness, including death and adverse environmental have been linked to land application of sewage sludge (Synder, 2005).

PREVENTIVE MEASURES FROM SEWAGE SLUDGE

Care should be taken while applying sewage sludge to soil to prevent any adverse environmental effect. The safe mode is that pathogenic microorganisms do not get into water courses and to ensure that there is no accumulation of heavy metals in the top soil (Olawoyin et al., 2012).

Electronic wastes include discarded electrical or electronic devices. The used appliances of electrical and electronics may contain contaminants such as lead, cadmium, beryllium, or brominated flame retardants. The processing of electronic waste in developing countries may cause serious health and pollution problems. Even in developed countries recycling and disposal of e-waste may involve significant risk to workers and communities and great care must be taken to avoid unsafe exposure in recycling operations and leaking of materials such as heavy metals from landfills (Sthiannopkao et al. 2012).

(A)

(B)

Fig. 2.11 (a) & (b): Pollution by Sewage Sludge
Sources: adlib.everysite.co.uk and www.stela.de

Fig. 2.12: Used Keyboards, Mouse
Sources: en wikipedia.org

PREVENTIVE MEASURES FROM ELECTRONIC WASTE

In European countries regulations have been introduced to prevent the dumping of e-waste in landfills the hazardous chemicals present in e-waste can leach into the land and have adverse effects on nearby communities and the environment. However the practice of dumping e-waste still persists in many countries. Even the e-waste of developed countries is exported to developing countries where it is recycled and then dumped. These toxic chemicals released during recycling cause unmanageable atmospheric pollution. A good way to protect soil from the pollution caused by e-waste is to increase their life span.

PRECAUTIONS TO RESTORE SOIL QUALITY

The scientists and the public should take responsibility to restore the soil quality. To avoid soil pollution environmental scientists utilize field measurement of soil chemicals and also apply computer models for analyzing transport and fate of soil chemicals. There are several principal strategies for remediation:

- Excavate soil and take it to a disposal site away from ready pathways for human or sensitive ecosystem contact.
- Aeration of soils at the contaminated site. However, in this case there is increased risk of air pollution.
- Thermal remediation by applying heat to raise subsurface temperatures sufficiently high to volatize chemical contaminants out of the soil for vapour extraction. Here also there is risk of air pollution.
- Bioremediation, involving microbial digestion of certain organic chemicals using commercially available micro flora.
- Extraction of soil vapor with an active electromechanical system, with subsequent stripping of the contaminants from the extract.

- Phytoremediation, or using plants to extract heavy metals
- Mycoremediation, or using fungus to metabolize contaminants and accumulate heavy metals
- Reducing chemical fertilizer and pesticide use
- Reusing of mater
- Recycling and recovery of materials
- Reforesting in the affected area

RESULTS AND DISCUSSION

Out of large number of factors responsible for soil pollution we have studied some of these factors viz. Acid rain, intensive farming, deforestation, genetically modified plants, nuclear wastes, agricultural practices, such as application of pesticides, herbicides and fertilizers mining, oil and fuel dumping , buried wastes, electronic waste etc. responsible for soil pollution. All these factors are the result of unethical or illegal activities of mankind. The need and greed in this materialistic world has worsened the conditions to an alarming situation. The increased concentration of pollutants in soil has reduced the soil fertility, reduced nitrogen fixation by plants, increased soil erosion, enhanced loss of soil and nutrients, increased deposition of silt in tanks and reservoirs, reduced crop yield, increased imbalance in soil fauna and flora.

The increased soil pollution is also responsible for water and air pollution because the dangerous chemicals from soil enter in the underground water and the pollutant gases are being released into the air. All these factors are affecting human, plants and animals health because all of us are dependent on earth for our survival. The pollutants present in soil are responsible for a number of diseases. The presence of heavy metals such as Pb, Hg, As, Mn, Cd, Cu, Ni, Zn etc as pollutants is responsible for a number of diseases such as memory loss, autism, itching, burning, pain, loss of hair, teeth, kidney disfunction etc. The polyaromatic hydrocarbons as pollutants are responsible for skin problems. The excess of pesticides and herbicides in soil is proving fatal both for the flora and fauna. Therefore proper preventive measures are necessary to avoid or minimize soil pollution otherwise the coming generations will have to face the consequences because life will become miserable on this planet.

REFERENCES

1. Barrow, C.J. (1995): Developing the Environment: Problems and Management, Longman, Harlow, pp. 326.
2. Murthy, D.B.N. (20040): Environment Awareness and Protection, Deep & Deep Publication, New Delhi, pp. 70-80.
3. Likens, Gene E., Keene, William C., Miller, John M. and Galloway, James N. (1987): Chemistry of Precipitation from a Remote, Terrestrial Site in Australia. Journal of Geophysical Research 92: 13299-314.

4 Rodhe, H., et al. (2002): The Global Distribution of Acidifying Wet Deposition. Environmental Science and Technology. 36(20): 4382-88.
5. US EPA: Effects of Acid Rain – Forests.
6. Likens, G.E., Driscoll, C.T. and Buso, D.C. (1996): Long-Term Effects of Acid Rain: Response and Recovery of a Forest Ecosystem Science, 272 (5259): 244-46.
7. Likens, G.E., Driscoll, C.T.; Buso, D.C., Mitchell, M.J., Lovett, G.M., Bailey, S.W., Siccama, T.G., Reiners, W.A. and Alewell, C. (2002): The Biogeochemistry of Sulfur at Hubbard Brook, Biogeochemistry, 60 (3): 235-316.
8. Reid, John F. (2011): The Impact of Mechanization on Agriculture, The Bridge on Agriculture and Information Technology 41 (3).
9. SAFnet Dictionary/Definition for Deforestation, Dictionary of Forestry.org (29-07-2008).
10. Ronald, Pamela (2011): Plant Genetics, Sustainable Agriculture and Global Food Security, Genetics 188 (1): 11-20.
11. Andrew Pollack for the New York Times. April 13, 2010 Study Says Overuse Threatens Gains from Modified Crops.
12. Attix, Frank H. (1986): Introduction to Radiological Physics and Radiation Dosimetry, New York, Wiley-VCH, pp. 2-15, 468, 474.
13. Anderson, Mary P. and Woessner, William W (1992): Applied Groundwater Modeling. San Diego, CA: Academic Press Inc. pp. 325-327.
14. Gullan, P.J. and Cranston, P.S. (2010): The Insects: An Outline of Entomology, 4th Edition. Blackwell Publishing UK: 584 pp.
15. Mileusnic, M., Mapani, B.S., et al (2014) Journal of Geochemical Exploration, Vol. 144, 409-420.
16. Rankin, W.J. (2014): Minerals, Metals and Sustainability: Meeting Future Material Needs, Collingwood Vic., CSIRO Pub.
17. Carls, Mark G. et al. (2001): "Persistence of Oiling in Mussel Beds After the Exxon Valdez Oil Spill." Marine Environmental Research 51, (2): 167-190.
18. Chauhan, Ravish K. (2013): Harmful Effects of Some Common Organic Compounds Used in Daily Life as Household, Int. J. Curr. Microbiol. App. Sci., 2(11): 283-289.
19. Chauhan, Ravish K. and Bhardwaj, Rakesh K. (2012): Physio-chemical Analysis of Sewage Water Before and After Treatment Using USAB, J. Adv. Sci. Res. 3(4): 42-44.
20. Snyder, C. (2005): The Dirty Work of Promoting "Recycling" of America's Sewage Sludge. Int J Occup Environ Health 11 (4): 415-27.
21. Olawoyin, R., Oyewole, S.A. Grayson, R.L. (2012): Potential Risk Effect from Elevated Levels of Soil Heavy Metals on Human Health in the Niger Delta, Ecotoxicol. Environ. Saf., Vol. 85: 120-130.
22. Sthiannopkao, S. and Wong MH. (2012): Handling e-waste in Developed and Developing Countries: Initiatives, Practices, and Consequences. Sci Total Environ.

Pages: 49-68

SOIL CHARACTERISTICS AND AGRO-ECOLOGY

Edited by: Dr. Avnish Chauhan; Dr. Pawan Kumar 'Bharti'

ISBN: 978-93-5056-758-6

Edition: 2015

Published by: Discovery Publishing House Pvt. Ltd., New Delhi (India)

3

Growth, Yield and Elemental Status of *Lycopersicum esculantum* L. Grown in Fly Ash Amended Soil

A. Leela Veni; Sabitri Nahak and **Rajani Kanta Sahu***

ABSTRACT

Fly ash (FA) from coal in Odisha (India) was used for amending soil at levels equivalent to 0, 5, 10, 20 40 and 80 T/H in which, tomato was grown and elemental residues of emended soil and plant parts were enumerated. FA amendments caused significant improvement in soil quality and germination percentage of tomato plants. Growth (Shoot length, leaf area, leaf number and yield (number of fruits, fruit weight and yield per plant) of tomato increased with an increase in FA amendments. In the present study fly neutralize the pH imbalance, increased EC, CEC, OC, P and some essential micro nutrients i.e. Fe, Mn, Pb, Co which help in micro nutrient deficiency soil and increases the productivity of the crop plants. Based on the data obtained we found that flooded-tomato plant soil amended at 5-40 metric tons FA per ha level of FA not only improved the physical properties of the soil but also contributed to better growth and yield of tomato crops.

P.G. Department of Botany, Berhampur University, Berhampur - 760 007, Odisha, (India).

INTRODUCTION

Coal-fired power plants generate fly ash (FA) whose elemental composition (both nutrient and toxic elements) varies due to types and source of used coal (Camberato et al., 1997). In most instances FA consists of plant macro-nutrients, Na, K, P, and Fe and micronutrients, Co, B, Zn, Cu, and Mn. The elements, Pb, Ni, Cr, Cd and a few more, also occur abundantly and have the potential to cause contamination/toxicity (Fytianos et al., 2001). Further, plant micro-nutrients at high concentrations can cause metal toxicity (Miller et al., 2000). Although mobilized elements from dumped FA masses are potential sources of plant nutrients there is a universal concern that heavy metal contaminations of terrestrial and aquatic ecosystems may also occur (Miller et al. 2000).

In India, about 80-million metric tons of FA is generated annually from thermal power stations with only a minor part used now for preparing bricks, ceramics and cements. Unclaimed FA occupies an additional 100 ha land each year. Through washouts in each rainy season adjacent areas, including rice fields, inevitably become contaminated, thus potentiating grave problems. Nevertheless FA and other coal combustion byproducts have been used as nutrients supplements to crop soil in the US (Miller et al., 2000). Lower amendment levels of FA caused enhancements of both growth and yield while adverse effects at higher levels were observed for several crops including maize, soybean, barley, cabbage, apple, alfalfa, beet (Korcak, 1995; Miller et al., 2000). However, there is no report on growth, yield or leaf metabolism of the rice plant or physico-chemical changes in the flooded rice-soil due to FA-amendment. It is obvious that research is needed to assess the possible contamination of heavy metals from FA (Korcak, 1995; Brown and Chaney, 2000).

The preliminary objectives of this study was to quantify the uptake and distribution of both nutrient and toxic elements in a popular and cultivar of tomato grown in FA amended soil. It is anticipated these results, couples with data on biological parameters that measure plant growth and yield, will assist in assessing FA as a nutrient supplements, and concomitantly clarify levels of contamination due to FA-leachates.

MATERIALS AND METHODS

Fly Ash

Electro-statically precipitated FA in an unweathered condition (Sample-lots less than 30 days old) obtained from Talcher thermal power station (Odisha) consists of the following (%) by weight : sand 15.5, silt 72.5 and clay 13, with pH 7.4 and the following elements (mg per kg): Na 800, K 840, Fe 425, P 68, Ni 190, Co 670, Pb 200, Zn 340, Mn 450, Cu 700, Cr 505 and Cd 131, by analysis with an absorption spectrophotometer (Model AA 1475 at RRL, Bhubaneswar).

Field Preparation and Fly Ash Treatment

The experimental fields were repeatedly ploughed to completely remove the rhizomes, roots of perennial grasses and shrubs. Then the field was left to be dried under sun for a week and then ploughed again. After 2-3 times thoroughly ploughed experimental plots of $1 \times 1m^2$ sizes were prepared. The experimental plots were uniformly spaced by 8 inch high and 1 feet wide ridge throughout. Soil samples were collected at a depth of 5-10cms, air dried and stored for further analysis. All the experimental plots were mixed thoroughly with cow dung compost @ of 7.5T/H. Then the plots were amended with fly ash produced from TTPS @ 5, 10, 20, 40, 80 TH and mixed thoroughly by a spade. The fields were watered by sprinkling lightly so as to leave the soil with enough moisture for germination.

Disease free healthy seed of test crops were procured from the agriculture office, Jeypore (District: Koraput), Odisha, India. Five replicates of 100seeds each were soaked overnight and next day sown in the fields. Sprouting was observed six days after sowing. Germination counts were recorded on each alternative day. 100 healthy seeds were selected from the soaked seeds. These seeds were sown in the respective experimental plots with uniform spacing as per agronomic practice. All the experimental plots as well as the control plots were maintained alike.

Soil Analysis

Soil of experimental plots was sandy loam, and pH of soil samples (with and without FA), was measured with a digital pH meter (Digison model D1-707) in a soil/water mixture at the ratio of 1: 2.5. Electrical conductivity (EC), expressed in µMho/cm of soil samples (FA/soil water at ratio of 1/5 suspension) was determined following 30 min equilibration in a mechanical shaker, by a digital conductivity meter (Digison model D1-909). For determining water-holding capacity (WHC) of soil, air-dried soil samples were uniformly packed into a pre-weighed WHC brass apparatus having whatman no.1 filter paper at its bottom, in triplicates, as described by piper (1994). The apparatus was immersed in water (1 cm depth) and left fro 12 h fro maintaining a water level throughout. The apparatus was subsequently surface-dried with the filter paper whose weight was recorded. Further, the apparatus was oven-dried at 105°C fro 24 h and subsequently, the dry weight of the apparatus and those of filter papers were recorded. WHC of soil is expressed in percent per gram weight of air-dried soil. Cation exchange capacity (CEC) of soil was determined by the methylene blue method. ; a lot of 2 g soil sample was equilibrated with 50ml of 1% $NaCO_3$, for titration against methylene blue as an indicator. The end point was noted by a light blue hallow circle a dark blue centre from a drop of solution on a whatman no.1 filter paper; CEC value was determined by multiplying the titration factor with 0.535 and expressed as C mol. Per kg. Organic Carbonic values of

30-days-old-soil samples were determined by oxidation with potassium dichromate in acid medium (Walkly and Black, 1934); to lots of 5g of air-dried and sieved soil/FA samples, aliquots of 10 ml of 1N $K_2Cr_2O_7$ solution, 20ml of 12 NH_2SO_4 and 1.25% $AgSO_4$ were added with constant stirring. After incubation for 30 min to each sample a volume of 200 ml distilled water was added followed by addition of 10ml phosphoric acid (85%) and 1 ml (0.42%). The indicator phenyl amine and titrated against 1N ferrous ammonium sulphate (Mishra et al., 2005).

Elemental Analysis

Digestions of soil samples with and without FA were done in 20 ml of mixed acids (10 N HNO_3: 12 NH_2SO_4; 60% $HClO_4$ in the ratio 5:0.5:1) (Mishra et al. 2005). Harvested leaves for tomato plants were thoroughly washed and oven dried at 90°C for 40 h, and the dried plant parts were ground to powders; lots of 1g of the powders were digested with 10 N HNO_3. Elemental analyses of digested soil and plant samples were done with an atomic absorption spectrophotometer and for determining Na and K contents a flame photometer was used.

RESULTS

Germination (Table 3.1)

Germination was recorded after 6 days of sowing and germination count was counted from 6th to 11th days. With an increase in duration of treatments, there was an increase in the (%) of germination irrespective of concentrations. The parameter exhibit a positive with correlation (r = -0.058) between FA treatment and % of germination of *Lycopersium esculentum* L.

Table 3.1: Effect of Different Concentrations of Fly Ash Emended Soil on Percentage of Germination in *Lycopersium esculentum* c.v. S-28

	Days After Sowing					
FA Treatment (T/H)	6	7	8	9	10	11
Cont.	35	39	40	40	40	41
5	15	21	35	45	46	56
10	29	30	41	49	57	61
20	19	30	41	50	54	62
40	20	32	40	46	58	63
80	16	26	31	40	54	66

FA : Flyash, T/H: Tones per hectare

Seedling Height (Table 3.2)

Seedling shoot length was recorded 11th days after the germination. FA application to soil affected the Seedling shoot length in both positive and negative directions with increase in FA concentration there is a significant increase in the Seedling shoot length up to 20 T/H ($p<0.001$). Whereas in 40 T/H treatment the result a same as in control. In 80 T/H the seedling shoot length increased a little from control but not significantly. There is a weak correlation between FA treatments and Seedling shoot length ($r=-0.64$).

Table 3.2: Effect of Different Concentrations of Fly Ash Emended Soil on Seedling Height of *Lycopersium esculentum* c.v. S-28

FA Treatment (T/H)	Height (cm)
Cont.	3.7 ± 0.1 ***(a)
5	2.60 ± 0.1 ***(a)
10	2.50 ± 0.2 ***(a)
20	2.50 ± 0.7 ***(a)
40	3.07 ± 0.1 NS(a)
80	3.80 ± 0.1 NS(a)

Probability level:*$p<0.05$, **$p<0.01$, ***$p<0.001$

NS: Not Significant, T/H: Tones per hectare

Shoot Length (Table 3.3)

Plant height was observed from 21th to 51th days at an interval of 10 days. With an increase in concentrations of FA the plant height decrease significantly increase in the shoot height in all the concentrations of FA ($p<0.05$, $p<0.01$, $p<0.001$). The parameter show strong positive correlation between FA treatments and shoot height ($r=-0.94$).

Table 3.3: Effect of Different Concentrations of Fly Ash Emended Soil on Shoot Length of *Lycopersium esculentum* c.v. S-28

FA Treatment (T/H)	Height (cm)			
	21DAS	31DAS	41DAS	51DAS
Cont.	5.95 ± 0.15 NS(a)	9.82 ± 0.28 NS(a)	16.25 ± 0.43 NS(a)	30.37 ± 0.63 *(a)
5	5.9 ± 0.13 ***(a)	9.78 ± 0.27 NS(a)	16.69 ± 0.04 NS(a)	32.05 ± 0.57 **(a)
10	7.49 ± 0.25 ***(a)	10.27 ± 0.43 NS(a)	16.39 ± 0.32 NS(a)	33.72 ± 0.92 NS(a)
20	7.93 ± 0.47 ***(a)	11.39 ± 0.59 ***(a)	17.01 ± 0.04 NS(a)	34.28 ± 1.7 ***(a)
40	7.09 ± 0.13 ***(a)	13.32 ± 0.38 ***(a)	17.23 ± 0.42 ***(a)	36.5 ± 1.2 ***(a)
80	7.09 ± 0.13	13.24 ± 0.16	20.25 ± 0.43	38.77 ± 0.44

*Probability level:**$p<0.05$, **$p<0.01$, ***$p<0.001$

NS: Not significant, *a*: Significant test between flyash and control soil

T/H: Tones per hectare, *DAS:* Days after sowing

Number of Leaves (Table 3.4)

Number of leaves was counted from 23th to 43th days at an interval of 10 days. Addition of FA increased the number of leaves in all the concentrations of FA treatments. With an increase in the concentrations of FA there is increase in the number of leaves significantly in comparison to its control ($p<0.05$, $p<0.01$, $p<0.001$) except 20 T/H which increased but not significantly. The parameter showed weak negative correlation between FA treatment and leaf number ($r=-0.41$).

Table 3.4: Effect of Different Concentrations of Fly Ash Emended Soil on Number of Leaves of *Lycopersium esculentum* c.v. S-28

FA Treatment (T/H)	Number of Leaves (DAS)		
	23	33	43
Cont.	4.6 ± 0.16 **(a)	7.6 ± 0.16 ***(a)	8.1 ± 0.31 **(a)
5	5.5 ± 0.22 ***(a)	8.7 ± 0.21 *(a)	10.0 ± 0.51 *(a)
10	5.7 ± 0.21 ***(a)	8.3 ± 0.21 NS(a)	9.7 ± 0.63 NS(a)
20	5.6 ± 0.16 ***(a)	7.9 ± 0.37 NS(a)	9.3 ± 0.71 *(a)
40	5.6 ± 0.16 NS(a)	7.4 ± 0.22 ***(a)	9.2 ± 0.29 ***(a)
80	4.7 ± 0.15	6.6 ± 0.16	10.0 ± 0.25

Probability level: *p<0.05, **p<0.01, ***p<0.001
NS: Not significant, *a:* Significant test between flyash and control soil
T/H: Tones per hectare, *DAS:* Days after sowing

Number of Flowers (Table 3.5)

Total number of Flowers was countered from 48th to 62th days at an interval of 2 days. FA treatment showed much increased in Flower number over control. The flower number increased progressively with an increase in the duration of treatments. There is weak positive correlation between FA treatment and flower number ($r=-0.59$).

Table 3.5: Effect of Different Concentrations of Fly Ash Emended Soil on Number of Flowers of *Lycopersium esculentum* c.v. S-28

FA Treatment (T/H)	Number of Flowers(DAS)							
	48	50	52	54	56	58	60	62
Cont.	0	0	0	0	0	0	0	11
5	0	0	1	3	8	18	27	17
10	1	0	2	2	5	16	22	23
20	2	3	8	13	20	36	41	32
40	0	1	3	10	25	42	43	47
80	0	1	2	4	10	24	26	31

FA: Flyash, *T/H:* Tones per hectare, *DAS:* Days after sowing.

Fruit Number (Table 3.6)

Total number of Fruit was observed from 60th to 80th days at an interval of 10 days and the observation has been presented. With an increase in the concentration of FA there is an increase in the fruit number except 20T/H which decrease from control and 40 and 80T/H FA treatment showed gradual increase in fruit number from control ($p<0.01$, $p<0.001$). This parameter shows positive correlation between FA and fruit number ($r=-0.91$).

Table 3.6: Effect of Different Concentrations of Fly Ash Emended on Number of Fruits of *Lycopersium esculentum* c.v. S-28

FA Treatment (T/H)	Number of Fruits (DAS)		
	60	70	80
Cont.	2.7 ± 0.26 NS(a)	5.7 ± 0.85 *(a)	7.2 ± 0.59 NS(a)
5	5.0 ± 1.3 NS(a)	10.0 ± 0.14 NS(a)	8.2 ± 0.48 NS(a)
10	4.0 ± 0.76 ***(a)	7.5 ± 0.93 *(a)	7.4 ± 0.47 NS(a)
20	8.7 ± 1.5 ***(a)	9.2 ± 1.2 ***(a)	6.9 ± 0.43 **(a)
40	7.8 ± 0.94 ***(a)	10.4 ± 0.52 ***(a)	10.72 ± 0.69 ***(a)
80	6.3 ± 1.0	9.9 ± 1.0	12.2 ± 0.4

Probability level: *p<0.05, **p<0.01, ***p<0.001
NS: Not significant, a: Significant test between flyash and control soil
T/H: Tones per hectare, *FA:* Flyash

Fruit Weight (Table 3.7)

The fruit weight was recorder after 84days after sowing. Fruit increased with increase in the duration of treatments. However, the increasing trend is not regular in the treatments. In the shows very weak correlation between FA treatments and weight of fruits ($r=-0.10$).

Table 3.7: Effect of Different Concentrations of Fly Ash Emended Soil on Fruit Weight/Plant of *Lycopersium esculentum* c.v. S-28

FA Treatment (T/H)	Fruit Weight/Plant (gm/m^2)
Cont.	312.47
5	418.29
10	426.3
20	429.12
40	419.85
80	362.16

FA: Flyash, *T/H:* Tones per hectare, *DAS:* Days after sowing

Harvest Root Length (Table 3.8)

Application of FA contribution to increase the after harvest root length in 5 and 10 T/H which increased significantly at 10T/H ($P<0.051$) rest of the treatments decreased but not significantly. There is a negative correlation between harvest root length and FA treatments ($r=-0.62$).

Table 3.8: Effect of Different Concentrations of Fly Ash Emended Soil On Root Length of *Lycopersium esculentum* c.v. S-28

FA Treatment (T/H)	Root Length(cm)
Cont.	17.25 ± 1.8 NS(a)
5	22.11 ± 2.3 *(a)
10	22.11 ± 0.92 NS(a)
20	17.27 ± 1.7 NS(a)
40	15.69 ± 1.6 NS(a)
80	15.89 ± 1.1

*Probability level:**$p<0.05$, **$p<0.01$, ***$p<0.001$

NS: Not Significant, *a:* Significant test between flyash and control soil

T/H: Tones per hectare, *FA:* Flyash, *DAS:* Days after sowing.

Plant Dry Weight (Table 3.9)

FA increased in plant dry weight significantly up to 40 T/H ($p<0.001$, $p<0.01$, $p<0.05$) except 5th which increase but not significantly, while in 80T/H decreased but not significantly over control. This parameter showed poor negative correlation between FA treatments and plant dry weight ($r=-0.48$).

Table 3.9: Effect of Different Concentrations of Fly Ash Emended on Plant Dry Weight of *Lycopersium esculentum* c.v. S-28

FA Treatment (T/H)	Dry Weight/Plant (gm/m^2)
Cont.	16.88 ± 1.0 NS(a)
5	20.79 ± 1.7 ***(a)
10	25.27 ± 1.5 **(a)
20	21.26 ± 1.0 *(a)
40	19.95 ± 0.99 NS(a)
80	16.15 ± 0.57

*Probability level:**$p<0.05$, **$p<0.01$, ***$p<0.001$

NS: Not significant, *a:* Significant test between flyash and control soil

T/H: Tones per hectare, *FA:* Flyash, *DAS:* Days after sowing.

Soil Texture (Table 3.10)

Texture of experimental soil of tomato field has improved further by fly ash application. FA application @ 80 T/H decreased sand% from 97.5 to 84.0 and simultaneously increased clay % from 0.5 to 14.0 in comparison to control.

Table 3.10: Texture of Fly Ash Amended Tomato Field

FA Treatment (T/H)	Texture (%)		
	Sand	Clay	Silt
Cont.	47.5	2	0.5
5	94.5	1.5	4
10	93.5	1.5	5
20	93	1	6
40	92	1.5	6.5
80	84	2	14

FA: Flyash, *T/H:* Tones per hectare, *DAS:* Days after sowing.

pH (Table 3.11)

Fly ash (pH 6.1) amendment to sandy soil (5.6 to 5.7) increased pH in all concentrations recorded after harvest of the crops. FA treatment increases the pH from (5.6 to 6.6) due to the buffering capacity of FA.

Table 3.11: pH of Fly Ash Amended Tomato Field

Cont.	5T/H	10/H	20T/H	40T/H	80T/H
B.C.(5.6-5.7)	(5.6-5.7)	(5.6-5.7)	(5.6-5.7)	(5.6-5.7)	(5.6-5.7)
A.C.(5.7-5.8)	(5.7-5.8)	(5.8-6.1)	(6.0-6.2)	(6.2-6.6)	(6.2-6.6)

B.C.: Before cropping, *A.C.:* After cropping

CEC (Table 3.12)

Cation exchange capacity in response to FA amendments was found to increase progressively with increasing FA concentrations. The maximum increase was observed in FA 80T/H.

Table 3.12: Cation Exchange Capacity of Fly Ash Amended Tomato Field

FA Treatment (T/H)	Cation Exchange Capacity
Cont.	3.67
5	5.45
10	5.8
20	3.67
40	3.14
80	3.8

FA: Flyash, *T/H:* Tones per hectare, *DAS:* Days after sowing.

EC (Table 3.13)

Electrical conductivity in FA treated soil increased in comparison to control. There was progressive increase in EC with an increase in the FA treatments. The maximum increase was recorded in FA 80T/H (0.41 to 0.47).

Table 3.13: Electrical Conductivity of Fly Ash Amended Tomato Field

Cont.	5T/H	10T/H	20T/H	40T/H	80 T/H
B.C.(0.28-0.32)	(0.28-0.32)	(0.28-0.32)	(0.28-0.32)	(0.28-0.32)	(0.28-0.32)
A.C.(0.35-0.38)	(0.35-0.38)	(0.39-0.40)	(0.40-0.42)	(0.38-0.46)	(0.41-0.47)

B.C.: Before cropping, *A.C.*: After cropping.

OC and Nitrogen (Tables 3.14 and 3.15)

Soil nitrogen was calculated from the organic carbon content of the soil increases due to FA treatments. A steady increase in the organic carbon and nitrogen was observed from 5 to 80 T/H. The maximum was observed at the highest concentrations.

Table 3.14: Organic Carbon Content of Fly Ash Amended Tomato Field

Organic Carbon Content (lb/acre)					
Cont.	5T/H	10T/H	20T/H	40T/H	80 T/H
B.C.(0.79-0.80)	(0.79-0.80)	(0.79-0.80)	(0.79-0.80)	(0.79-0.80)	(0.79-0.80)
A.C.(0.81-0.82)	(0.82-0.83)	(0.86-0.85)	(0.85-0.87)	(0.86-0.88)	(0.87-0.89)

B.C.: Before cropping, *A.C.*: After cropping

Table 3.15: Nitrogen Content of Fly Ash Amended Tomato Field

Nitrogen Content (lb/acre)					
Cont.	5T/H	10T/H	20T/H	40T/H	80T/H
B.C.(0.079-0.080)	(0.079-0.080)	(0.079-0.080)	(0.079-0.080)	(0.079-0.080)	(0.079-0.080)
A.C.(0.081-0.082)	(0.082-0.083)	(0.086-0.085)	(0.085-0.087)	(0.086-0.088)	(0.087-0.089)

B.C.: Before cropping, *A.C.*: After cropping.

Phosphate (Table 3.16)

Phosphorous content in the range of 63.83 to 70.02 (lb/acre) was observed in all the experimental fields before cropping. Addition of FA @ 5 to 80T/H progressively increases the phosphorous content in the fields ranging from 83.95-98.08 after cropping. Maximum was observed at 80 T/H.

Table 3.16: Phosphate Content of Fly Ash Amended Tomato Field

Phosphate Content (lb/acre)					
Cont.	5T/H	10T/H	20T/H	40T/H	80 T/H
B.C.(63.83-70.02)	(63.83-70.02)	(63.83-70.02)	(63.83-70.02)	(63.83-70.02)	(63.83-70.02)
A.C.(83.95-84.62)	(89.7-90.98)	(89.88-91.63)	(90.98-92.89)	(97.05-98.08)	(97.55-98.35)

B.C.: Before cropping, *A.C.*: After cropping

Potassium (Table 3.17)

FA is a good source of Potassium as a result of which K content of the experimental soil increased in the FA treated soils remarkably soil increased in the FA treated soils remarkably over the control field. Maximum K was observed at 80T/H FA treatment.

Table 3.17: Potassium Content of Flyash Amended Tomato Field

Potassium Content (lb/acre)					
Cont.	5T/H	10T/H	20T/H	40T/H	80 T/H
B.C.(388-398)	(388-398)	(388-398)	(388-398)	(388-398)	(388-398)
A.C.(390-400)	(390-420)	(410-448)	(423-456)	(490-560)	(618-697)

B.C.: Before cropping, *A.C.:* After cropping

Elemental Status (Table 3.18)

Leaf elemental analysis of *Lycopersium esculentum* L. showed accumulation of elements like Fe, Mn, Pb and Co in fly ash treatments. The contents were higher in almost all treatments than the control, but exceptionally decreased in almost all treatments than the control, but exceptionally decreased in higher dosages (40 and 80 T/H of FA 40+ and 80+ T/H treatments). However, the accumulation trend differed for each element. Fe and Mn showed increased concentrations, in plants grown in fly ash amended soil in comparison to control soil. The accumulation of Fe and Mn increased from 650 to 811 ppm (40 T/H) and 18.8 to 45.0 ppm (5T/H). Pb content increased in 5, 10 and 20 T/H fly ash treatments but remarkably less than control in 40 T/H and 80 T/H treatments applied than the other treatments. However, any of the metals have not given any regular trend of uptake in increase or decrease in FA or FA+ treatments.

Table 3.18: Effect of Different Concentrations of Fly Ash Emended Soil on Heavy Metal Uptake of Leaves of *Lycopersium esculentum* c.v. S-28

FA Treatment (T/H)	Heavy Metal Uptake (ppm)			
	Fe	Mn	Pb	Co
Cont.	650	18.8	2.8	1.4
5	720	45	8.8	3.2
10	686	42.4	5.4	1.8
20	795	31.6	5.8	1.6
40	811	20.8	1.8	1.2
80	664	19.4	1.6	1.1

FA: Flyash, *T/H:* Tones per hectare

DISCUSSION

Tomato plants grown in different concentrations of fly ash amended soil germination increased by 36.58%, 48.78%, 51.21%, 53.654% and 60.97% at 5, 10, 20, 40 and 80 T/H respectively. Shoot length increased by 5.53% ($P<0.05$), 11.03% ($P<0.01$), 12.87% ($P<0.05$), 20.18% ($P<0.001$) and 27.65% ($P<0.001$) at 5, 10, 20, 40 and 80T/H. Similarly the leaf number increased by 23.45% ($P<0.01$), 19.75% ($P<0.05$), 14.81% ($P<0.05$), 13.58% ($P<0.05$) and 23.45% ($P<0.001$) at 5, 10, 20, 40 and 80 T/H. Flower number increased by 54.54%, 109.09%, 190.90%, 327.27%, 181.81% at 5, 10,20, 40 and 80T/H. The number of fruits increased by 13.88%, 48.88%, ($P<0.01$), 69.44% ($P<0.001$), at 5, 10, 20, 40 and 80 T/H. The fruit weight increased by 33.86%, 36.42%, 37.33%, 34.36% and 15.90% at 5, 10, 20, 40 and 80 T/H. The root length increased by 28.17%, 28.17%, ($P<0.05$) at 5 and 10T/H. The dry weight increased by 23.16%, 49.70%, ($P<0.001$), 25.94% ($P<0.01$), 18.18% ($P<0.05$) at 5, 10, 20 and 40 T/H. The increased growth of *Lycopersium esculentum* L. by Fly ash application in soil is due to a qualitative change in the physical and chemical properties of the soil.

Metal are known to induce biophasic dose-response curves which allows a gross division in to 2 general regions (Vallee and Ulmer, 1972). The stimulatory effect of low concentrations against a background of a deficiency state constitutes phase one of the dose-response curve. For some metals, the requirement may be at such low concentrations that experimental production of a deficiency state may be technically difficult. As a result, little is known of the possible stimulatory effect of metals at low concentrations. On the other hand, the inhibitory toxic effect of high concentrations that constitute phase two of the dose-response curve has been found for most metals about which adequate information exists, including mercury (Davis et al., 1978; Lepp, 1981; Dash and Panda, 1988).

Direction and magnitude of these responses will depend on the sensitivity of the individual, the intensity the form in which it is present. From experimental studies, it is possible to construct yield-dose response curves, where yield can represent a growth parameter ranging from biomass production in the long term. The precise for of the response curve will determine their usefulness in bioassay studies for any particular metal toxicity. Differential effects of an appropriate metal concentration or concentration range, on the performance of different species, population or both genotypes can therefore be used to quantify both sensitivity and tolerance. For most heavy metals, a dose-response curve can be constructed in order to observe impact on plant growth. The shape of these curves will depend on both metal essentiality/toxicity and species sensitivity. A feature of many such response curves, even for non essential heavy metals is a stimulatory response in growth or yield at very low external concentrations, followed by inhibitory effects at higher concentrations. Many workers have not detected this low-level stimulatory response because of the metal concentrations chosen in tolerance tests. However, there is some evidence to suggest that in tolerance plants the metals concentrations producing both stimulatory and inhibitory effects are higher than for normal (Non-tolerance) plants. The effect is manifested by an apparent "need" for otherwise toxic metals, but in reality the response curve has been shifted upscale towards higher treatment concentrations.

In our experiment, soil emended with 5, 10, 20, 40 and 80 T/H of fly ash increased growth and yield of tomato is a stimulatory phase. In stimulatory phase in tomato very low dose (5 and 10 T/H) cause increase in the shoot I height. The stimulatory dose is followed a tolerance phase where the increment in the plant growth remains steadily for some time. In tomato there was in abrupt in plant growth in 20 and 40 T/H under goes through a toxic phase. Finally declines towards toxic phase in higher dose (80T/H). The fruit number also increased at very low dosages (5 and 10 T/H) and steadily decreased from stimulatory phase to toxic phase. Whereas in shoot dry weight, in very was an abrupt increase in yield then declined under toxic phase (80 T/H), but in root dry weight it decreased at very low control, while at (5 T/H) and gives similar result at 10T/H like control, while at (20 T/H) it induced better increment in root dry weight.

In tomato the fruit number increased at very low dose (5 and 10T/H) but decreased at 20 T/H, and at the rate of treatments. Similarly the fruit weight increased from very low dosages (5 and 10 T/H) to stimulatory phase (20 and 40T/H) than declined but increased from the control. The plant dry weight increased at very low dosages (5 and 10 T/H) and at stimulatory dose is followed by a tolerance phase where the increment in plant dry weight increased abruptly and 80T/H under goes through a toxic phase where the plant dry weight declined. Composition of the growth pattern and yield indicates their susceptibility to the metal concentrations in the fly ash as well as the susceptibility of the test crop. Results indicate is a tolerance plant with a wide range of tolerance zone as well as it can withstand higher metal concentrations of the soil (80 T/H).The growth and yield pattern of tomato demonstrates increase in at a much higher dose. Thus the dose response relationship in different sciences gives useful information on the assessment of external metal concentrations of the plant growth and yield performance.

Response of Plant Root to Heavy Metals

Response of plants to the impact of heavy metals depend on the sensitivity of the individual plant, the intensity of the stress, the form of metal applied and several additional condition.

(a) Change in root Biomass

Most studies found a reduction, e.g. For *Beta vulgaries* or *Holcus lanatus*. Sometimes an increase occurred. The shoot/Root ratio of biomass can decrease or increase (Baker and Walker, 1989). In the present study, vegetable crops of tomato grown in different concentrations of Fly ash show an increased root biomass (Dry Weight) except at higher concentration (80 T/H) which is phytotoxic. In the harvesting stage root length increases in response to fly ash treatment, however in the mature stage the differences are most significant, the root length increased at low dosages at 5 and 10 T/H ($P<0.05$).

(b) Changes in the Architecture of the whole root system

A freshly observed phenomenon is enhanced lateral root formation as a consequence of toxic concentrations of Al, Cu, Cr, Cd, Mn, Pb, and Zn. This leads to a denser and compact root system, through a decrease in lateral root initiation has also been observed. The root axis is compressed and a reduced distance between root and youngest lateral roots has been reported (Pung and Speghardt, 1979). In our study fly ash treated soil induced profuse lateral rooting in tomato. Simultaneously the preliminary root elongation is suppressed along with lateral root growth which is responsible for increased root biomass. Flay ash contains a host of heavy metals like Al, Fe, Cr, Cd, Mn, Pb, Zn etc. The heavy metal concentrations induced dense and impact root system in our experiment too.

(c) Changes in growth rate

These are very common responses and have been used as a test of tolerance. There are many general considerations and also many special studies e.g. Pb, Cu, Ni, Al, Co on this aspect of metals response (Baker et al., 1964).

(d) Initiation of root elongation

This is commonly observed as a result of interference with cell division. Perhaps by initiating cytokinesis or to nucleic acids or by a more general inhibition of cell division/mitosis, cell elongation (By Pb), distributed mitosis (For *Zea mays*), reduced mitotic rate (Allium/ *Zea mays*) or decreased extension of the cell wall (by Zn) and decreased cell wall synthesis (Punz and Sieghardt, 1993).

Effect of FA on Chemical Properties of Soil

An increase in fly ash application rate caused a considerable increase in both pH and EC of soils. The increases were more obvious for sandy soil. The pH shifted from 5.7-5.8 to 6.2-6.6 in all the fly ash applied plots of at the largest application rate 80 T/H. But after application of fly ash the EC shifted from (0.35-0.38) for control soil and (0.41-0.47) at the largest application rate 80 T/H FA.

The initial increase in soil pH after amendment was attributed to the release of Ca, Mg, and OH ions from fly ash (Hodgson et al., 1982). It has been suggested that Ca was the major element soluble in water. Calcium oxide in ash is respectively constant and in contact with water, CO_2 is absorbed leading to the precipitation of $CaCO_3$. Residual pH effect after cropping was found to be more obvious for sandy soil than for sandy loam. A dramatic increase in EC after ash amendment was noted for both soils.

Comparable findings have been reported for natural soil after ash amendment. The measurement of EC reflects the total concentration of soluble cations or anioins in solution and the two parameters are quantitatively related. Hence 80% ash amended sandy soil could be considered as an acidic and soil which might seriously affect the growth of sensitive plants. According to Singh et al., (1994) sandy loam soil amended with fly ash of the Panki thermal power plant, Kanpur (India) under goes various changes. An upwards shift in soil pH was not pronounced at 2%, 4% and 8% of bean field.

Similarly the ECE, OC P_2O_5 and K_2O also changed after application of fly ash. Copping increased the ECE of the soil 3.67 to 5.80 Meq $100g^{-1}$ of tomato field. The OC increases from 0.81-0.82 to 0.87-0.89 lb/acre (80 T/H) of tomato field. Similarly the phosphate content increased from 83.95-84.62 to 97.55-98.35 lb/acre of tomato field. After cropping the potassium content also increased from 390-400 lb/acre to 618-647 lb/acre of tomato field.

Fly Ash Toxicity

Environmental factors are only ecologically relevant if they result in a stress and thus, effects on the individual, the population and the ecosystem. But environmental stress can damage plants at all biological levels from molecules to ecosystems. Therefore, damage will be defined as a situation when the stress has passed beyond the repair system operating at each biological level as soon as final result will affect the fitness of an individual and/or population and the structure and/or function of an ecosystem. Due to the various kinetics and reaction velocities at each level, from disturbance of a biomembrane; up to changes of the genetically composition of a population. Damage at the higher organization level can often be related to visible parameters of plant performance; i.e. plant colour, plant structure, plant growth and reproduction. Visible damage is the 1st registration by eye of a chain of changed biochemical and physiological processes at the sub cellular, cellular, tissue and whole plant level.

Plants exhibited differential toxic responses; Mn being more toxic than Fe. This could be with the organic components of the plants. This conforms to our previous report on Fe and Mn toxicity and accumulation in *Hydrodictycyon reticulatum*. Mishra and Shukla (1986) have reported the enrichment of soils and plants with trace elements by fly ash application. However, metal uptake by the plant from the soil depends on the concentration of the metal in the metal in soil and on the physiological requirement for the metal by plant. The retarded growth of plants grown in soils with higher applications of fly ash as reflected by decreased leaf number, leaf area, root length and its diameter as well as phytomass of the above and below ground parts was probably due to decreased levels of chlorophyll and toxic effects of heavy metals coupled with undesirable changes in the chemical properties of the soils (Mishra and Shukla, 1986; Wong and Wong, 1990) Thus may also influence the plant growth adversely.

Field and green house studies both indicates that many chemical constituents of fly ash may benefits plant growth and can improve agronomic properties of the soil (Chang et al., 1977). The effects on plants were preliminary due to a shifted equilibrium induced by the fly ash derived from high-s coal would influence the chemistry of amended soils in a manner different from that of the fly ash with alkaline pH. The weathering of fly ash in storage lagoons stabilizes the fluctuating pH and precipitates soluble minerals which could minimize the overall impacts. The interactions between plants and fly ash amended soils are further complicated by varying edaphic factors and plant species.

Literature on fly ash toxic effects of on plants are available, however no attempt was made to separate the effect by species, soil characteristics, or experimental conditions, of the essential plant nutrients, the concentrations of S, Mo and B in plant tissues have been shown to increase consistently with ash applications to soil. Concentrations of the nonessential trace elements Al, Mn and Sr were also consistently increased. There were instances when increases in dry matter yields were obtained in the flyash-amended soils but these were associated preliminary with correction of either macro or micronutrient deficiencies. These increases, are primarily caused by increased plant nutrient availability (i.e., Ca^2, Mg^{2+}), also prevented the toxic effects of Al and Mn^+ and other metallic ions by neutralizing the so acidity. (Fail and Wochok, 1977; Kovaecic and Hardy, 1972; Capp and Engle, 1967; Mahalingam, 1973) observed substantial increases in rice (*Oryza sativa*) yield by applying low rates of flyash to a saline alkali soil thus lowering the soil pH from 9.1 to 7.5. Because the N content of flyash is usually nil and P contents is quite insoluble, these nutrients should asses to sustain good growth when fly ash is applied. Increased N concentrations in plant tissues have been observed in some cases, especially when poorly burned coal was used (Page et al., 1977; Adriano et al., 1978). The major plant nutrients (P, K, Ca and Mg) were affected inconstantly by ash application.

The affected plants are further demonstrated by the enrichment ratio (ER). ER of chemical element is calculated plant tissue with that of the unaffected plant tissue. The higher ER of a chemical element indicates greater degree of plant tissue enrichment in the effected soils. An enrichment ratio or 0<1 would be indicative of the reduced plant uptake or that element by plants. Most chemical elements examined exhibited little tendency of plant tissue enrichment (ER=1.0) in fly ash-amended soils. However many potentially hazardous elements such as As, Ba, Be, Mo, Se and V all showed remarkable concentrating of effects when plants are grown in fly ash effected substrates. 15 and 20 T/H increases the growth and yield suggesting the stimulatory effect of low concentrations of essential and nonessential metals in the fly ash .possible explanations for the stimulatory responses in tolerant plant are not yet fully understood. It is unlikely that trace metals. It has greater absolute requirements of essential trace metals. It is more probable that the efficiency of the tolerance mechanism in detoxifying the metal may be so great it prevents the metals from being internally available. Explanations of the stimulatory effects of nonessential metals are yet to be found and further research in this area should be rewarding.

Edaphic Factors and Metal Toxicity

Acidic soil tested with fly ash caused unfavorable changes in the soil's chemical equilibrium, including pH, EC and available toxic metals. As a result of the hydrolysis of CaO and MgO (Fly ash that are high in Ca and Mg oxides), the soil pH and EC were found to increase in relation to the amounts of fly ash added to the soil columns.

Results showed that there is accumulation of the heavy metals in the fly ash treated tomato plants varied with evidence are available that greater concentration of available and lower concentration of total metals in acidic soil than in natural soils have been observed. The available content of heavy metals measured seems to vary with pH of the soil. It has been observed that, as the pH of the soil was increased, the amounts of available heavy metals like Fe, Mn, Pb and Co contents decreased. One of the heavy metal s most salient features is the effect of pH on the reaction between heavy metals and soils. The tendency of metal ion to hydrolysis could also be responsible for part of the observed response to pH change (Beveridge and Pickering, 1980).

The texture of a given soil is important in evaluating the contribution of heavy metals by that soil. ECE is the most important parameter to be considered in determining the release and behavior of heavy metals from flyash/soil to the water environment. Christopherson and his team have constructed a mathematical model based on ion-exchange and demonstrated that the residence time of the Fe uptake in *Phaseolus vulgaris* in relation to pH of soil amended with different concentrations of fly ash.

Water which percolates through layers of soil also becomes very important it is obvious that once the heavy metals are related from fly ashes, with increasing contact period with acidic water, their percolation through soil layers would also follow the same mechanism and higher contents of these heavy metals will occurs within smaller pores of soils than in larger pores of soils. Thus, the total contents of heavy metals measured varied at different depths due to varying levels of ECE at different depths of the soils.

Another most important parameter is the organic matter content in the soil. Organic matter is a very variable medium, a rather large sample to sample variation has been observed for the small soil sample to samples used for the analysis. Bolter (1971) have studied the mechanisms of organic matter in soils and reported that a uniformly distributed throughout the soils. The extent to which heavy metals ions bind vary with the solution pH concentrations of competing cations, nature of the organic material and the complexing power of any ligands present. However, the absorptive capacity of the humic substances for metals ions was found greater than that of many types of clay and varied more with changes in pH (Beveridge and Pickering, 1980).

In a leaching experiment it has been observed that a pozzolanic reaction resulted after 25 days and 32 days of continuous leaching/percolation through 5% and 10% fly ash applied soil columns, respectively. After that, the residence time of percolating water in the fly ash/ soil columns increased, although the percolation of water was continued up to a period of 40 days. The exact reasons for such a pozzolanic reactions are yet not known, but more effective reactions can occur in acidic soils (Sharma et al., 1989). However this occurrence may be due to the acidity of applied water on the cementing nature of fly ash and such a situation enhances the adsorption and subsequent mobility of heavy metals in fly ash soil columns.

However, from the above results and discussion it is assumed that the release of these heavy metals into the ground water by the action of acidic rain on a fly ash soil bed, the condition which is prevailing near coal-fried power plants of fly ash disposal sites in India, would be highly dependent on the texture of soil i.e. pH, O.M., CEC adsorption precipitation and mobility of heavy metals in soils. Wherever necessary, the data obtained may be carefully interpreted and used for the disposal of fly ash on land, bearing in mind the conditions prevailing in the actual environment.

CONCLUSION

Fly ash contains good number of plant nutrients. It was planned to evaluate its utility in agriculture particularly in an acidic soil as a substitute of lime to raise the pH of the soil and study its effect on growth and yield of tomato. In agro climatic condition of Berhampur, Odisha; results of graded levels of FA treatment in tomato, all the dosage increase the growth parameters but only 40 and 80 T/H increase the yield of tomato. Fly ash increased the soil physical properties to some extent while metal uptake has correlation with soil pH. Metal toxicity is observed in crops applied with high dose of fly ash. While fly ash show promise as a source of plant nutrients, several factors need to be explored before its extensive utilization in agriculture can be recommended.

REFERENCES

1. Adriano, D.C., Woolford T.A. and Ciravolo T.G. (1978): Growth and Elemental Composition of Corn and Bean Seedling as Influenced by Soil Application of Coal Ash. J. Eniron. Qual., 7: 416-421.
2. Baker, A.J.M. and Walker P.L. (1989): Physiological Responses of Plants to Heavy Metals and the Quantification of Tolerance and Toxicity. Bioavailability., 1: 7-12.
3. Beveridge, A. and Pickering W.I., (1980): Influence of Humantesolute Interactions on Aqueous Heavy Metal Ion Levels. Water, Air and Soil Pollution., 14: 171-185.
4. Bolter, Water E.A. (1971): Geochemistry of Mining, Milling, Retention Ponds in the New Lead Belt of Southeast Missouri (unpublished) Water Resources Research Report.

5. Brown, S., Chaney R.L. (2000): Beneficial Uses Flue Gas Desulfurization by-products: Examples and Case Studies of Land Application. In: Dick W.A. et al. (eds) Land Application of Agricultural, Industrial and Municipal Byproducts, SSSA Book Series: 6, SSSA, Madison, W.I., pp. 33-360.
6. Calmano, W., Hong J., Forstner U., (1993): Binding and Mobilization of Heavy Metals in Contaminated Sediments Affected by pH and Redox Potential, Wat. Sci. Tech., 28: 53-58.
7. Capp, J.P. and Engle C.F. (1967): Fly Ash in Agriculture Bur, Mines Inf. Cir C 8348. U.S. Dep. Interior Washington D.C. P. 210-220.
8. Chang, A.C., Lund L.J., Page A.L. and Warneke J.E. (1977): Physical Properties of Flyash Amended Soils. J. Environ. Qual., 6: 267-270.
9. Dash, S. and Panda B.B. (1988): Biomonitoring of Low Levels of Mercurial Derivatives in Water and Soil by Allium Micronucleus Assay. Mutation Res., 203: 11-12.
10. Davis, R.D., Beckett P.H.T. and Wollan E. (1978): Critical Levels of Twenty Potential Toxic Elements in Young Spring Barley. Pl. Soil., 49: 395-408.
11. Dubois, M., Gilles K.A., Hamilton J.K., Rebers P.A., Smith F. (1956): Colormetric Method for Determination of Sugars and Related Substances. Anal Chem., 28: 350-356.
12. Fail, J.L., Jr. and Wochok Z.S. (1977): Soybean Growth on Fly Ash Amended Strip Mine Soil. Pl. Soil., 48: 473-484.
13. Fulekar, M.H. and Dave J.M., "Environmental Impact Assessment of Fly Ash from Coal Fired Power Plants" Ecological (in press).
14. Fytianos, K., Katsianis G., Triantafyllou P., Zachariadis G. (2001): Accumulation of Heavy Metals in Vegetables Grown in an Industrial Area in Relation to Soil, Bulletin of Environmental Contamination and Toxicology., 67(3): 423-430.
15. Hodgson, L., Dyer, D. and Brown, D.A. (1982): Neutralization and Dissolution of High Calcium Fly Ash. J. Environ. Quality., 11: 93-98.
16. Korcak, R.F. (1995): Utilization of Coal Combustion By-products in Agriculture and Horticulture. In: Karlen DL et al (eds) Agricultural Utilization of Urban and Industrial By-products. ASA Spec Publ 58, ASA, CSSA and SSSA, Madison, W.I., pp. 107-130.
17. Kovaecic, W., and Hardy R.G. (1972): Progress Report: Utilization of Fly Ash in the Reclamation of Coal Mine Spoil Banks in South Eastern Kansas Geol. Surv. Bull., 204: 29-31.
18. Lepp, N.W. (Ed) (1981): Effect of Heavy Metal Pollution on Plants.Vol. 2. Applied Science Publishers, London.
19. Lowry, O.M., Rosenbrough N.J., Farr A.I., Randall R.L. (1951): Protein Measurement with the Folin Phenol Reagent. J Biol. Chem., 194: 245-275.
20. Maehaly, A.C., Chance B. (1967): The Assay of Catalase and Peroxidases. In Glick D (ed) Methods of Biochemical Analysis, Vol. 1. Interscience Publishers, New York., pp. 357-427.
21. Mahalingam, P.K. (1973): Ameliorative Properties of Lignite Fly Ash in Reclaiming Saline and Alkali Soils. Madras Amer. Proc., 34: 453-456.
22. Miller, D.M., Miller W.P., Dudka S. and Sumner M.E. (2000): Characterization of Industrial By-products. In: Dick WA et al (eds) Land Application of Agricultural, Industrial, and Municipal By-Products. SSSA Book Series: 6, SSSA, Madisoon, W.I., pp. 107-119.
23. Mishra, M., Sahu R.K., Padhy R.N. (2005): Effect of Vermicomposted Municipal Solid Waste on Growth, Yield and Heavy Metal Contents of Rice (*Oryza sativa*). Fresenius Environ Bull., 14: 584-590.
24. Mishra, L.C. and Shukla K.N. (1986): Edaphic Properties of Fly Ash from a Coal Fired Power Plant at Kanpur, India. Environ. Pollut., Ser (B), 11: 55-66.
25. Page, A.L., Bingham F.T., Lund L.J., Braford G.R. and Elseewi A.A. (1977) Consequences of Trace Element Enrichment of Soils and Vegetation from the Combustion of Fuels Used in Power Generation. S. Calif. Edition Res. Dev., Ser 77-RD-29.
26. Piper, C.S. (1944): Soil and Plant Analysis. Inter Sci. Publishers, New York.

27. Punz, W.F and Sieghardt H. (1993): The Responses of Roots to Herbaceous Plant Species to Heavy Metals. Environ. Exp. Bot., 53(1): 85-98.

28. Sharma, S., Fulekar M.H. and Jayalakshmi C.P., (1989): "Flyash Dynamics in Soil-water System" CRC Critical Revs. Environ Control, 19(3): 251-275.

29. Singh, N., Singh S.N., Yunus M. and Ahmad K.J. (1994): Growth Response and Element Accumulation in Beta Vulgaris L. Raised in Flyash Amended Soils. Ecotoxicology., 5: 287-98.

30. Valle, B.L. and Ulmer, D.D. (1972): Biochemical Effects of Mercury, Cadmium and Lead. Annual Review of Biochemistry, 41: 91-127.

31. Walkley, Y.A. and Black I.A. (1934): An Examination of Digestion Method for Determining Soil Organic Matter and a Proposed Modification of the Chromic Acid Titration Method. Soil Sci., 37: 29-38.

32. Wong, J.W.C. and Wong M.H. (1990): Effects of Flyash on Yields and Elemental Composition of Two Vegetables, *Brassica parachinensis* and B. *chinensis*. Agric. Ecosystems Environ., 30: 251-264.

Pages: 69-91

SOIL CHARACTERISTICS AND AGRO-ECOLOGY

Edited by: Dr. Avnish Chauhan; Dr. Pawan Kumar 'Bharti'

ISBN: 978-93-5056-758-6

Edition: 2015

Published by: Discovery Publishing House Pvt. Ltd., New Delhi (India)

Engineering Techniques for Increasing Water Use Efficiency Under Arid Zones Conditions

Dr. Abdelraouf Ramadan Eid Abdelghany

ABSTRACT

To alleviate the suffering resulting from the shortage of water resources in arid zones must apply all possible techniques to improve water use efficiency, starting from the mouth of EL-RAYAH passing through main canals then branch canals until reaching the irrigation water to plant and not to the field only. There are some engineering techniques proved positive impacts on raising of water use efficiency, including: (1) Appling zero and minimum tillage technique, (2) Laser land leveling, (3) Appling surge irrigation technique with developed surface irrigation with clay soils, (4) Modern techniques with drip irrigation system (new designs, pulse irrigation and using irregular volumetric distribution of compost along laterals and (5) Using of deficit irrigation concept and partial root drying irrigation in water management.

Associated Professor at Water Relations and Field Irrigation Department, Agricultural and Biological Research Division, National Research Center- Giza- Egypt.

Corresponding Address: Abdelraouf Ramadan, 33 El-Buhouth St., Dokki, Cairo, Egypt.

INTRODUCTION

Water scarcity is a global problem. As cities grow and populations increase, the problem worsens since needs for water increase in households, industry and agriculture. Climate change has also contributed significantly to the water scarcity problem. Rising temperatures increase the rate of evaporation from land and surface water resources; this has caused reductions in river run-off in several areas. The rise in temperatures has also greatly affected areas that rely on snowmelt and mountain glaciers as a water source. Water scarcity does not only occur in arid and semi-arid areas but also occurs in areas that receive ample rainfall and/or have abundant fresh water resources. How the available water is used, managed and conserved, determines if there is enough to meet household, agricultural, industrial and environmental demands (WHO, 2009).

Maximizing irrigation water use efficiency is a common concept used by irrigation project managers; also, the visual quality of the crop yield is the primary criteria on used to assess irrigation systems effectiveness. In recent years, however, growing competition for scarce water resources has led to applying modified techniques for maximizing water use efficiency and improving crop yields and quality, particularly in arid and semi arid regions.

The main objective of this chapter is focusing on the important of engineering techniques in increasing of water use efficiency under arid zones conditions. Some of engineering techniques to improve water-use efficiency including: (1) Zero and minimum tillage, (2) Laser land leveling, (3) Appling surge irrigation technique with developed surface irrigation, (4) Improvement of solid set Sprinkler irrigation system, (5) Modern techniques with drip irrigation system and (6) Importance of deficit irrigation concept and partial root drying irrigation.

WHAT IS THE MEANING OF WATER USE EFFICIENCY ?

Water use efficiency is a term commonly used to describe the relationship between water (input) and agriculture product (output). When used in this way the term is, strictly speaking, a water use *index*. Water use efficiency is also often used to express the effectiveness of irrigation water delivery and use.

Hillel (2000) the term efficiency is used to quantify the relative output obtainable from a given input. Referring to the use of water in irrigation, efficiency may be defined in various ways, depending on the nature of the inputs and outputs to be considered. Water use efficiency may be combined in a single concept, the *overall agronomic efficiency of water use*, F_{ag}: $F_{ag} = P/U$

where P is crop production (total dry matter or the marketable product, as the case may be) and U is the volume of water applied. As only a fraction of the applied water is actually absorbed and utilized by the crop.

ENGINEERING TECHNIQUES FOR INCREASING WATER USE EFFICIENCY UNDER ARID ZONES CONDITIONS

Zero and Minimum Tillage

No-till is sowing a crop without prior cultivation and with very little soil disturbance at seeding. The term minimum tillage is confusing as it can mean all of these things except multiple tillage and therefore it should be dropped. Conservation tillage such as no-till and zero-till are promoted by WANTFA as these seeding systems have the least amount of soil disturbance and the greatest soil cover remaining from previous crop residues. Alongside other factors, degradation of the natural resource-base as a result of intensive farming and inappropriate use of inputs has been widely documented as the root-cause of the problem (Hira, 2009). This has compelled many agricultural scientists and policy makers to look toward a more sustainable path of cereal production viz., conservation agriculture (CA) and the associated resource conservation technologies (RCTs) (Chauhan et al., 2012). The CA technology ensemble is based on principles of minimal soil disturbances, residue retention, rational crop rotations, and controlled traffic, while the term RCT covers all farming practices/technologies that facilitate conservation and enhancement of resource use efficiency in farming (FAO, 2010). The CA alternatives are often heralded as more sustainable than the conventional tillage practices, leading to a paradigm shift in tillage and land preparation options, while helping farmers reduce the cost of production. Examples for CA-based RCTs include zero tillage (ZT) in wheat and direct seeding in rice in South Asia (Erenstein and Laxmi, 2008). The key machinery component of the ZT technology is a tractor drawn seed drill that allows the seeds to be sown directly in the un ploughed fields with a single pass of tractor, often with simultaneous basal fertilizer application. The present study aims to examine the on-farm economic impacts of ZT adoption in wheat cultivation.

No-till or zero till is an important element in the CA framework, which has been adopted across more than 100 million hectares worldwide (Derpsch et al., 2010). In this practice, seeds are placed directly in the untilled soil that has retained crop or cover crop residues from the previous season, with minimum soil disturbance. It is also known as direct seeding and direct drilling (Derpsch et al., 2011). Conservation tillage is another term commonly used in this context to describe a number of tillage options that result in reduced soil disturbance, which include no-tillage or ZT, minimum tillage and/or ridge tillage. On the other hand, conventional tillage (CT) implies all other land preparation practices that typically involve "intensive tillage with multiple passes of the tractor to accomplish ploughing, harrowing, planking and seeding operations" (Erenstein and Laxmi, 2008).

On the other hand, machineries used for CT vary across the cropping systems, from bullock-drawn wooden ploughs to tractor-drawn iron harrows and motivators. The details of the different types of machinery used for CT and their rate of adoption in Haryana and the rest of the Indo-Gangetic Plains "IGP" are given by Krishna et al. (2012a). Around the world, conservation tillage practices have been shown to result in sustainable farming in diversified agricultural environments (Reicosky and Saxton, 2007). Several studies conducted across the production systems of South Asia have revealed the potential benefits of CA-based crop management practices in resource conservation, input use efficiency, reduced consumption of fossil fuels, productivity enhancement and production cost-savings, lower weed infestation, soil health improvement, and better climate adaptability (Gathala et al., 2013). The positive farm profitability effect of ZT wheat adoption in India is estimated to be to the tune of US$96 per hectare, which can be decomposed into (i) production cost-savings and (ii) yield increase, with limited spillover effect in the subsequent rice crop (Erenstein and Laxmi, 2008).

Laser Land Leveling

Jat, et. al. (2006) indicated that land leveling is done to enhance use efficiency of water and fertilizer nutrients, and to improve the crop stand and yields. However in the initial years crop yields at times are adversely affected, that can be avoided if some of the relevant conditions described below are taken into considerations. Level maintenance: With appropriate tillage practices, Fertilizer needs of cut areas: Cut areas require additional nutrition. Compound fertilizer (N and P) can be applied at around 50-100 kg/ha Subsoil considerations: Make sure that exposed subsoil is not problematic (acidity, salinity, sodicity, higher percolation rate, etc.) while going for heavy cuts, Efficiency: Identify higher and lower level grades in the field to minimize soil movement, Operator's skill: Efficient land leveling depends on operator's skill and experience.

Traditionally farmers level their fields using animal drawn or tractor-drawn levelers (Fig. 4.1). These levelers are implements consisting of a blade acting as a small bucket for shifting the soil from higher to the low-lying positions. It is seen that even the best leveled fields using traditional land leveling practices are not precisely leveled (Fig. 4.2) and this leads to uneven distribution of irrigation water. The common practices of irrigation in intensively cultivated irrigated areas are flood basin and check basin irrigation systems. These practices on traditionally leveled or unleveled lands lead to water logging conditions in low-lying areas and soil water deficit at higher spots (Fig. 4.3). Significant amounts (10-25%) of irrigation water is lost during application at the farm due to poor management and uneven fields (Fig. 4.4) (Kahlown et al. 2000).

Benefits of Laser land leveling: (1) *Saving in irrigation water:* A significant reduction in total water use in wheat as well as rice was recorded due to precision land leveling compared to traditional land leveling.

Fig. 4.1 (a): Traditional Method of Land Leveling Using Animal-drawn Wooden Log. (b) Mechanised Land Leveling Using Tractor-drawn Planker

Fig. 4.2: Water Logging in a Wheat Field

Fig. 4.3: Non-uniform Crop Stand in an Undulated Field

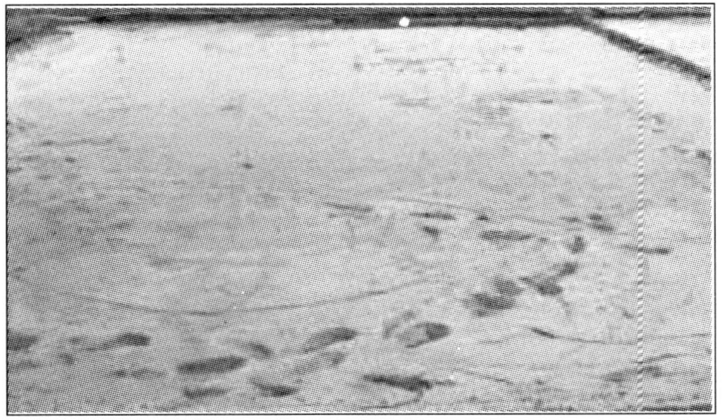

Fig. 4.4: Uneven Distribution of Irrigation Water Under Traditional Land Leveling

The total water use in wheat and rice in laser leveled field was reduced to 49.5% and 31.7%, respectively (Jat et al. 2003). The estimated total water use of wheat crop was 5270 m^3 ha^{-1} and 3525 m^3 ha^{-1} in traditionally leveled field and laser leveled fields respectively (Fig. 4.5). In raised bed planted wheat, about 26% water can be saved through laser land leveling (Fig. 4.6). In rice, total water use was estimated as 6950 m3 ha-1 and 9150 m3 ha-1 under precision land leveling and traditional land leveling respectively (Figs. 4.7, 4.8). From other on-farm investigations on wheat in villages Masauta and Lakhan, 338 to 808 m^3 ha^{-1} saving in total water use was found (Rajput & Patel, 2003). Studies conducted by RWC and PDCSR, Modipuram at the 71 farmers' fields of western Uttar Pradesh revealed that more than 61 farmers saved about 5-10 ha-cm water in wheat crop and about 10-15 ha-cm water in transplanted rice crop. Tyagi (1984) reported the application depth values of 3.9 and 9.7 cm at leveling index (LI) of 0.75 cm. and 6.75 cm, respectively in wheat crop under sodic soils of Haryana. Further, the distribution efficiency obtained with various depths of application (4 to 12 cm) showed that distribution was more uniform (> 90%) in plots with an average LI of 0.75 cm and poor (< 50%) in plots with an average LI of 6.75 cm. However, with increasing depth of water application, the distribution improved in poorly leveled plots as well. *(2) Improvement in irrigation efficiency:* The foremost objective of laser land leveling is to improve application and distribution efficiencies of irrigation which ultimately leads to higher water productivity (fig. 4.9). The distribution efficiency of applied. (3) *Enhancement of water productivity:* In an on-station investigation at PDCSR, Modipuram, a significant reduction in water use, and marked improvement in water productivity in rice-wheat cropping system was recorded due to precision land leveling compared to traditional leveling. It was recorded (Jat et al. 2005) that with similar fertility levels and land configurations, the water productivity of rice and wheat increased from 0.55 and 0.82 to 0.91 and 1.31 kg grain m-3 water, respectively. Raised bed planting further improved the productivity of wheat in laser leveled fields (Fig. 4.10).

Appling Surge Irrigation Technique with Developed Surface Irrigation

Surface irrigation is the most common executed irrigation system in Egypt as well as world wide. This wide spread implementation might be due to its low capital cost, no special technical experience regarding operation and maintenance is needed and no specific equipment are required as well as the long practical background among local farmers regarding usage of such system. On the other hand, surface irrigation among other methods has the lowest irrigation efficiency. Deep percolation particularly in the upper part of the irrigated field as well as the less-uniformity of irrigation water above soil surface are the main causes of the lower efficiency of surface irrigation.

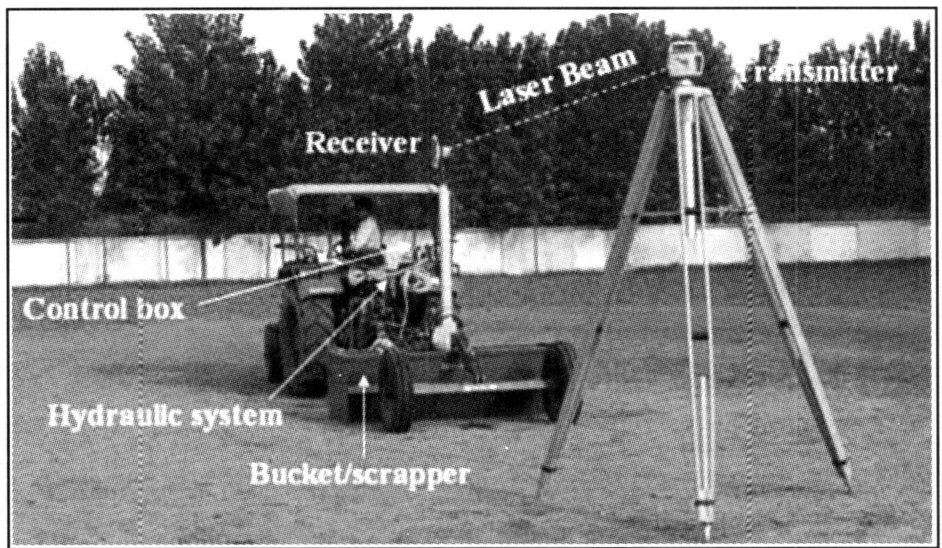

Fig. 4.5: Functioning of Laser Land Leveler

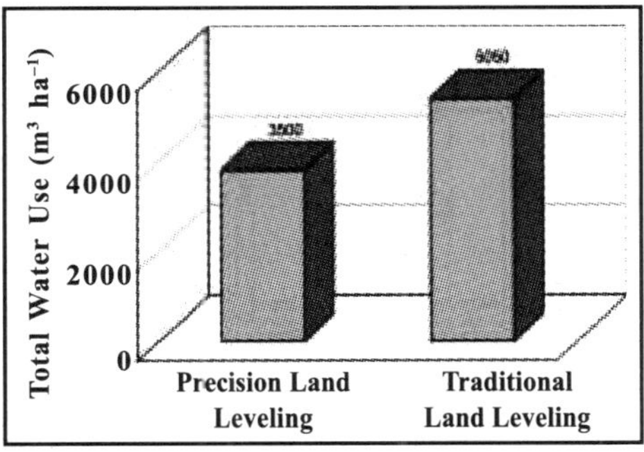

Fig. 4.6: Total Water Use (m^3 ha^{-1}) in Wheat Under Precision and Traditional Land Leveling

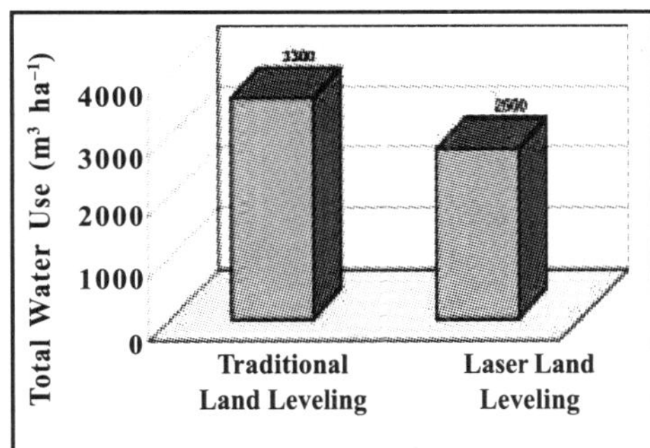

Fig. 4.7: Effect of Laser Land Leveling on Total Water Use (m^3 ha^{-1}) in Raised Bed Planted Wheat

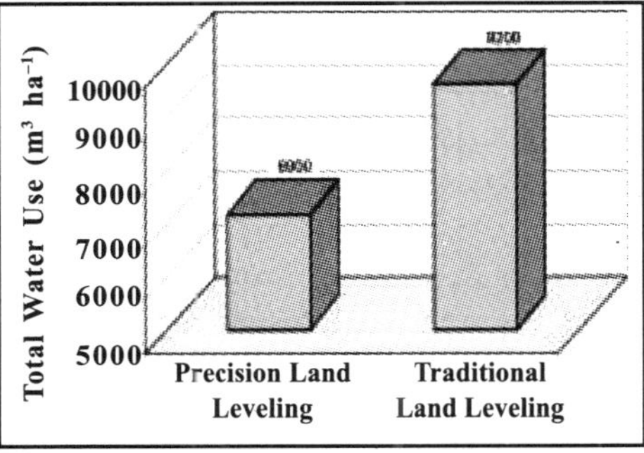

Fig. 4.8: Effect of Land Leveling on Water Use (m^3 ha^{-1}) of Rice in a Sandy Loam Soil

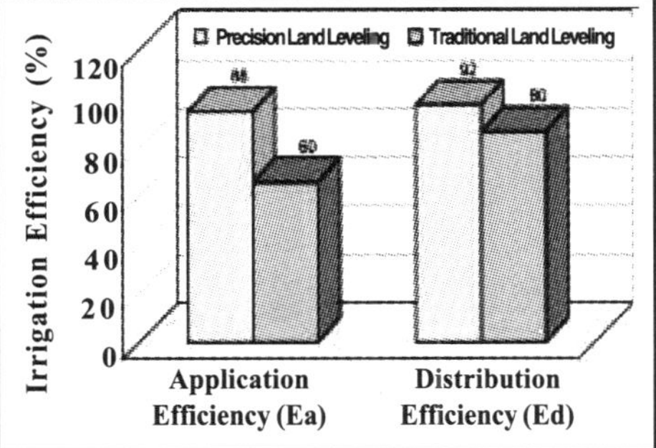

Fig. 4.9: Effect of Land Leveling on Irrigation Efficiencies in Wheat

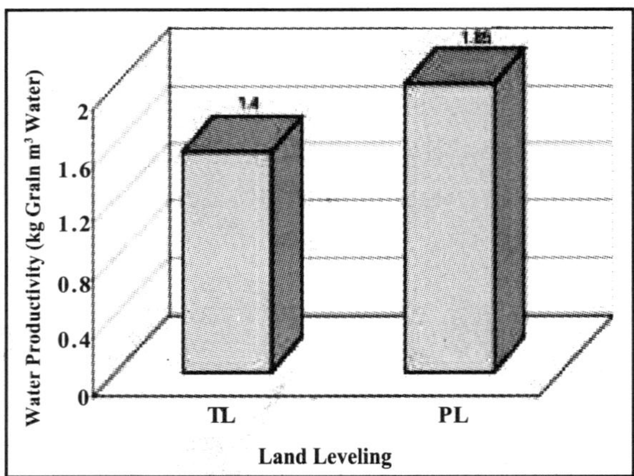

Fig. 4.10: Effect of Laser Leveling on Water Productivity of Raised Bed Planted Wheat

(PL: Precision Leveling and TL: Traditional Leveling)

In average, losses of irrigation water under this method is about 45% causing several acute problems such as leaching of nutrient elements and raising of water table. Consequently, reduction in crop yield, crop-water and/or fertilizer productivity could be predicted. Therefore, tremendous efforts should be implemented to minimizing water losses in irrigated agriculture particularly under surface irrigation system. Among these ways; preparing good seedbed environment, good leveling of soil surface with proper slope using laser technique, tail water reuse, cut-back irrigation(surge irrigation) as well as alternative or one by one furrow irrigation as shown in (fig. 4.11). However, improving the performance of surface irrigation should be economical, practical or even desirable (Ibrahim and Emara, 2010).

Matter (2001) studied the effect of surge furrow irrigation compared with continues irrigation on water management at different ploughing methods, showed that, surge flow treatments required less time for completion the advance phase than with those continuous flow treatments at different ploughing treatments. Surface irrigation using furrow is the most widely used irrigation method in the clay soil. Studies done at the Malheur Experiment Station and elsewhere have shown significant benefits to surge irrigation: (1) More uniform application of irrigation water (2) Reduced water use through reductions in deep percolation and runoff (3) Reduced costs through reductions in water use and labor (4) Reduced nitrogen leaching (5) Reduced sediment loss (6) Reduced surface water contamination (Shock and Welch, 2011). Surged water advances to the end of the field at least as rapidly as continuous flow irrigation with the same inflow rates but with a smaller volume of water, thus greatly improving the uniformity of application during the advance phase.

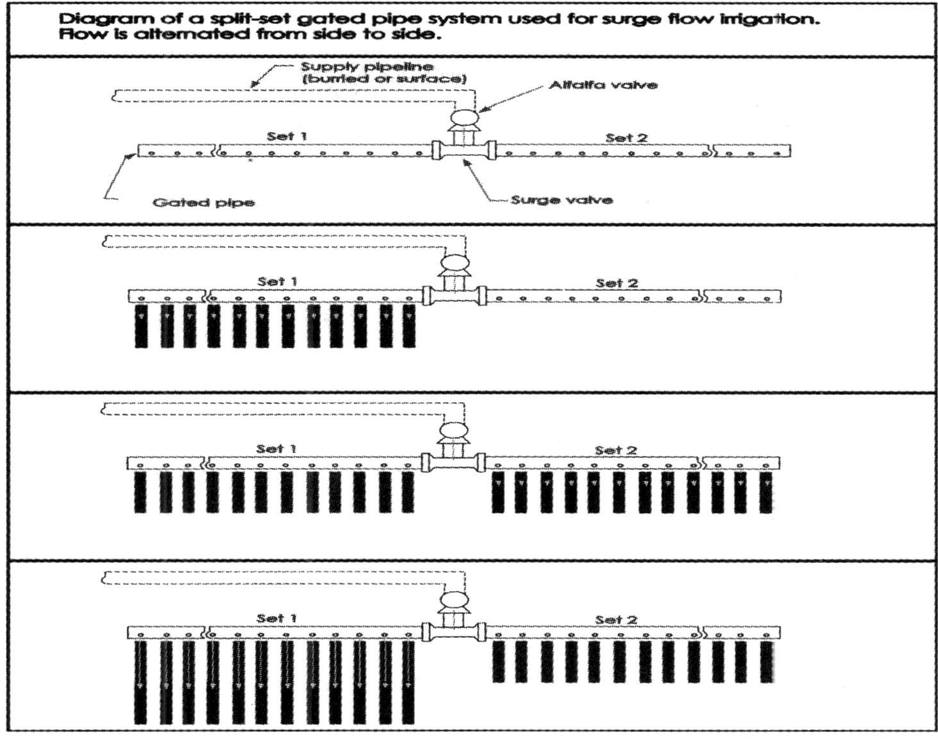

Fig. 4.11: Cut-back Irrigation or Surge Irrigation of Furrow Irrigation

Surge irrigation is one of the famous methods in irrigation management and has been studied in many articles, which some of them will be described in the following. Mostafazadeh-Fard *et al.* (2006) developed and evaluated an automatic surge irrigation system in furrow irrigation. The results showed that the system was able to accurately and automatically irrigate the furrows by surge method based on information were given to the system. For the same discharge and volume of water applied to the furrows the water advance along the furrows were faster for surge flow as compared to the continuous flow. Valipour and Montazar (2012) determined number of required observation data for rainfall forecasting to agricultural water management. Sial *et al.* (2006) studied performance of surge irrigation under borders. Keeping in view different parameters like volume of water, distribution uniformity, application efficiency, deep percolation losses and yield of wheat, the surge mode of irrigation was convincingly better compared with conventional/continuous irrigation even under the border irrigation. As shown in (fig. 4.12).

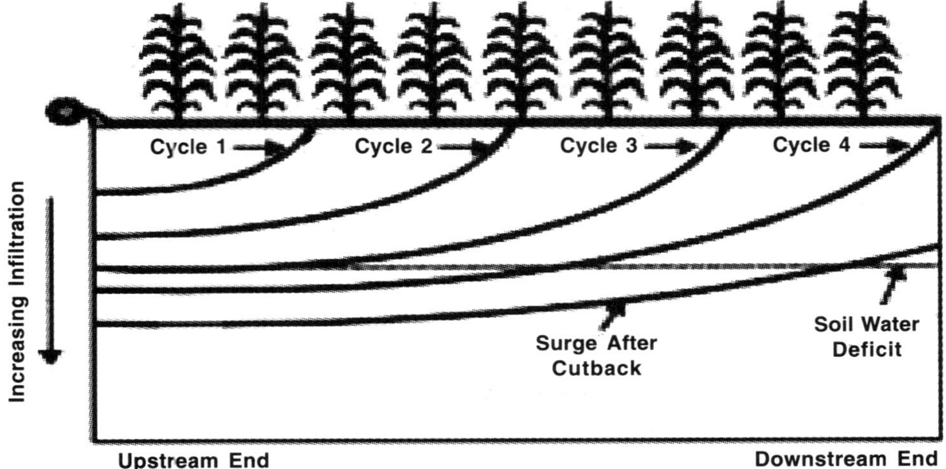

Fig. 4.12: The Positive Effect of Surge Irrigation Technique

Modern Techniques with Drip Irrigation System

New Designs

Abdelraouf, (2014 a) reported that maximizing irrigation water use efficiency is a common concept should be used in Egypt due to limited water resources. The performance of new design for drip irrigation system compared with two traditional designs to maximize water and fertilizers use efficiency under desert environment conditions. (1) Design 1: drip irrigation system (control), (2) Design 2: drip irrigation system with PRD technique (partial root drying; one emitter will irrigate one part of the root system and emitters of other lateral will irrigate other half of root system) with the same direction for main lines and laterals and (3) New design: drip irrigation system with PRD technique with opposite direction for main lines and laterals. The following parameters were studied to evaluate the effect of different irrigation methods on (1) emission uniformity, (2) soil moisture distribution (3) application efficiency (4) Growth characteristics of maize plant (5) yield of maize (6) irrigation water use efficiency of maize "$IWUE_{maize}$". (7) economical evaluation. Statistical analysis indicated that the maximum values of growth, yield, $IWUE_{maize}$ and total income were detected under new design of drip irrigation system with PRD technique with opposite direction for manifolds lines and laterals. Fig. 4.13 indicated the impact of new design on average of emitters discharge along laterals and (figs. 4.14, 4.15 and 4.16) Soil moisture distribution along laterals under three designs.

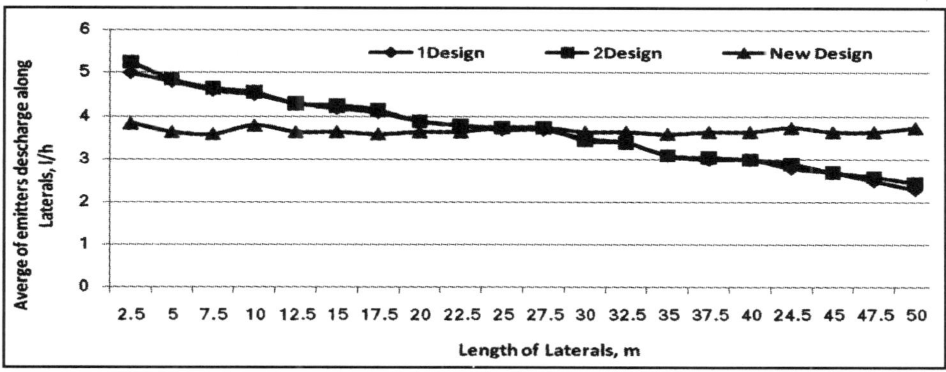

Fig. 4.13: The Impact of New Design on Average of Emitters Discharge Along Laterals

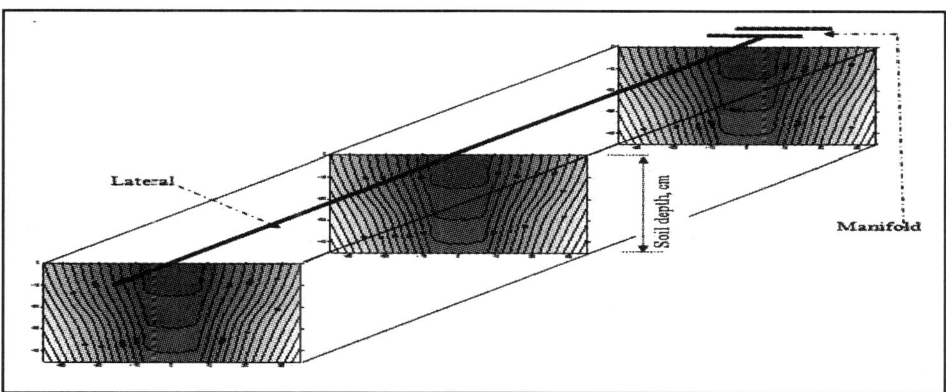

Fig. 4.14: Soil Moisture Distribution Along Laterals Under Design 1 [Drip Irrigation System (control)]

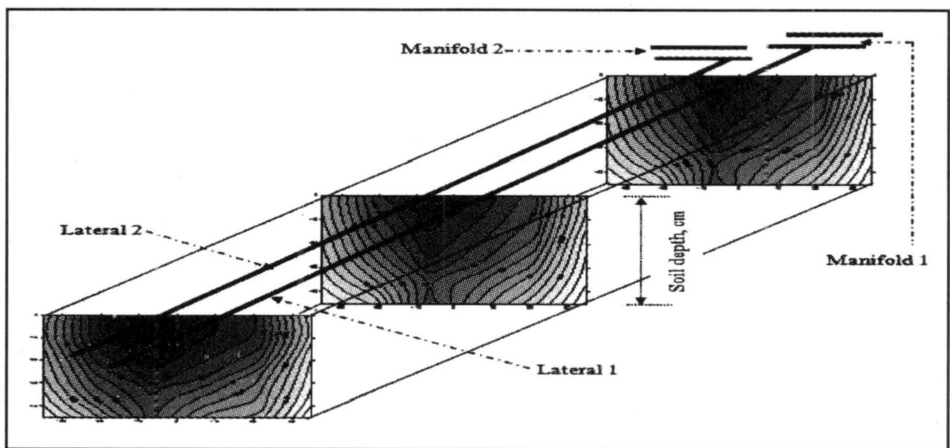

Fig. 4.15: Soil Moisture Distribution Along Laterals Under Design 2 (Drip Irrigation System with PRD Technique with the Same Direction for Manifolds and Laterals)

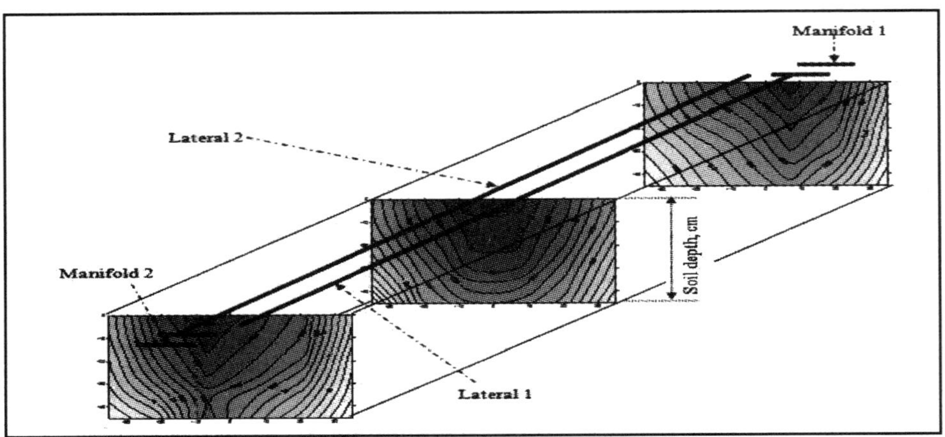

Fig. 4.16: Soil Moisture Distribution Along Laterals Under New Design (Drip Irrigation System with PRD Technique with Opposite Direction for Manifolds and Laterals)

Pulse Irrigation

Pulsing irrigation refer to the practice of irrigating for a short period then waiting for another short period, and repeating this on-off cycle until the entire irrigation water is applied (Eric *et al.*, 2004). Where drip irrigation is used, you may need to irrigate more than once a day to meet peak water requirements. If the drip system drains out after each irrigation, break the irrigation down into the longest pulses possible to reduce losses to drainage. Redesign the irrigation system if the wetted area is too small (limiting) and pulsing is not an option (Helen, 2007). Based on reports from other states (where soil types are different), it is often believed that the size of the wetted zone can be increased if irrigation is pulsed (Eric *et al.*, 2004). For most crops, the soil in the root zone should be kept near field capacity at all times. This means that irrigation should be frequent, and the amount of water applied each time should be equal to the amount used by the plants since the last irrigation. In general, short irrigation cycles with high application rates help promote lateral movement of water, resulting in better wetting patterns for light soils. "Pulse irrigation," where the system is operated several times a day for short durations, can further widen the wetted pattern. Long duration at a low application rate results in better infiltration of water in heavy (high clay content) soils. Irrigation frequency is one of the most important factors in drip irrigation scheduling. Due to the differences in soil moisture and wetting pattern, crop yields may be different when the same quantity of water is applied under different irrigation frequencies. Irrigation frequency might provide desirable conditions for water movement in soil and for uptake by roots (Segal *et al.*, 2000).

Applying irrigation water in stages or pulses rather than all at one time can save water by giving the media time to moisten from the first pulse of water thereby allowing it to absorb subsequent irrigation more readily and reducing the total amount of water required. (Scott, 2000). The benefits of pulse irrigation method, such as reducing surface soil water evaporation, decreasing fertilizers leaching, enhancing yield and so on, have been documented by different researchers. Drip irrigation with over irrigation, valuable nutrients may be leached out of the root zone and become unavailable for the plants, while contaminating the groundwater (Zin El-Abedin, 2006). Total potato tuber yield was highest for the Soil Water Balance scheduling method. Irrigation frequency influenced yield differently for the different scheduling methods. Tuber relative density was improved by pulse irrigation (Steyn *et al.*, 2005).

Abdelraouf (2009) stated that pulse drip irrigation technique has many positive effects. The most important results could be summarized as follow: (1) Moisture content in the root zone and wetted soil volume (more than or equal 100% of field capacity) in root zone increased by increasing number of irrigation pulses and this is maybe due to increasing number of pulses cause increasing in water movement in horizontal direction than vertical direction. Not only soil moisture content in the root zone increased by increasing number of pulses but also pulse technique made enhancement in soil moisture distribution inside root zone and increased from wetted soil volume (more than or equal 100% of field capacity) "$WSV_{>100\%FC}$". The best conditions were determined according to the highest values of $WSV_{>100\%FC}$. Where increasing in $WSV_{>100\%FC}$ means increasing in volume of available water in root zone as shown in (fig. 4.17) compared with control treatment in (fig. 4.18) (2) Application efficiency increased from 89% under continuous drip irrigation to maximum value where it become 94% after applying pulse technique with 4 pulses under surface drip irrigation, recording an increase of 5.3%. (3) Clogging ratio of emitters decreased from 9.79% under continuous drip irrigation to minimum value, where it become 5.38% after applying pulse technique on 4 pulses under surface drip irrigation, recording a decrease 45%. (4) Emission uniformity increased from 85.02% under continuous drip irrigation to maximum value, where it become 90.48 % after applying pulse technique on 4 pulses under surface drip irrigation, recording an increase 6.4%. (5) Yield of potato increased from 4.70 (ton/fed.) under continuous drip irrigation to maximum value, where it become 6.57 (ton/fed.) after applying pulse technique with 4 pulses under subsurface drip irrigation, recording an increase 40% (6) To get maximum yield, best quality characters of potato tuber and net income, we must apply pulse technique on 4 pulses under subsurface drip irrigation.

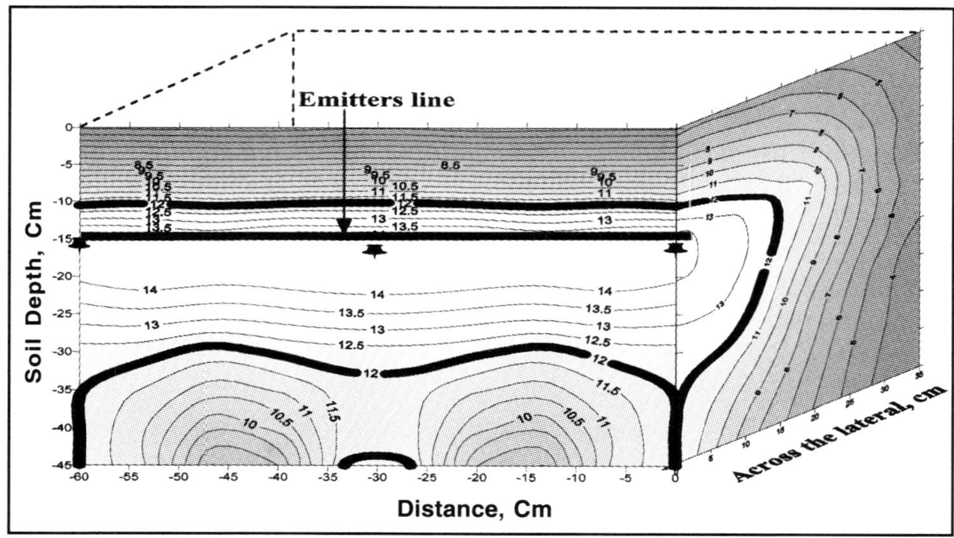

Fig. 4.17: Three Dimensional Soil Moisture Distribution and Wetted Soil Volume (More than or Equal 100% of Field Capacity) for Sandy Soil Under Subsurface Drip Irrigation at 100% from Peak Actual Water Requirements on 4 Pulses

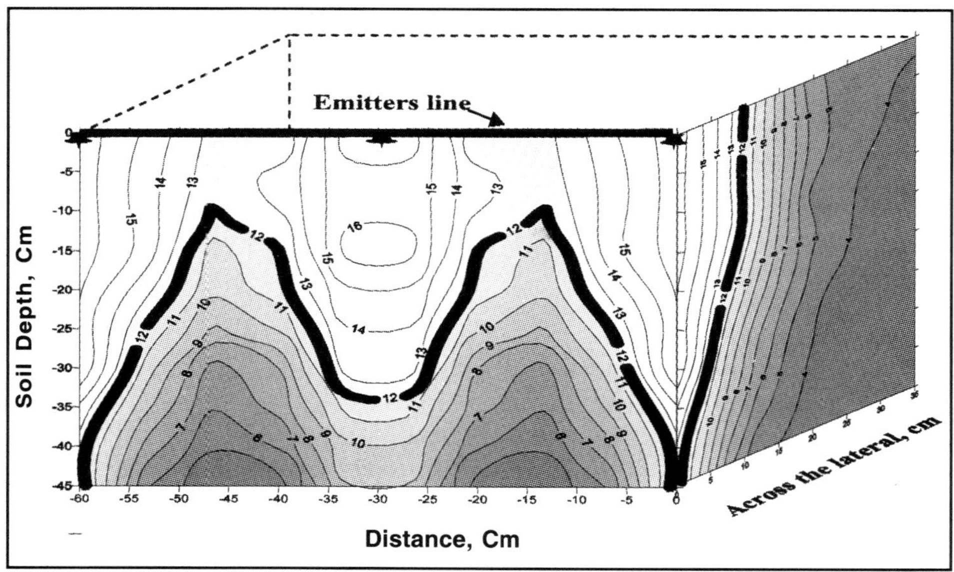

Fig. 4.18: Three Dimensional Soil Moisture Distribution and Wetted Soil Volume (More than or Equal 100% of Field Capacity) for Sandy Soil Under Surface Drip Irrigation at 100% from Peak Actual Water Requirements Under Continuous Drip

Using Irregular Volumetric Distribution of Compost Along Laterals

Abdelraouf, (2014 b) stated that, Egypt is one of the countries facing great challenges due to its limited water resources represented mainly by its fixed share of the Nile water and its aridity as a general characteristic. So, we had to innovate any technique to increase from water use efficiency on farm to achieve this goal, two field experiments were carried out during growing seasons 2012 and 2013, it executed in Research Farm of National Research Center (NRC) in EL-NUBARYA region, Egypt to study the effect of new engineering method for irregular volumetric distribution ratios of compost under reduction of emission uniformity on yield and water use efficiency of maize crop (Zea mays-L, HF-10 Varity). Study factors were irregular volumetric distribution ratios of compost on four zones along lateral were [D1= (25%, 25%, 25%, 25% compost), D2= (20%, 20%, 25%, 35% compost), D3= (15%, 15%, 30%, 40 compost) and D4= (10%, 10%, 35%, 45% compost)] under reduction of emission uniformity and emitter discharge along lateral, EU [EU1= 90%, EU2 = 80%, and EU3 = 70%]. The following parameters were studied to evaluate the effect of study factors on: (1) Application efficiency along lateral. (2) Water stress along lateral (3) Yield of maize, (4) Irrigation water use efficiency of maize "IWUE maize. Statistical analysis of the effect of irregular volumetric distribution ratios of compost on along laterals under reduction of emission uniformity indicated that, maximum values of yield and irrigation water use efficiency of maize were obtained under D1, D2 with EU1and D2 appropriate with EU2 and D3 appropriate with EU3. Fig. 4.19 represented the Irregular volumetric distribution ratios of compost on four zones along laterals and (fig. 4.20 represented the impact of D1, D2 and D3 under EU1, EU2 and EU3 on irrigation water use efficiency of maize.

Importance of Deficit Irrigation Concept and Partial Root Drying Irrigation

Deficit Irrigation

The manager needs to know the level of transpiration deficiency allowable without significant reduction in crop yields. The main objective of deficit irrigation is to increase the WUE of a crop by eliminating irrigations that have little impact on yield. Before implementing a deficit irrigation programme, it is necessary to know crop yield responses to water stress, (Kirda and Kanber, 1999). Agronomic measures such as varying tillage practices, mulching and anti-transpirants can reduce the demand for irrigation water. Another option is deficit irrigation, with plants exposed to certain levels of water stress during either a particular growth period or throughout the whole growth season, without significant reduction in yields. Much published research has evaluated the feasibility of deficit irrigation and whether significant savings in irrigation water are possible without significant yield penalties. Stegman (1982) reported that the yield of maize, sprinkler irrigated to induce a 30-40 percent depletion of available water between irrigations, was not statistically different from the yield obtained with trickle irrigation maintaining near zero water potential in the root zone.

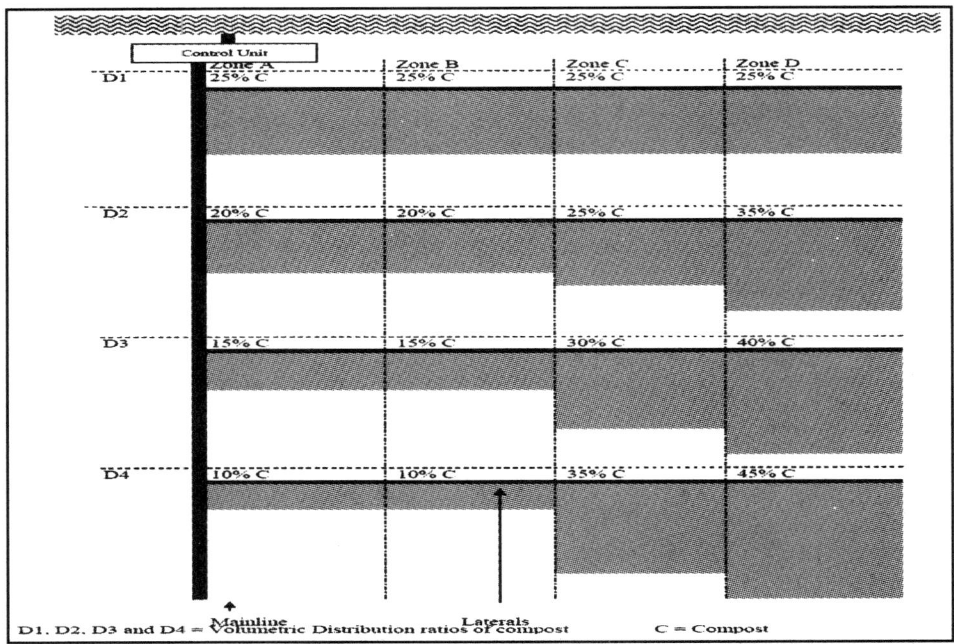

Fig. 4.19: Irregular Volumetric Distribution Ratios of Compost on Four Zones Along Laterals

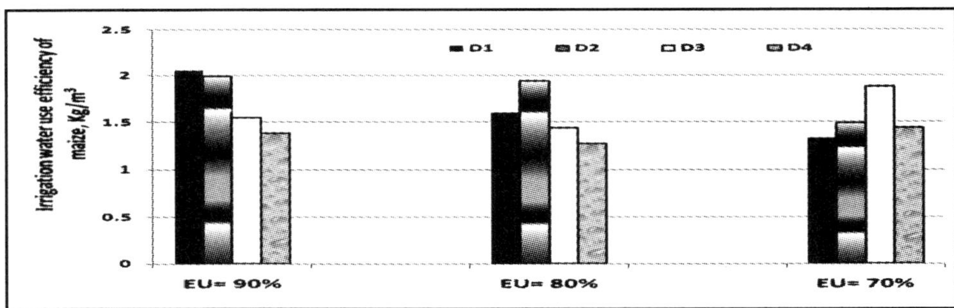

Fig. 4.20: Effect of Volumetric Distribution Ratios of Compost on Irrigation Water Use Efficiency of Maize Under 90%, 80% and 70% Emission Uniformity

Furthermore, yield reductions from disease and pests, losses during harvest and storage, and arising from insufficient applications of fertilizer are much greater than reductions in yields expected from deficit irrigation. On the other hand, deficit irrigation, where properly practiced, may increase crop quality. For example, the protein content and baking quality of wheat, the length and strength of cotton fibres, and the sucrose concentration of sugar beet and grape all increase under deficit irrigation. The resulting yield reduction may be small compared with the benefits gained through diverting the saved water to irrigate other crops for which water would normally be insufficient under traditional irrigation practices. The proper application of deficit irrigation practices can generate significant savings in irrigation water allocation. Among field crops, groundnut, soybean, common bean and sugar cane show proportionately less yield reduction than the relative evapotraspiration deficit imposed at certain growth stages. Crops such as cotton, maize, wheat, sunflower, sugar beet and potato are well suited for deficit irrigation applied either throughout the growing season or at pre-determined growth stages. For example, deficit irrigation imposed during flowering and boll formation stages in cotton, during vegetative growth of soybean, flowering and grain filling stages of wheat, vegetative and yielding stages of sunflower and sugar beet will provide acceptable and feasible irrigation options for minimal yield reductions with limited supplies of irrigation water. This work may provide guidelines for practicing deficit irrigation for identifying likely growth stages for imposing reduced ET, and for assessing the economic feasibility and acceptability of deficit irrigation through the estimation of expected relative yield decreases. (FAO, 2002). Irrigators can respond to limited water supplies by: (1) reducing water applications to the same crop and incurring water deficits during all or part of the growing season, (2) growing crops that match the water supply, (3) growing the same crop on a reduced area in combination with irrigated crops that have smaller water use requirements, or (4) reducing the irrigated area and substituting dry land crops or fallow periods (Klocke et al., 2006).

Smith and Kivumbi, (2002) reported that, Dwindling water resources and increasing food requirements require greater efficiency in water use, both in rainfed and in irrigated agriculture. Regulated deficit irrigation provides a means of reducing water consumption while minimizing adverse effects on yield. Models can play a useful role in developing practical recommendations for optimizing crop production under conditions of scarce water supply. To assess the applicability of the FAO CROPWAT model for deficit irrigation scheduling, a study utilized data provided in studies from a joint FAO/IAEA coordinated research project (CRP) on "The use of nuclear and related techniques in assessment of irrigation schedules of field crops to increase effective use of water in irrigation projects," Stress conditions in the root zone are defined by the critical soil water content, expressed as the fraction of total available soil water between field capacity and wilting point that is readily available for crop transpiration, and characterizes a soil moisture condition in which crop transpiration is not limited by any flow restrictions in the root zone. The critical soil water content varies for different crops and different crop stages and is determined by the rooting density characteristics of the crop, evaporation rate and, to some extent, by the soil type FAO (1998) as shown in (fig. 4.21). Optimal irrigation, i.e. no stress, was applied by allowing depletion to 60 percent of total available soil moisture. Fig. 4.22 represents the soil water balance for optimal irrigation of cotton in Turkey (eight irrigation applications). The cotton crop was subjected to deficit irrigation by imposing water stress in one or more growth stages. This was achieved by adapting the full irrigation treatment to achieve water stress in the specific stages of growth. Fig. 4.23 shows an example where water stress was imposed on the cotton crop during flowering. In the various treatments, irrigation was withheld until the water content was depleted to 20 percent of total available soil moisture. Stress applied in the flowering stage resulted in irrigation on days 75, 92, and 111 after sowing.

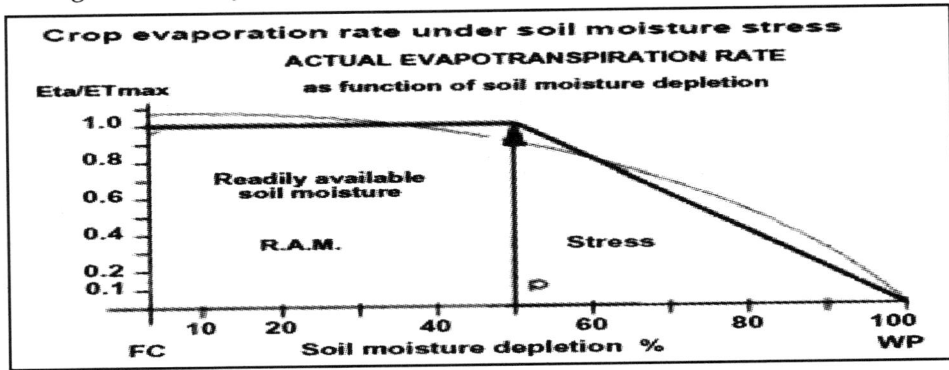

Fig. 4.21: Crop Evaporation Rate Under Different Allowable Soil Moisture Depletion

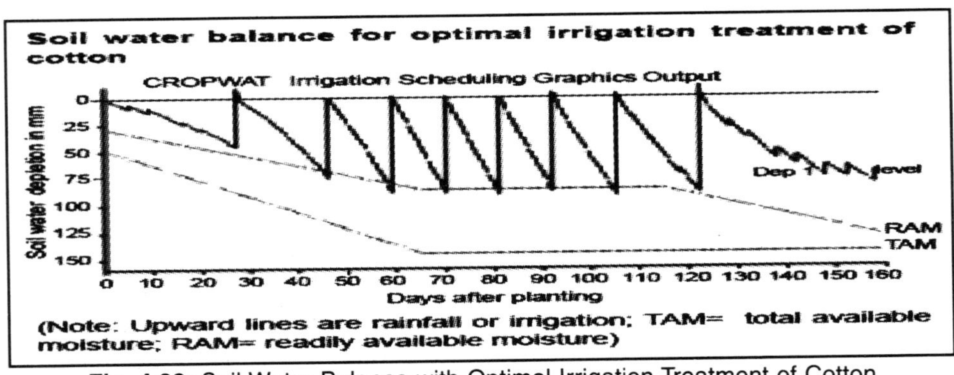

Fig. 4.22: Soil Water Balance with Optimal Irrigation Treatment of Cotton

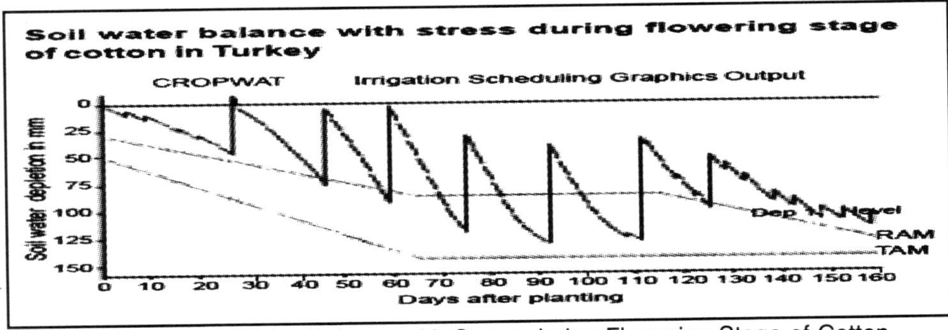

Fig. 4.23: Soil Water Balance with Stress during Flowering Stage of Cotton

Partial Root Drying Irrigation

Full irrigation (FI) is used by farmers in non-limited or even water-limited areas. In this method, crops receive full evapotranspiration requirements to result the maximum yield. Nowadays, full irrigation is considered a luxury use of water that can be reduced with minor or no effect on profitable yield (Kang and Zhang, 2004). Water-saving irrigations are used to improve the water productivity (WP) in recent years. Deficit irrigation (DI) and partial root-zone drying irrigation (PRD) are the water-saving irrigation methods that cut down irrigation amounts of full irrigation to crops. The amounts of irrigation reduction is crop-dependent and generally accompanied by no or minor yield loss that increases the water productivity (Ahmadi et al., 2010b). Partial root-zone drying (PRD) is a modified form of deficit irrigation (DI) (English et al., 1990), which involves irrigating only one part of the root zone in each irrigation event, leaving another part to dry to certain soil water content before rewetting by shifting irrigation to the dry side; therefore, PRD is a novel irrigation strategy since half of the roots is placed in drying soil and the other half is growing in irrigated soil (Ahmadi et al., 2010a). Schematic diagram of FI, DI and PRD are shown in (fig. 4.24). (Davies and Hartung, 2004).

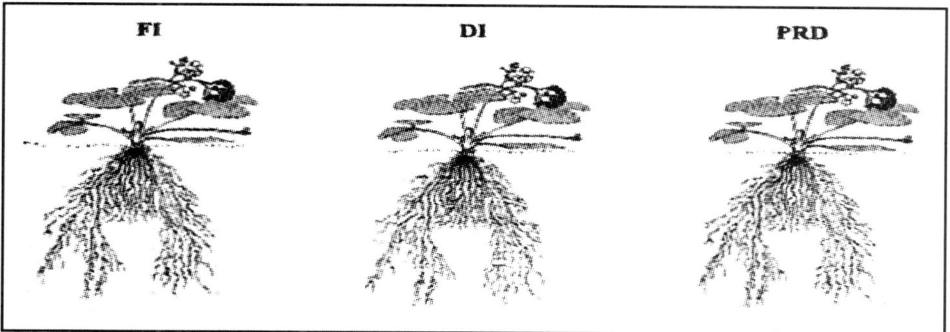

Fig. 4.24: Schematic of the Irrigation Pattern in FI, DI, and PRD (After Davies and Hartung, 2004)

Wetting and drying each side of roots are dependent on crops, growing stage, evaporative demands, soil texture and soil water balance (Saeed et al., 2008). Yet there is little understanding on mechanism of PRD effects on crop growth, therefore, no definite solid procedure exist on determining the optimum timing of irrigation for each side. Kriedmann and Goodwin (2003) indicated that when soil water extraction from dry side is negligible, wetting should be changed from irrigated side to non-irrigated side. Furthermore, Liu et al. (2008) stated that switching should be based on threshold soil water content in which the maximum xylem abscisic acid (ABA) concentration is produced. ABA is a plant hormone that is produced in the roots in drying soils and is transported by water flow in xylem to the shoot for regulating the shoot physiology (Kang and Zhang, 2004). Therefore, in PRD roots sense the soil drying and induce ABA that reduce leaf expansion and stomatal conductance and simultaneously the roots in wet soil absorb sufficient water to maintain a high water status in shoot (Ahmadi et al., 2010a). Practical results showed that crops under PRD yielded better than under DI when the same amount of water is applied. This resulted in higher water productivity (WP) and even better fruit quality (Shahnazari et al., 2007).

Alternate-furrow irrigation consists of irrigating every other furrow of a field while leaving the off furrow dry. Several investigators studied alternate-furrow irrigation in the 1960s and early 1970s with much the same results: water was saved as compared to every furrow irrigation and yield was usually, but not always, unaffected. Fig. 4.25 represented the layout of alternate-furrow irrigation technique for two field experiments were executed at Gemmiza Agricultural Research Station during 2003/ 2004 and 2004/2005 seasons in clay soil to find out the extent to which alternate-furrow irrigation technique and distance between seedlings affected yield of onion crop and water utilization and from the obtained results was volumes of applied water under alternate-furrow irrigation (AFI) treatments were reduced in comparison with those under every- furrow irrigation, and these results were true in the two seasons of study (El- Sharkawy, 2006).

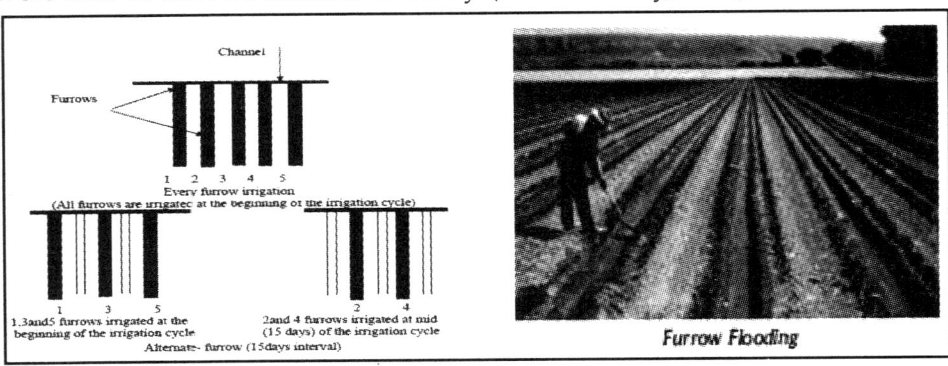

Fig. 4.25: Layout of Alternate-furrow Irrigation Technique

Ying Hua and ShoaZhong (2000) stated that alternate- furrow irrigation (AFI) compared with conventional furrow irrigation (CFI), decreased deep percolation of irrigation water, decreased evapotranspiration rate and increased evapotranspiration efficiency for maize crop, Abdel–Maksoud et al. (2002) found that significant reductions in applied water due to the alternate-furrow irrigation at 7 and 14 days interval and water saving were about 8% and 30%, respectively, comparable to common furrow irrigation. Moreover, alternate- furrow irrigation at 14 days interval seems to decrease the yield insignificantly, whereas, under alternate- furrow at 7 days interval, the figure was increased by 14.5%, as compared with every- furrow irrigation.

The authors also found that water utilization efficiency (WUtE) values were improved under alternate- furrow irrigation, either at 7 or 14 days interval compared to every furrow irrigation.

REFERENCES

Abdel-Maksoud, H.H.; S.A. Othman and A.Y. El-Tawil (2002): Improving Water and N-use Utilization for Field Crops via Alternate Furrow Irrigation Technique 1-Maize crop. J.of Agric. Sci., Mansoura Univ., 27(12): 8761-8769.

Abdelraouf, R.E.(2009): Study the Performance of Pulse Drip Irrigation in Organic Agriculture for Potato Crop in Sandy Soils. Ph.D. Thesis. Department of Agricultural Engineering, Faculty of Agriculture, Cairo University, Egypt.

Abdelraouf, R. E. (2014 a): New Design for Drip Irrigation System to Maximize Water and Fertilizers Use Efficiency. Accepted in Middle East Journal of Applied Sciences and will be Published in Vol. 3 No (4), July-Sep. (2014)

Abdelraouf, R.E. (2014 b): New Engineering Method to Improve Water Use Efficiency of Maize Under Drip Irrigation System Using Irregular Volumetric Distribution of Compost along Laterals. Middle East Journal of Agriculture Research, 3(3): 383-394.

Ahmad, S. (1992): Handbook of Sprinkler Irrigation Systems. Water Resources Research Institute National Agricultural Research Centre Islamabad.

Ahmadi, S.H.; M.N. Andersen; F. Plauborg; R.T. Poulsen; C,R. Jensen; A.R. Sepaskhah ands. Hansen (2010a): Effects of Irrigation Strategies and Soils on Field Grown Potatoes: Gas Exchange and Xylem [ABA]. Agri. Water Management, 97: 1486-1494.

Ahmadi, S.H.; M.N.Andersen; F. Plauborg; R.T. Poulsen; C.R. Jensen; A.R. Sepaskhah and S. Hansen (2010b): Effects of Irrigation Strategies and Soils on Field Grown Potatoes: Yield and Water Productivity. Agri. Water Management. DOI 10.1'016/j.agwat.2010.07.007.

Barrett P. and Associates (1999): Determining a Framework, Terms and Definitions for Water Use Efficiency in Irrigation. Report to Land and Water Resources Research and Development Corporation, September 1999. 26p. Land & Water Australia, www.lwa.gov au

Chauhan, B.S.; G. Mahajan; V. Sardana; J. Timsina and M.L. Jat (2012): Productivity and Sustainability of the Rice-wheat Cropping System in the Indo-Gangetic Plains of the Indian Subcontinent: Problems, Opportunities, and Strategies. Adv. Agron. 117, 315-369.

Davies, W.J. and W. Hartung, (2004): Has Extrapolation from Biochemistry to Crop Functioning Worked to Sustain Plant Production Under Water Scarcity? Proceeding of the 4th International Crop Science Congress, Brisbane, Australia, Published on CDROM, Published on CDROM, http://www.cropscience.org.au/icsc2004/.

Derpsch, R.; T. Friedrich; A. Kassam and H. Li (2010): Current Status of Adoption of No Till Farming in the World and Some of its Main Benefits. Int. J. Agric. Biol. Eng. 3 (1), 1-25.

Derpsch, R.; T. Friedrich; J.N. Landers; R. Rainbow, D.C. Reicosky; J.C.M., Sturny; P. Wall; R.C.Ward and K.Weiss (2011): About the Necessity of Adequately Defining No-tillage-a Discussion Paper. In: Proceedings of the 5th World Congress of Conservation Agriculture, Brisbane, Australia, pp. 26-29.

English, M.J; J.T. Musick and V.V.N. Murty (1990): Deficit Irrigation. In: Management of Farm Irrigation Systems (Hoffman, G.J., Howell, T.A., and Solomon, K.H., Editors). ASAE Monograph No. 9. American Society of Agricultural Engineers Publisher, 1020p.

Erenstein, O. and V. Laxmi (2008): Zero Tillage Impacts in India's Rice-wheat Systems: A Review. Soil Till. Res. 100, 1-14.

Eric, S.; S. David and H. Robert (2004): To Pulse or not to Pulse Drip Irrigation that is the Question UF/ IFAS - Horticultural Sciences Department. Florida, USA NFREC-SV-Vegetarian (04-05).

FAO (2002): Deficit Irrigation Practices. ISSN 1020-1203. FAO, Rome. Water Reports 22. pp. 1-23.

FAO (2010): Conservation Agriculture. Website: <http://www.fao.org/ag/ca/>. Fre, R., Grosskopf, S., Lovell, C.A.K., 1994. Production Frontiers. Cambridge University Press, London.

Gathala, M.K.; V. Kumar; P.C. Sharma; Y.S. Saharawat; H.S. Jat; M.Singh; A. Kumar; M.L. Jat; E. Humphreys; D.E. Sharma and J. K. Ladha (2013): Optimizing Intensive Cereal-based Systems Addresssing Current and Future Drivers of Agricultural Change in the Northwestern Indo-Gangetic Plains of India. Agric. Ecosyst. Environ. 177, 85-97.

Helen, R. (2007): Citrus Irrigation. Department of Agriculture and Food, Waroona. State of Western Australia. www. Agric.wa.gov.au

Hernández Navarro M.L. (2002). Frecuencia e intensidad del viento en Zaragoza. Geographicalia, 2ª época. 27: 63-75.

Hillel, D: (2000). Improving Water-use Efficiency, Title: Small-scale Irrigation for Arid Zones: Principles and Options. Produced by: Natural Resources Management and Environment Department.

Hira, G.S., (2009): Water Management in Northern States and the Food Security of India. J. Crop Improv. 23 (2), 136-157.

Ibrahim M.A.M and T.K. Emara (2010): Water Saving Under Alternative Furrows Surface Irrigation in Clay Soils of North Nile Delta. Fourteenth International Water Technology Conference, IWTC 14 2010, Cairo, Egypt.

Jat, M.L.; C. Parvesh; S.K. Raj Gupta and M.A. Gill (2006): Laser Land Leveling: A Precursor Technology for Resource Conservation. Project Directorate for Cropping Systems Research, Modipuram Rice-Wheat Consortium for the Indo-Gangetic Plains CG Block, National Agriculture Science Centre (NASC) Complex, DPS Marg, Pusa Campus, New Delhi - 110 012, India.

Jat, M.L., S.S. Pal; A.V.M.Subba Rao and S.K.Sharma (2003): Improving Resource Use Efficiency in Wheat Through Laser Land Leveling in an Ustochrept of Indo-Gangetic Plain. In: National Seminar on Developments in Soil Science, 68th Annual Convention of the Indian Society of Soil Science, November 4-8, 2003, CSAUAT, Kanpur (UP).

Jat, M.L.; S.K. Sharma; R. Gupta; K. Sirohi and P. Chandana (2005): Laser Land Leveling: the Precursor Technology for Resource Conservation in Irrigated Ecosystem of India. In: Conservation Agriculture-status and Prospects (Eds., Abrol, I.P., Gupta, Raj K. and Malik, R.K.), CASA, New Delhi, pp. 145-154.

Kahlon, M.S.; R. Lal and M. Ann-Varughese (2013): Twenty Two Years of Tillage and Mulching Impacts on Soil Physical Characteristics and Carbon Sequestration in Central Ohio. Soil Till. Res. 126, 151-158.

Kang, S.Z. and J.H. Zhang (2004): Controlled Alternate Partial Root-zone Irrigation: Its Physiological Consequences and Impact on Water Use Efficiency. Jour. of Experimental Botany, 55: 2437-2446.

Kirda, C. and R. Kanber (1999): Water, No Longer a Plentiful Resource, Should be Used Sparingly in Irrigated Agriculture. In: C. Kirda, P. Moutonnet, C. Hera & D.R. Nielsen, eds. Crop Yield Response to Deficit Irrigation, Dordrecht, The Netherlands, Kluwer Academic Publishers.

Klocke, N.L.; L.R. Stone; G.A. Clark; T.J. Dumler and S. Briggeman (2006): Water Allocation Model for Limited Irrigation. Applied Eng. in Agric. 22(3): 381-389.

Kriedmann, P.E. and I. Goodwin (2003): Regulated Deficit Irrigation and Partial Rootzone Drying. Irrigation Insights no. 4, Land and Water Australia, Canberra, 102p.

Krishna, V.; M.M. Bhatia; N. Teufel and D. Bashnoi (2012a): Characterizing the Cereal Systems and Identifying the Potential of Conservation Agriculture in South Asia. In: CIMMYT Socio-Economics Working Paper 5, CIMMYT, Mexico, D.F.

Li, J. and M. Rao (2003): Field Evaluation of Crop Yield as Affected by Nonuniformity of Sprinkler-applied Water and Fertilizers. Agricultural Water Manage., 59: 1-13.

Liu, F.; R. Song; X. Zhang; A. Shahnazari; M.N. Andersen; F. Plauborg; S.E. Jacobsen and C.R. Jensen (2008): Measurement and Modeling of ABA Signaling in Potato (Solanum tuberosum L.) during Partial Root-zone Drying. Environ. and Experimental Botany, 63: 385-391.

Matter, M.A. (2001): Relationship Between Ploughing Methods and Surge Irrigation and its Effect on Water Rationalization M.Sc. Thesis. Fac. of Agric. Kafr El- Sheikh. Tanta Univ. Egypt.

Mostafazadeh-Fard; B.Y. Osroosh and S. Eslamian (2006): Development and Evaluation of an Automatic Surge Flow Irrigation System. Journal of Agriculture and Social Sciences, 2(3): 129-132.

Rajput, T.B.S. and N. Patel (2003): Laser Land Leveler se khet samatal karayiye pani bachayiye aur paidavar badhayiye. Folder (Hindi). Water Technology Centre, Indian Agricultural Research Institute, Pusa New Delhi.

Reicosky, D.C. and K.E. Saxton (2007): The Benefits of No-tillage. In: Baker, C J. and Saxton, K.E. (Eds.), No-tillage Seeding in Conservation Agriculture, Second ed. FAO and CAB International, pp. 11-20.

Saeed, H.; I.G. Grove; P.S. Kettlewell and N.W. Hall (2008): Potential of Partial Root Zone Drying as an Alternative Irrigation Technique for Potatoes (Solanum tuberosum). Annals of Applied Botany, 152: 71-80.

Scott, C. (2000): Pulse Irrigation. Water Savings Indiana Flower Growers Association. Vol. 14, No. 1. Cooperating with the Department of Horticulture and Landscape Architecture Cooperative Extension Service Purdue University West Lafayette, 120 pp.

Segal, E.; A. Ben-Gal and Shani, U. (2000): Water Availability and Yield Response to High-frequency Micro-irrigation in Sunflowers. 6th International Micro-irrigation Congress. Micro-irrigation Technology for Developing Agriculture'. South Africa, 22-27 October, E-mail alonben-gal@rd.ardom.co.il.

Shahnazari, A.; F. Liu; M.N. Andersen; S.E. Jacobsen and C.R. Jensen (2007): Effects of Partial Root-zone Drying on Yield, Tuber Size and Water Use Efficiency in Potato Under Field Conditions. Field Crops Research, 100: 117-124.

Shock, C.C. and T. Welch (2011): Surge Irrigation, Sustainable Agriculture Techniques, Oregon State University, Department of Crop and Soil Science Ext/CrS pp: 135.

Sial, J.K.; M.A. Khan and N. Ahmad (2006): Performance of Surge Irrigation Under Borders. Pak. J. Agric. Sci., 43(3-4): 186-192.

Sigman, M.; S. Whaley; M. Kamore; N. Bwibo and C. Neumann (2005): Supplementation Increases Physical Activity and Selected Behaviors in Rural Kenyan Schoolchildren. CRSP Research Brief 05-04-CNP. University of California, GlobalLivestock Collaborative Research Support Programme, Davis, Calif.

Smith, M. and D. Kivumbi (2002): Use of the FAO CROPWAT Model in Deficit Irrigation Studies Land and Water Development Division, Food and Agriculture Organization, Rome, Italy L.K. Heng, Joint FAO/IAEA Division, International Atomic Energy Agency, Vienna, Austria.

Stegman, E.C. (1982): Corn Grain Yield as Influenced by Timing of Evapotranspiration. Irrigation Science 3: 75-87.

Stephens, W. and T. Hess (1999): Systems Approach to Water Management. Agricultural Water Management. 40: 3-13.

Tyagi, N.K. (1984): Effect of Land Surface Uniformity on Irrigation Quality and Economic Parameters in Sodic Soils Under Reclamation, *Irrigation Sci.* 5: 151-166.

Valipour, M. and A.A. Montazar (2012): Optimize of All Effective Infiltration Parameters in Furrow Irrigation Using Visual Basic and Genetic Algorithm Programming. Australian Journal of Basic and Applied Sciences, 6(6): 132-137.

WHO, (2009): 10 Facts About Water Scarcity. Available at: http://www.who. nt/features/factfiles/water/en/index.html. Accessed on 28 Jan. 2013.

Ying Hua, P. and K. Shaozhong (2000): Irrigation Water Infiltration into Furrows and Crop Water Use Under Alternate Furrow Irrigation. Transactions of the Chinese Society of Agricultural Engineering 16(1): 9-43.

Zin El-Abedin, T.K. (2006): Effect of Pulse Drip Irrigation on Soil Moisture Distribution and Maize Production in Clay Soil. The 14th Annual Conference of Misr Society of Agr. Eng., 22 Nov., 2006 pp. 1058-1076.

Pages: 92-104

SOIL CHARACTERISTICS AND AGRO-ECOLOGY

Edited by: Dr. Avnish Chauhan; Dr. Pawan Kumar 'Bharti'

ISBN: 978-93-5056-758-6

Edition: 2015

Published by: Discovery Publishing House Pvt. Ltd., New Delhi (India)

5

Impact of Information Technology on Farmers and Traders in Regulated Markets

A Case Premise to Regulated Market at Solan (Himachal Pradesh), India

Mehta, Piyush[1*] and Madhanraj S.[2]

ABSTRACT

Farmers and traders should know the present scenario of information technology for efficient optimization of agricultural regulated markets. Information technology gives abundant knowledge of past and future performance of marketing of their agricultural products and brings plentiful opportunities for traders to develop their agriculture trading business. Solan area is a production site of wide ranging commercially grown vegetables like tomato, pea, cabbage, garlic etc. Farming in Solan is commercial and farmers grow for the markets. There is need for remunerative marketing of farming produce. The use of information technology will help farmers for getting higher competitive prices of their produce. The present study will bring out how farmers and traders utilize the information technology. The existing level of use of IT by the farmers and traders will be assessed along with the benefits drawn. It is necessary to get the feedback about the information technology from farmers

1 Assistant Professor, Department of Business Management, College of Horticulture, Dr. YS Parmar University of Horticulture & Forestry, Nauni, Solan - 173 230 (H.P.), India.

2 MBA Student, Department of Business Management, College of Horticulture, Dr. YS Parmar University of Horticulture & Forestry, Nauni, Solan - 173 230 (H.P.), India.

and traders to improve and develop information technology in Agriculture Regulated Market, Solan. The concerned study has provided the deeper insight of farmers and traders attitude towards information technology in the regulated market and further the study has examined the benefits of information technology perceived by traders and farmers.

Key words: Information Technology, Agriculture Regulated Market, Agricultural products.

INTRODUCTION

The regulated market is defined as "one which aims at the elimination of theunhealthy and unscrupulous practices, reducing marketing charges and providing facilities toproducer-sellers in the market" (*Acharya and Agarwal, 2007*). Historically in the year I886, British Government launched cotton regulated market in Hyderabad to supply cotton fromIndia to Britain through fair price practice. Later on endorsement by the Central Bank Enquiry Committee in I931, Regulated Market for Agriculture Products was established inIndia by the recommendation of Royal Commission on Agriculture (*Anonymous, 2011*). It aims to give fair price for the agriculture product of farmers through strengthening of farmers' community and avoidance of intermediates and exploitation of farmers. Regulated market is purely democratic organization that occupies a place of paramount importance in the contemporary agricultural marketing scenario in India. It emerged as the most powerful instrument to revamp and radicalize the age-old and tradition-bound system of agricultural marketing in India (*Singh, 1995*).

Agriculture has been greatly influenced by information technology. Information Technology is rapidly becoming more and more visible in society and agriculture. Information technology refers to how we use information, how we compute information and how we communicate information to people (*Wirekoon, 2009*).

Information Technology is defined as "the science or practice of collecting, storing, using and sending out information by means of computer system and telecommunication to people" (*Longman Dictionary for Contemporary English*). The information technology can help an average Indian farmer to get relevant information regarding agro-inputs, crop production technologies, agro processing, market support, agro-finance and management of farm agri-business.

The information technology approach for commercial crops, horticultural crops or floriculture has to focus on Integrated System which may be for plant nutrition or plant protection (*Chauhan, 2003*).

The important agricultural portals in India are:

DAC Portal (*http://agricoop.nic.in*): provides information on schemes and programmes of the department, etc.

AGMARKNET Portal (*http://agmarknet.nic.in*): linking important agricultural produce markets, the State Agriculture Marketing Boards and Directorates on a daily basis.

DACNET Portal (*http://dacnet.nic.in*): agriculture online central scheme to provide information and services to the farming community.

INTRADAC (*http://intradac.nic.in*): The INTRADAC facilitates information dissemination within the department.

SEEDNET (*http://seednet.gov.in* bring allseeds users under a closed-user-·oup and establish 'Seed Informatics Online'.

AGRISNET: Agriculture Resource Information Systems Strengthening/ Promoting Agricultural Informatics & Communications.

Kisan Call Centre: deliver extension services and marketing information.

Solan Regulated Market (*SolanSubziMandi*)

A Market Committee in Solan was established in the year 1975. There are 13 regulated markets operational in Solan district which also include regulated market atSolan. Vegetables and fruit commodities are marketed under the AgricultureProduce Marketing Act -1969 and Horticultural Produce Marketing Act 2005. Vegetables like cauliflower, tomato, pea, etc occupy the major position of cultivatedland. The average daily outgoing of agro product is 270 tonnes in Solan and it may vary in peakseason up to 470 tonnes (*Anonymous, 2011*).

Objectives of the Study

1. To examine the present status and existing use of information technology amongst farmers and traders in agricultural regulated market of Solan.
2. To examine the benefits of information technology perceived by traders and farmers.
3. To study the attitude of farmers and traders towards information technology in the regulated market.
4. To suggest policy issues for improved use and disseminating of information technology tothe traders and farmers.

REVIEW OF RELATED LITERATURE

Agricultural Information Systems and Services overviewed the networking issues related to Agricultural Research Information System (ARIS) of ICAR in India. Agricultural libraries and information centers play a vital role in the service of the nation [*Vayyavuru et al.* (*2001*)]. A wide information gap exists between research and practice. Indian farmers need timely expert advice to make them more productive and competitive. An effort was made to execute the information gap by exploiting advances in information technology. The framework for a cost-effective agricultural information dissemination system for disseminating expert agricultural knowledge to the farming community is needed [*Reddy et al.* (*2005*)]. Globalization as one of the reasons for possible widening of the gap between the poor and the rich nations was examined and the emerging concept of "digital slavery" was carefully evaluated [*Ogunsola et al.* (*2005*)]. IT has improvised the marketing activities of retail business in agricultural areas in Indian economy [*Matani* (*2007*)]. There is a substantial purpose of using ICT among Agri-based entrepreneurs and the level of ICT usage among Agri-based entrepreneurs toward Agri-based entrepreneur's productivity [*Hassan et al.* (*2008*)]. Companies deal with market intelligence to facilitate the identification of customer needs and to generate the appropriate response to IT needs [*Borges et al.* (*2009*)]. Researchers estimated the impact of a change in procurement strategy of a private buyer in the central Indian state of Madhya Pradesh. Beginning in October 2000, Internet kiosks and warehouses were established that provide wholesale price information and an alternative marketing channel to soy farmers in the state. Using a new market level dataset brings significant increase in soy price after the introduction of kiosks. The results point toward an improvement in the functioning of rural agricultural markets [*Aparajita et al.* (*2010*)].

Okwoche *et al.* (2010) evaluated agricultural marketing information system among members of farmers' community based organizations in Benue state. A total of 173 farmers were randomly selected and interviewed. Some 35% of the respondents sought information on storage and sales of produce. While only 3% of the respondents shared Information on production, processing, storage and sales. Friends; family and neighbours were the most useful sources of agricultural marketing information in the area.

Subhash *et al.* (2010) studied the role of information technologies at the rural level in various parts of the country and showed that less than 10 percent of the KrishiVigyan Kendra's and other extension scheme activity adopted use digital Content contributes digital content for general Use. Authors identified the need for 'easier knowledge flow method information exchange, storage and rescue mechanisms in rural areas. He also focused on knowledge achievement, knowledge institute and knowledge idea in agriculture and rural livelihood for rural development.

Barakade *et al.* (2011) argued thatthe current models of agriculture knowledge transfer in India were mainly based on extension activities through person to person contacts, publications, radio and television discussions and exhibits of products, fertilizers and seeds at farmers fairs. The authors studied the advances in information and communication technologies and their penetration and impact on Indian agriculture sector.

Goel *et al.* (2011) argued that the impact that technology is going to have on rural marketing initiatives in the next few years be tremendous.

Technology is likely to make a huge difference to the way we look at rural India. The authors tried to address different queries like how can information technology (IT) contribute to rural development? What are the channels through which impacts can be realized and what are the practical means for realizing potential benefits? The author also examined several ongoing projects that aim to provide IT-based services to rural populations in India.

Ali *et al.* (2011) made a case study of the Indian Tobacco Company's (ITC) e-Choupal initiative and analyzed the role of information delivery through Information and Communication Technology (ICT) in enhancing decision-making capabilities of Indian farmers.Users of e-Choupal show significantly better decision-making aptitudes, as compared to non-users. on various agricultural practices across the agricultural supply chain. Further socio demographic backgrounds of the users such as education levels, the social category they belong to income levels. and land holding size also played a significant role in determining decision-making aptitudes The study emphasized the importance of designing [CT enabled information systems to suit the socio- demographic profile of the user groups.

Staatz *et al.* (2011) while evaluating the impact on market performance of investments in agricultural Market Information Systems (MIS) faced several methodological challenges. The methodological challenge were into two broad categories: (a) defining the dimensions of market performance to measure and identifying reliable indicators of those performance dimensions, and (b) identifying the causal effects of the MIS. The authors discussed these challenges and identified approaches that may be useful in developing a "convergence of evidence" concerning whether investment in a given MIS is socially worthwhile.

Chengappa *et al.* (2012) studied application of Information Technology (IT) in the form of introduction of E-tender system in the selected regulated agricultural markets of Karnataka. The use of IT was found to improve the marketing efficiency through competitive and transparent bidding mechanism and by minimization of manipulations in trading practices. It was suggested that efficiency of the system can be enhanced if end-to-end IT applications are introduced.

Liang Wu (2012) argued that the process of promoting agricultural information, "Last Mile" problem was to adopt information technology problems for farmers. The author analyzed the impact on farmers' adoption of information technology services. The results showed that the main factors were effort expect, performance expect, social influence and facilitating conditions.

Kwadwo *et al.* (*2012*) looked at the evidence on the role of emerging ICTs in the agricultural sector in Africa with respect to farmers' access to information and other services that would help improve agricultural productivity, practices, and farmer livelihoods. It suggests that countries should avoid monopoly situations and encourage pluralistic providers to induce competition for higher efficiency and lower costs to consumers.

Kumar *et al.* (*2012*) outlined the level of attitudes of the farmers on ICT application in agriculture, impact of ICT application in agriculture activities and problems in accessing the ICT application has been discussed in Ramanathapuram district. Various planners and administrators of the agriculture department of the government must consider the threats faced by farmers to protect their interests as well as the interest of the nation.

Kizito *et al.* (2012) analyzed the impact of agricultural market information systems (MIS) activities on market performance in Mozambique. The study found the initiation of improved agricultural market information include: (a) growing maize and large and small groundnuts; (b) owning a radio; (c) presence of a cell phone network in the village; (d) membership in a farmer association; (e) access to extension services; (f) proximity to a road with public transport; (g) being nearer to a village administrative post; (h) level of education; and (i) the agro-ecological zone in which the household is located.

Premakumara *et al.* (2013) argued that the impact of information was not same for all the farmers and it differs due to difference in age education, crop type and source of information. It was observed that the timely availability and reliable information plays a major role in efficient and systematic development of agriculture.

Alfatni *et al.* (2013) reviewed established as well as emerging visualization techniques utilized in the quality assessment of food products. In this discourse the authors set out to underscore some of the most novel signal processing techniques employed in the non destructive grading of agricultural products by way of an automated quality verification system utilize advanced engineering principles to accomplish the grading task.

Harbans *et al.* (2013) examined the performance and investment in regulated markets in Kullu district of Himachal Pradesh by selecting three regulated markets (thirty traders and sixty Farmers). The study revealed that the compound growth rates of arrivals for vegetables were significant and positive in all the markets except in the Bhunter market. All the markets lack facilities like mechanical graders and cold storage, cafeteria/restaurant and rest house. The market fee was the major source of income in the Bandrol and Patlikuhl markets. These markets lack basic infrastructure to handle the increasing arrival of fruits and vegetables and therefore volume of trade was not sufficient. Hence, there was a need to develop the basic infrastructural facilities including shops for traders parking, etc in these markets.

RESEARCH METHODOLOGY

The area selected for the study was Regulated Market in Solan town locally called as Solan Subzi Mandi, purposively selected due to its growing popularity amongst fruit and vegetable growers of Solan districts and increasing dissemination of information through information technology. A sample of 70 respondents were taken by Simple Random Sampling Technique, which include 50 farmers and 20 traders visiting the regulated market in Solan. Data was collected on scheduled questionnaires through personal interview method and analyzed with simple tabular analysis.

RESULTS AND DISCUSSION

Major important agriculture products sold by sampled farmers in regulated market-Solan where information technology plays vital role to know the price of product in other regulated market was studied and examined in the table 5.1.

Table 5.1: Major Agriculture Products Marketed by Sampled Farmers

Sl. No.	Name of the Products	No. of Farmers Selling the Product in Market	Farmers in Percentage
1.	Apple	4	8
2.	Cauliflower	4	8
3.	Cabbage	3	6
4.	Garlic	3	6
5.	Tomato	13	26
6.	Capsicum	10	20
7.	Peas	8	16
8.	Potato	2	4
9.	Pomegranate	2	4
10.	Others	1	2
	Total	50	100

Source: Primary proble.

Tomato (26%), capsicum (20%) and peas (16%) and were the most dominating crops sold in the Solan regulated market by sampled farmers.

Alternative Marketing Places

Most of farmers (38%) preferred to sell their produce in other state regulated market as a choice of alternative place to sell their products.

Table 5.2: Different Alternative Marketing Places for Sampled Farmers

Sl. No.	Alternative Places	No. of Farmer Choosing Alternative Markets	Farmers in Percentage
1.	Direct Selling	4	8
2.	Retailers	9	18
3.	Sub-Districts RM	7	14
4.	otters state RM	19	38
5.	Private market	3	6
6.	No Alternatives	8	16
	Total	50	100

Source: Primary proble.

Farmers' Perecption for the Usage of Information Techology Enabled Services

View of information technology in marketing agriculture products among farmers and traders were percived to be helpful to market agriculture produce and in procuring and marketing of the produce. Thus, largely farmers (52%) have positive idea about IT. Two third of traders (70%) believes that IT is helpful in marketing.

Table 5.3: Farmers' Perecption for IT in Marketing Products Among Sampled Farmers and Traders

Sl. No.	Observations	No. of Farmers	No. of Traders	Farmers in Percentage	Traders in Percentage
1.	Helpful in deriving information	26	14	52	70
2.	Not helpful in deriving informations	24	6	48	30
	Total	50	20	100	100

Source: Primary proble.

Preferences of Information to Accessed by Sampled Farmers and Traders Using IT

73.91 per cent of farmers and 78.57 per cent of traders preferred to know price of the products, followed by 13.04 per cent of farmers' preferred to know about new cultivation practices. Thus, information pertained to price of products is the larger content of information accessed through information technology enabled services.

Table 5.4: Preferences of Information to Accessed by Sampled Farmers and Traders Using IT

Sl. No.	Details of Information	No. of Farmers Access	No.of Traders Access	Farmers in Percentage	Traders in Percentage
1.	Price of the Products	17	11	73.91	78.58
2.	Weather Data	2	1	8.70	7.14
3.	Quality of Products	0	0	0.00	0.00
4.	Trader Profile	1	1	4.35	7.14
5.	Schemes	0	1	0.00	7.14
6.	New Cultivation practices	3	0	13.04	0.0
	Total	23	14	100.00	100.00

Source: Primary proble.

Modes to Access Information by Sampled Farmers and Traders Using IT

Largely Mobile and Television plays vital role among sampled farmers (69.57%) and traders (78.57%) to get agriculture information which is mostly preferred to use as IT tool by both farmers and traders.

Table 5.5: Modes to Access Information by Sampled Farmers and Traders Using IT

Sl. No.	Modes of IT	No. of Farmers Using the Tool	No. of Traders Using Tools	Farmers in Percentage	Traders in Percentage
1.	Mobile	10	8	43.48	57.14
2.	Laptop/Computer	2	2	8.70	14.29
3.	Television	6	3	26.08	21.43
4.	News Paper	3	1	13.04	7.14
5.	Agriculture Block/ University/SMS	2	0	8.70	0.00
	Total	23	14	100.00	100.00

Source: Primary proble.

Benefits Gained

Certain benefits gained using information technology by farmers and traders illustrated in table 6 states that 35.71 per cent of traders and 39.13 per cent of farmers learned knowledge of market through IT tools, followed by 28.57 per cent of traders more than 13.04 per cent of farmers said gained profit as follows 21.54 per cent of farmers more than 14.29 per cent of farmers get knowledge of cultivation practice.

Table 5.6: Benefits Gained by Sampled Farmers and Traders Using IT

Sl. No.	Benefits Gained	No.of Farmers Acquired Benefits	No. of Traders Acquired Benefits	Farmers in Percentage	Traders in Percentage
1.	Good Profit	3	4	13.04	28.57
2.	Good Yield	4	0	17.39	0
3.	Knowledge of market	9	5	39.13	35.71
4.	Knowledge of cultivation practice	5	2	21.74	14.29
5.	Easy fund transfer	2	3	8.70	21.43
	Total	23	14	100.00	100.00

Source: Primary proble.

Suggestion for IT

Farmers and traders gave suggestion to improve and disseminate information technology, wherein 34 per cent offarmers and 30 per cent traders suggested television advertisement is substantially recognised as the larger source of extending the IT accessibility followed by 24 per cent of sampled farmers and 25 per cent suggested camp training to be provided to get the best use of IT enabled services.

Table 5.7: Suggestions to Improve and Disseminate IT by Sampled Farmers and Traders

Sl. No.	Methods	No. of Farmers Suggest	No. of Traders Suggest	Farmers in Percentage	Traders in Percentage
1.	Camps/Training	12	5	24	25
2.	Programmes/Schemes	10	4	20	20
3.	Television/Advertisement	17	6	34	30
4.	Education	10	4	20	20
5.	New software invention for agriculture	1	1	2	5
	Total	50	20	100	100

Source: Primary proble.

SUMMARY AND CONCLUSION

Nearly half of the sampled farmers (52%) had a positive usage inclinationtowards IT. Two third of traders (70%) believes that IT is helpful in marketing. IT usage level of sampled traders (70%) is higher than the sampled farmers (46%). Most of sampled farmers (73.91%) and traders (78.58%) prefer to know the price of products in other regulated market.

Mobile and Television plays vital role among sampled farmers (69.57%) and traders (78.57%) to get agriculture information which is mostly preferred to use as IT tool by both the sampled community. Though traders were satisfied with the quality of required information and its usefulness in decision making, as largely farmers and traders were gained from the use of information technology. The most importance attribute was knowledge about the market as examined, moreover, traders suggested for improvement in information technology by inserting trainingsto improve and disseminate the use of IT.

Around Solan town, Farmers' carries their agriculture products to sell in regulated market, thus availability of required information farmers decides their crop cultivation period and adjusting the harvest time until the rise of price in market and also helps in various different aspects of agriculture. Although some farmers' were unsatisfied with the use of IT. Usage of IT among small and medium land owners is quite in lower level even though mobile phone have been a part of everyone life which is a globalized tool of information technology but utilizing it as a sources of getting information is low among illiterate farmers. Most of the farmers' get information from fellow farmers, friends and commission agents who may have chance to give non reliable information so the farmer may face problem and get poor price for the products. In aspect of Traders in regulated market-Solan information technology is boon to their agriculture trading in terms of getting more information price of various agriculture products around country and develops their agriculture business and grooms it to another level. It was observed during the study that in order to maintain the relationship with whole sale customers, social networkingaccount are being commonly used to exchange details about markets and financial transaction. Though, the impact of Information Technology on farmers is less than traders in the regulated market-Solanthat calls an urgent need of incucating the larger usage of information technology enabled services for the betterment of trade, traders and farmers at large.

SUGGESTIONS

It was suggested by the farmers and traders that separate block for Information technology should be open within the regulated market, which may help farmers to access the information with the guidance of officers and also easy to afford, Implemented programmes and schemes for IT should be regularly inspected by the concern inspection authority to avoid the lack of service to farmers and traders, New agriculture programmes about information technology in agriculture should be telecasted in both public and private channels which is being a wide and strong media to reach the people, New software in easy mode should be invented by information technologist particularly in regional language where farmers can create their own account ask their quires and clear their doubts via mailing, Meetings should be conducted at every week with farmers, traders and officer to discuss about the status of market thus improving the communication between them and Digital display in regulated market about current price and arrival of products of regulated market and other markets would help to know the present status of market which helps to make spot decisions.

REFERENCES

Aparajita Goyal, 2010. Information Direct Access to Farmers and Rural Market Performance in Central India. *American Economic Journal: Applied Economics*, 22-45.

Azamllamidi and Maryam Safabakhsh. 2011. Impact of Information Technology on e-Marketing. Procedia Computer Science, World Conference on Information Technology 3: 365-368.

Barakade, A.J., Lokhande, T.N., (*et al.*). 2011. Impact of Globalization Information Technology in Agriculture. *International Referred Research Journal*. 2: 54-57.

Chengappa, P.G, (*et al.*). 2012. IT Application in Agricultural Marketing Service. *Institute for Social and Economic Change. Nagarabhavi. Bangalore*. 25: 359-372.

G. Kumar and R. Sankarakumar. 2012. Impact of Information and Communication Technology in Agriculture–Perception of the Farmers in Ramanathapuram District. *International Journal of Statistika and Mathematika.* 4 (2): 33-41.

Jabir Ali and Sushil Kumar, 2011. Information and Communication Technologies and Farmers' Decision-Making. *International Journal of Information Management.* 3: 149-159.

Janet Kaaya. 1999. Role of Information Technology in Agriculture. *FoA Conference*. Vol. 4.

Kapoor, B, Sindhi, V., (*et al.*). 2011. Impact of Information Communication Technologies (ICTs) on Rural Marketing & Development. *VSRD International Journal of Computer Science and Information Technology*. 1(6): 396-407.

KwadwoAsenso-Okyere and Daniel Ayalew Mekonnen, 2012. The Importance of ICTs in the Provision of Information for Improving Agricultural Productivity and Rural Incomes in Africa. *United Nation Development Programme*. 1-30.

Lalllarbans, Gupta Varsha, Kumar Virender, (*et al.*).2013. Regulated Markets in Kullu District of Himachal Pradesh: Economic Analysis of Performance and Investment. *Agriculture Economics Research Review: Indian Journal*. 26: 208.

Liang Wu. 2012. Imperial Research on Poor Rural Agricultural Information Technology Services to Adopt. *International Workshop on Information and Electronics Engineering*. 29: 1578-1583.

Matani, A.G. 2007. Information Technology Improving Retail Marketing in Agriculture Co-operative. *Indian Institute of Management, Kozhikode*. 185-186.

MdSalleh Hassan, Musa Abu Hassan, (*et al.*). 2008. Use of Information and Communication Technology (ICT) Among Agri-based Entrepreneurs in Malaysia. *World Conference on Agricultural Information and IT*. 753-762.

Mauro Borges, Norberto Hoppen, (et al.). 2009. Information Technology Impact on Market Orientation in e-business. *Journal of Business Research, Balas*. 883-890.

M.S.M., Alfatni and A.R.M. Shariff, (et al.). 2013. Application of Internal Grading System Technologies. *Journal of Food Engineering*. 116: 703-725.

Ogunsola, L.A., 2005. Information and Communication Technologies and the Effects of Globalization Electronic. *Journal of Academic and Special Librarianship.* 6: 1-2.

Okwoche, V.A.O., Obinne, C.P.O (*et al.*). 2010. Evaluation of Agricultural Marketing Information System Among Members of Farmers' Community-Based Organic ... *Indian Agricultural Journal*. 5: 338-34.

Premakumara, G.S and Usharani, N.D., 2013. Impact of Information and Agricultural Development. *Indian Journal of Research*. 3: 43-45.

Rasheed Sulaiman, V., Andy Hall. (*et al.*). 2011. Necessary but not Sufficient: Information and Communication Technology ... *Research into Use*. Paper 16.

Reddy, P.K and Ankaiah. R. 2005. Framework of Information Technology-Based Agriculture Information Dissemination System to Improve Crop Productivity.

Shankaraiah, N., Shashekala, (*et al.*). 2012. Dissemination of Farm Information Through AgriPortals. *International Journal of Advanced Biological Research.* 2(3): 382-391.

Subhash Singh Parihar, Bharat Mishra, (*et al.*). 2010. Sustainable Models of Information Technology for Agriculture and Rural Development. *Indian Research Journal.* 10(1): 20-23.

Surabhi Mittal and Gaurav Tripathi. 2009. Role of Mobile Phone Technology in Improving Small Farm Productivity. *Agricultural Economics Research Review.* 22: 451-459.

Umang Goel, Ankit Bajpai, (*et al.*). 2011. Changes in Rural Marketing Through Information and Communication Technology. *International Journal of Innovation, Management and Technology.* 2 (2): 152-155.

Vadivelu.A and Kiran, B.R. 2013. Problems and Prospects of Agricultural Marketing in India: An Overview ... *International Journal of Agricultural and Food Science.* 3(3): 108-118.

Vayyavuru Sreenivasulu and H.B. Nandwana, 2001. Networking of Agricultural Information Systems and Services in India. *INSPEL.* 35 (4): 226-235.

Pages: 105-125

SOIL CHARACTERISTICS AND AGRO-ECOLOGY

Edited by: Dr. Avnish Chauhan; Dr. Pawan Kumar 'Bharti'

ISBN: 978-93-5056-758-6

Edition: 2015

Published by: Discovery Publishing House Pvt. Ltd., New Delhi (India)

Impact of Climate Change on Agriculture Production and Food Security

Tawfik*, M.M., Wafaa M. Haggag**, Nabila M. Zaki*, M.S. Hassanein* Amany, A. Bahr* and Amal, G. Ahmed*

ABSTRACT

Climate changes are believed to be contributing to an increase in average global temperatures. This is caused primarily by increases in "greenhouse" gases. Climate change threat lives in the world by affecting water resources, agriculture, coastal regions, freshwater habitats, vegetation, forests, snow cover and geological processes such as landslide, desertification and floods, and has long-term effects on food security as well as in human health. Over the next decades, it is predicted that billions of people, particularly those in developing countries, face shortages of water and food as a result of climate change. Concerted global action is needed to adapt to the effects of climate change that are happening now and will worsen in the future. Concerted global action is needed to adapt to the effects of climate change that are happening now and will worsen in the future.

Egypt is considered a developing country burdened by the scarcity of natural resources associated with extreme population growth. Egypt considered one

* Field Crops Research Department, National Research Centre, Egypt.

** Plant Pathology Department, National Research Centre, Egypt.

of the top five countries expected to be mostly impacted with climate changes. Climate change will probably affect water resources requiring reduction in irrigation water and that might pose another problem for agricultural production. Also, the increase of temperature and frequency of extreme events expected to affect crop yield as well as causing changes in the agricultural distribution of crops. Furthermore, it will negatively affect marginal land and force farmers to abandon them increasing desertification.

Key words: climate change - Agriculture production - Food security.

INTRODUCTION

Climate changes refer to an increase in average global temperatures. Natural events and human activities are believed to be contributing to an increase in average global temperatures. This is caused primarily by increases in "greenhouse" gases such as Carbon Dioxide (CO_2), Methane (CH_4), Nitrous Oxide (NO_2) and Chloro-Floro-Carbon (CFC_s) (Bates *et al.*, 2008). It resulting variations in solar energy, temperature and precipitation. It is a real threat to the lives in the world that largely affects water resources, agriculture, coastal regions, freshwater habitats, vegetation, forests, snow cover and geological processes such as landslide, desertification and floods, and has long-term affects on food security as well as in human health (Varshney *et al.*, 2011).

Over the next 100 years, accelerated warming and expansion of water in the oceans, and increased melting rates of low-lying glaciers and ice caps will have major consequences for low-lying farmland across the world (Medellín-Azuara *et al.*, 2008). This will lead to global variation in mean precipitation and drought. This suggests that the increase in atmospheric CO_2 and other greenhouse gases will potentially affect future climate (IPCC, 2007). Climate change is one of humanity's greatest challenges, affecting both current and future generations. Without urgent and concerted action, it will damage fragile ecosystems, impede development efforts, increase risks to public health, frustrate poverty alleviation programmes, and force large-scale migration from water or food-scarce regions. The environmental, economic, and social costs of inaction will far exceed the cost of taking immediate steps to address climate change (Campbell and Mann, 2011).

Over the next decades, it is predicted that billions of people, particularly those in developing countries, face shortages of water and food as a result of climate change. Concerted global action is needed to adapt to the effects of climate change that are happening now and will worsen in the future. Global climate change is a critical global issue with a range of potential effects on community infrastructure, ecosystems, agriculture and economic activity, no one country or group of countries can provide its remedy. The cooperation of countries and coordination of national efforts will be central in any solution to the problem. (Branca and McCarthy, 2011). The high sensitivity of field crops to climate conditions and the great uncertainty on the combined effects of increasing CO_2 concentration and projected changes in temperature and especially in rainfall patterns on crops reveals the necessity to better understand the impacts of future climate for implement appropriate adaptation and mitigation strategies in agriculture, to increase production and food security. The impact of climate change in many parts of the world has been explored for different crops (Thomson *et al.*, 2010). It has been suggested that some effects of climate change are likely to be beneficial in some agricultural regions (IPCC, 2007). The impact of climate change on agricultural production is related to three major specific factors which are atmospheric carbon dioxide concentration, precipitation and temperature (Branca and McCarthy, 2011).

There are two counteractive effects from increasing atmospheric CO_2 concentration and climate change. Atmospheric CO_2 concentration increase will have positive effects on crop production especially for C3 plants through stimulation of photosynthesis and improvement of water use efficiency (Holst *et al.*, 2010). However, under-water deficit and higher temperatures will usually shorten the growth cycle of a given cultivar (Ngigi, 2009), and together with reduced water supply are likely to reduce crop production (Gornall *et al.*, 2010). A number of climate change impact studies on field crop production around the world have reported varying results. Attri and Rathore (2003) found further increases in temperature beyond 38 ° C would negate the beneficial impacts of enhanced CO_2, and wheat yield would decrease by 20%. Wheat, barley, corn, and rice will be vulnerable to heat waves due to global warming during their reproductive phase, resulting in lower yields (Patil *et al.*, 2010). Crop breeding is immediately needed to cope with climate change adaptation. In addition, research is needed on responses to simultaneous increases in temperature and carbon dioxide levels and effects on water use efficiency (Clements *et al.*, 2011).

IMPACT OF CLIMATE CHANGE ON AGRICULTURE PRODUCTION

Climate change and agriculture is interrelated processes, both of which take place on a global scale (Cayan *et al.*, 2008). They added that, global warming is projected to have significant impacts on conditions affecting agriculture, including temperature, precipitation and glacial run-off. These conditions determine the carrying capacity of the biosphere to produce enough food for the human population. Rising carbon dioxide levels would also have effects, both detrimental and beneficial, on crop yields. The overall effect of climate change on agriculture will depend on the balance of these effects. Assessment of the effects of global climate changes on agriculture might help to properly anticipate and adapt farming to maximize agricultural production (IPCC, 2007). Both positive and negative impact of climate change on crops production is presented in (Fig. 6.1).

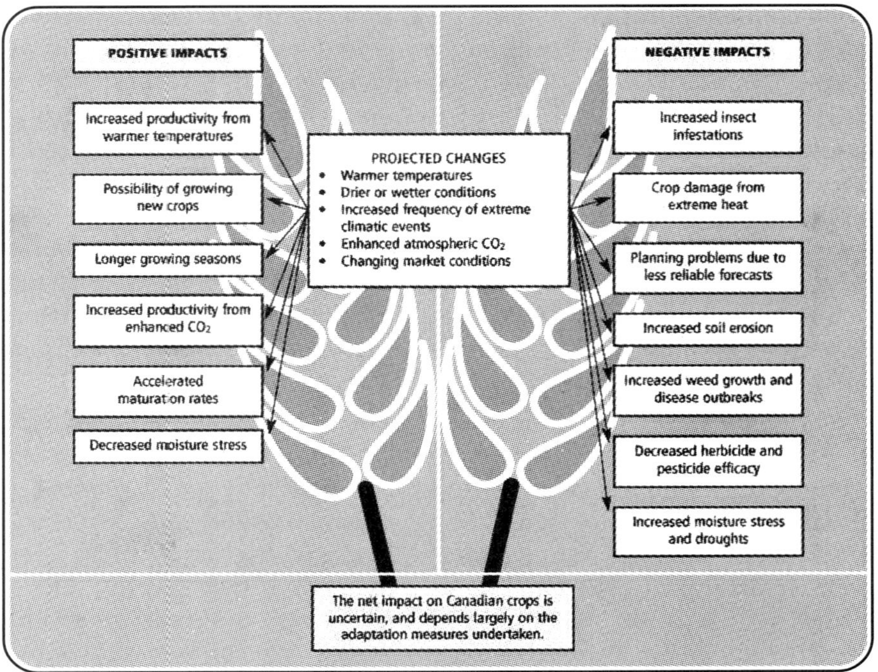

Fig. 6.1: Positive and Negative Impact of Climate Change on Crops Production (IPCC, 2007)

Changes in Temperature

Global warming is likely to bring local shifts in temperature and in the amount and seasonal distribution of precipitation. It is also likely to result in more extreme weather such as droughts and periods of heavy precipitation. Such changes can affect field crop growth, the spread of pests and diseases and water availability in both positive and negative ways. In many countries this will enable earlier sowing and more crop species to be grown, but generally greater opportunities for increased disease pressure (Peltonen *et al.*, 2009). Because each plant has an upper and lower threshold temperature which controls its range, temperature is one of the main factors governing plant migration to new areas under the various climate change scenarios, as well as the survival of plants within their current ranges (Clements *et al.*, 2011).

They added that field crops vary considerably in their tolerance to high temperatures. In general, field crops are less well adapted to high temperatures than wild plants and they are less able to use avoidance or escape mechanisms. Moreover, rising temperatures will cause shifts in crop growing seasons which affects food security and changes in the distribution of disease vectors putting more people at risk from diseases such as malaria and dengue fever. The effect of global warming on the incidence of extreme heat is illustrated in figure 6.2. Adverse effects of elevated temperature on crop plants may result from increases in average temperatures, high maximum temperatures or increases in the diurnal temperature range (Campbell and Mann, 2011). These effects may also be modifying by other factors such as water availability. Temperature effects on crop plants may be manifested indirectly. For example, high temperatures may cause increased mortality of pollinators and affect populations of pests and diseases and natural enemies (Deal and Henikoff, 2011). These effects may be positive or negative depending on the cropping system.

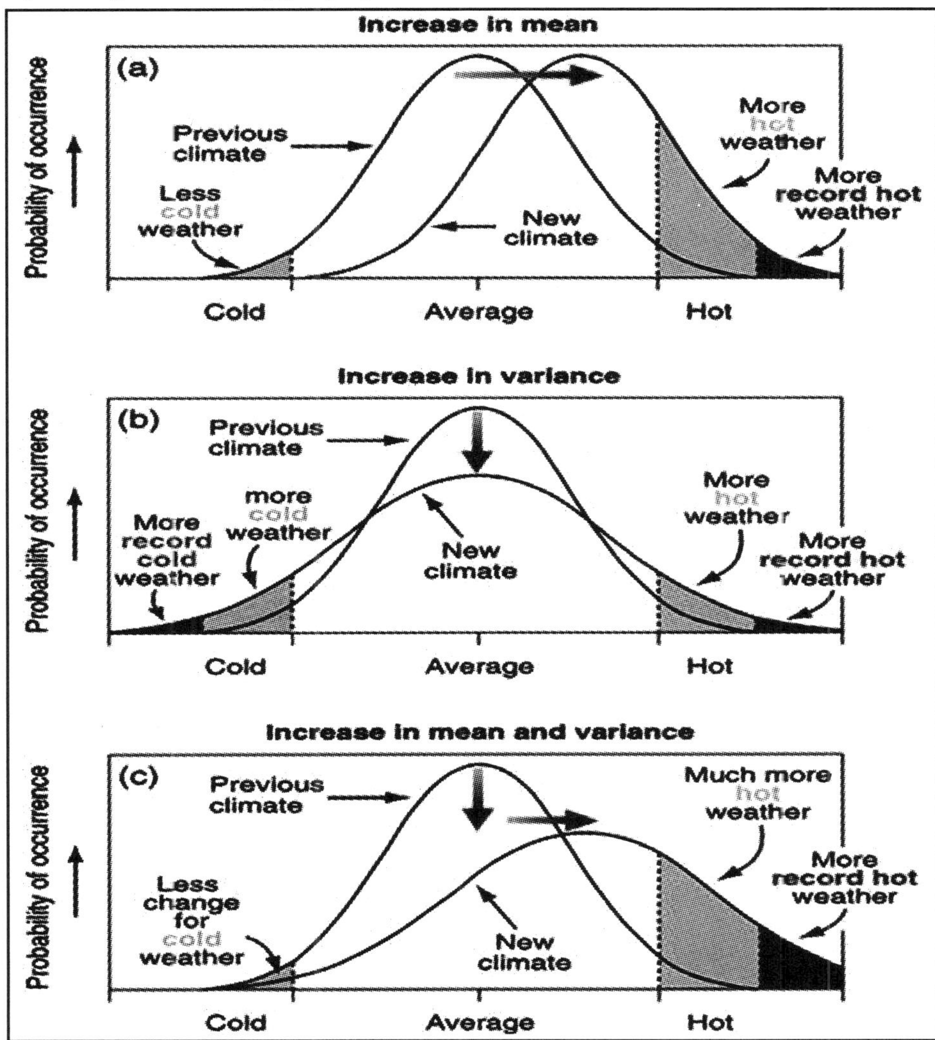

Fig. 6.2: Illustration of Effect on Extreme Temperature when (a) the Mean Increases, Leading to more Record hot Weather, (b) the Variance Increase, and (c) when both the Mean and the Variance Increase, Leading to much more Record Hot Weather. (IPCC, 2007)

Increased temperatures may also favour the growth of weed species enabling them to compete more effectively with crop plants (Clements *et al.*, 2011). They added that, the response of plants to temperature stress depends upon several factors include the crop growth stage, the type of plant tissue and the nature of temperature stress. For example, high soil temperatures may affect the seedling stage of certain crops such as cotton (Nabi and Mullins, 2008). In a recent study, historical temperature data were compared with projected future temperatures in each of the countries in Africa and the implications for three cereal crops (maize, wheat and sorghum) were examined (Burke *et al.*, 2009). The model projections revealed that, for each of the three cereal crops examined, temperatures within their current range are likely to increase significantly. On average, by 2050 temperatures in most years are predicted to be higher than those in any year that has been experienced to date. One of the consequences will be marked changes in the suitability of land for cultivation of particular crops (Devereux and Edwards, 2004).

Modest increases in temperature may lead to increased yields of cereal crops in temperate regions. By contrast, in tropical regions even a modest temperature (increase of 1-2 °C) is likely to result in yield losses in rice, maize and wheat, although the use of adaptation measures may modify this response (Tubiello *et al.*, 2007). In this concern, Hatfield (2010) summarized the temperature responses for maize (*Zea mays* L.) and sorghum (*Sorghum bicolor* L.). Each crop species responds differently to temperature throughout their life cycles with the vegetative period of growth having a higher temperature optimum than the reproductive stage. Exposure to higher temperatures during vegetative growth causes growth to progress at its fastest rate. Above the optimum, growth rates slow and cease when plants are exposed to their maximum temperature (Clements *et al.*, 2011).

Increasing Carbon Dioxide

Increases in CO_2 levels, will singly and together with temperature and changes in precipitation patterns, act to change crop ranges and productivities in more complex but generally negative ways (Leakey *et al.*, 2009). There is debate within the scientific literature as to the relative order of importance of these effects. Although they all operate in the same general way, using sunlight to convert CO_2 and H_2O to energy in the form of glucose, the three biochemical pathways of photosynthesis (C_3, C_4 and CAM) Figs. 6.3 and 6.4, depending on the plant environment, and are defined by the nature of the first product of CO_2 assimilation (Cowie, 2007).

Many tropical crops are C_4 photosynthesizes, including maize, sorghum and sugar cane, whilst temperate environments suit C_3 crops as wheat and barley (Sadava *et al.*, 2008). They added that, Crassulacean Acid Metabolism (CAM) evolved independently in plants such as the cacti and other succulents, suited to semi-arid environments while C_4 plants are more efficient at lower concentrations of atmospheric CO_2. However, assessing and predicting plant photosynthetic response to increases in CO_2 is difficult and the results are sometimes contradictory. C_3 plants respond with increased photosynthetic rates but with decreased leaf nitrogen levels when grown under enriched CO_2 levels (Clements *et al.*, 2011). They added that, under controlled conditions, C_3 plants show increased growth under increasing CO_2 concentrations, compared to C_4 plants, but this is less evident at higher temperatures.

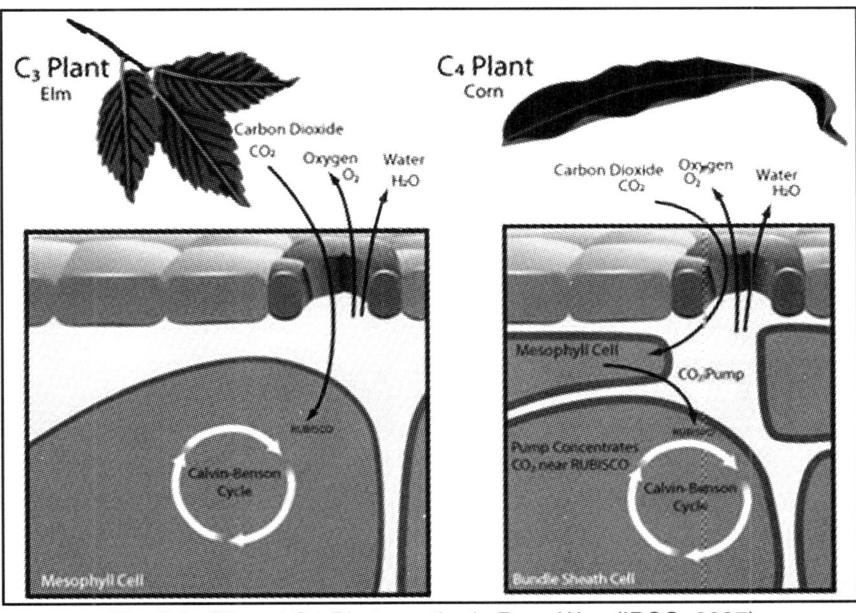

Fig. 6.3: C3 and C4 Photosynthetic Pass Way (IPCC, 2007)

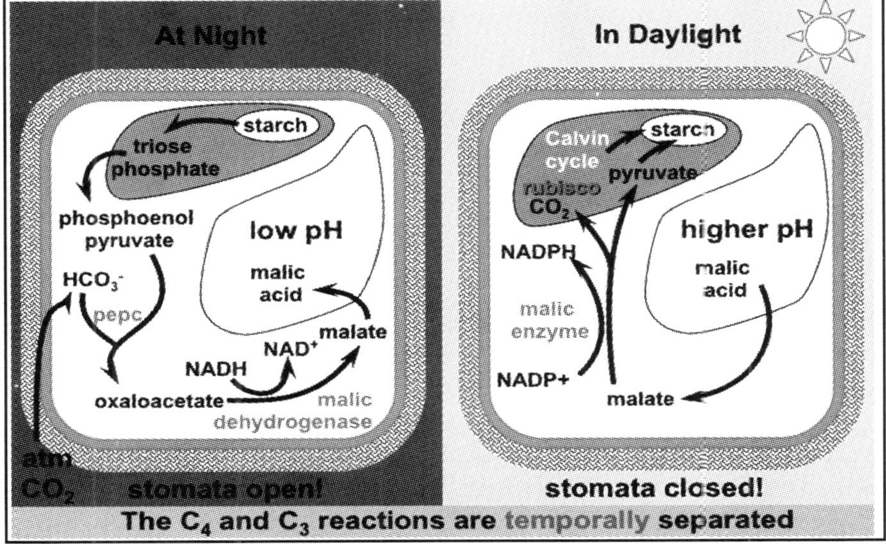

Fig. 6.4: CAM Photosynthesis: Crassulacean Acid Metabolism (IPCC, 2007)

Some C_4 crops respond less vigorously to increase CO_2 than others do and these include maize and sorghum. Moreover, Taub *et al*., (2008) studied the effects of high levels of CO_2 on five crops (barley, rice, wheat, soybean and potato). All of these crops had lower protein concentrations when grown at the higher CO_2 levels. For wheat, barley, rice and potatoes, elevated CO_2 cut protein concentration by 10-15%. Soybean showed a smaller reduction of 1.4%. Furthermore, Hogy *et al*., (2009) reported lower protein content, amino acids and minerals in wheat grains under elevated CO_2. In this concern, Hatfield (2010) stated that, increasing CO_2 will also cause plants to become more water use efficient. This latter response will help offset some of the potential limitations caused by the increased probability of drought during the growing season. They added that, improvement in water use efficiency is a direct result from reduced stomatal conductance and reduced transpiration relative to CO_2 uptake.

Changes in Precipitation

The availability of water is fundamental to agriculture. There is a direct influence of global warming on precipitation. Increased heating leads to greater evaporation and thus surface drying, thereby increasing the intensity and duration of drought. However, the water holding capacity of air increases by about 7% per 1°C warming, which leads to increased water vapor in the atmosphere (Trenberth, 2011). He added that the observed warming over several decades has been linked to changes in the large-scale hydrological cycle such as increasing atmospheric water vapour content, changing precipitation patterns, intensity and extremes, reduced snow cover and widespread melting of ice and changes in soil moisture and runoff.

Precipitation changes show substantial spatial and inter-decadal variability, the impact of climate change can occur through three major routes: drought, which is a lack of water for a period of time causing severe physiological stress to plants, flooding which is an excess of water for a period of time causing physiological and direct physical stress to plants and timing of water availability (Falloon and Betts, 2009). There is much less certainty attached to rainfall projections under different climate change scenarios. However, an increased frequency in drought events is likely to be one of the most serious consequences of projected global warming (IPCC, 2007).

A shortage of water affects plants by reducing the rate of photosynthesis, either through a direct effect of dehydration or through stomatal closure which reduces CO_2 intake (Blum, 2009). An increased frequency and severity of drought events will mean that some areas which are currently marginal for the production of some rainfed crops will no longer be suitable for production. For example, in some areas of maize production in southern Africa there is already a high risk of significant yield loss or crop failure. An increase in the number of dry days or in the frequency of the early seasons of rains would make maize production unsustainable (Tadross *et al.*, 2005). Where this is feasible, supplementary irrigation will be needed to counterbalance the higher soil moisture deficits. It has been estimated that globally, even taking into account greater water use efficiency resulting from higher levels of CO_2, there will be an increase of around 20% in net irrigation requirements by 2080 (Sharad, 2012). Figure 6.5 demonstrates projected water scarcity in 2025.

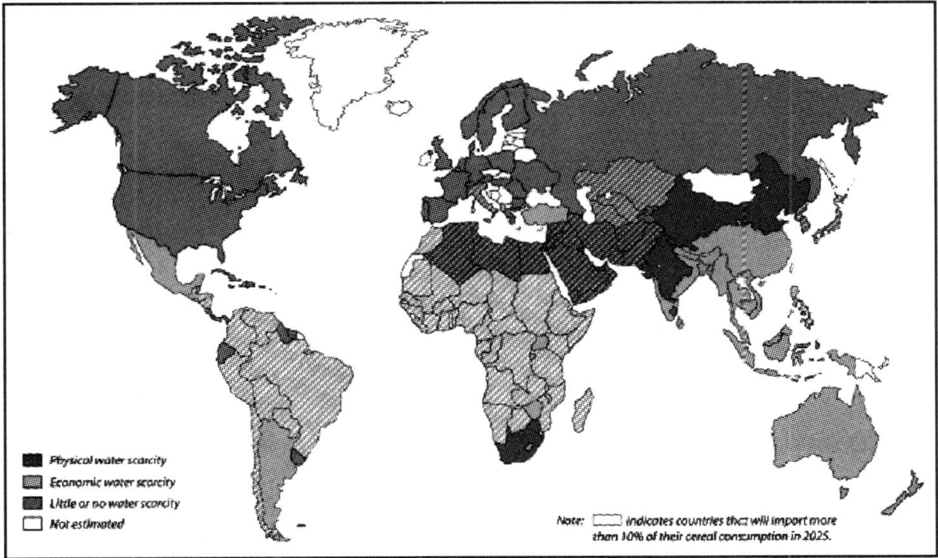

Fig. 6.5: Projected Water Scarcity in 2025 (IPCC, 2007)

Climate Variability, Extreme Events and Sea-level Rise

Climate change may be characterized by an increase in climate variability (IPCC, 2007). This may heighten the risks of crop failures, often connected to specific extreme events during critical crop phases, such as heat waves or late frosts during flowering. Another predicted effect of global warming, will caused increased flooding, salt-water intrusion, and rising water tables in agricultural soils located near coastlines. This is particularly crucial in tropical countries with large agricultural regions and high rural population. In this regard Campbell and Mann (2011) stated that, sea level is rising, during the 20th century, sea level rose about 15 cm (6 inches) due to melting glacier ice and expansion of warmer seawater. They predict that sea level may rise as much as 59 cm (23 inches) during the 21st Century, threatening coastal communities, wetlands, and coral reefs figure 6.6.

Moreover, Clements *et al.*, (2011) stated that, Arctic sea ice is melting and the summer thickness of sea ice is about half of what it was in 1950. This may lead to changes in ocean circulation. They added that over the past 100 years, mountain glaciers in all areas of the world have decreased in size and so has the amount of permafrost in the Arctic. Greenland's ice sheet is melting faster too. Mid-latitude storm tracks are projected to shift toward the poles, with increased intensity in some areas but reduced frequency. Tropical storms and hurricanes are likely to become more intense, produce stronger peak winds, and produce increased rainfall over some areas due to warming sea surface temperatures which can energize these storms (IPCC, 2007).

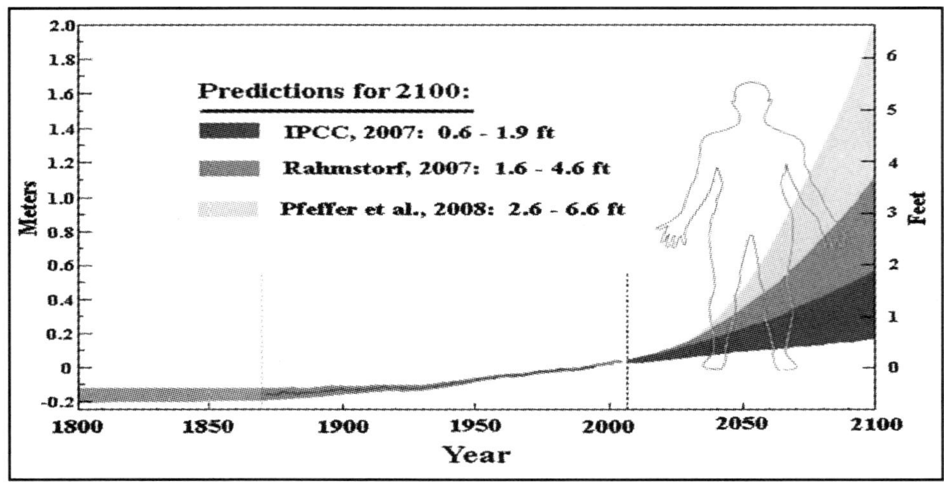

Fig. 6.6: Observed and Predicted Sea Level Rise in the 21st Century

Hydrological extreme events are typically defined as floods and droughts. Floods are associated with extremes in rainfall (from tropical storms, thunderstorms, orographic rainfall, widespread extra tropical cyclones, etc.), while droughts are associated with a lack of precipitation and often extremely high temperatures that contribute to drying. Floods are often fairly local and develop on short time scales, while droughts are extensive and develop over months or years (Trenberth, 2011). Data in Table 6.1 shows the most affected country by Climate variability, extreme events and sea-level rise.

Agricultural Pests

Climate change has the potential to reduce the effectiveness of current pest management strategies, requiring the dedication of additional resources for developing new knowledge systems and appropriate measures to counter new pests or the intensification of existing pests (IPCC, 2007). Warmer temperatures may speed development rates of some insect species, resulting in shortened times between generations and improved capacity for over-wintering at northern latitudes (Rosenzweig *et al.*, 2002). He added that, some insects populations may further become established and thrive earlier in the growing season, during more vulnerable crop stages.

Table 6.1: The most Affected Country by Climate Variability, Extreme Events and Sea-level Rise

Droughts	Floods	Storms	Sea Level rise
Malawi	Bangladesh	Philippines	Vietnam
Ethiopia	China	Bangladesh	Egypt
Zimbabwe	India	Madagascar	Tunisia
India	Cambodia	Viet Nam	Indonesia
Mozambique	Mozambique	Moldova	Mauritania
Niger	Rwanda	Mongolia	China
Mauritania	Pakistan	Haiti	Mexico
Eritrea	Sri Lanka	Samoa	Myanmar
Sudan	Thailand	Tonga	Bangladesh
Chad	Viet Nam	China	Senegal
Kenya	Benin	Honduras	Libya

In addition to these direct effects on pests, climate change will alter the seasonal patterns and chemistry of crop plants, indirectly affecting the pests that feed on the plants, for example, elevated CO_2 levels may change the nutritional content of some crops, increasing the feeding requirements for insect pests, even if pest numbers do not change each pest may become more destructive and more intense infestations may occur (Patterson *et al.*, 1999). They added that, climate change could firstly affect disease directly by either decreasing or increasing the encounter rate between pathogen and host by changing rates of the two species. However, both of these effects on disease will be mediated by host resistance and encounter rates, which in turn are potentially affected by climate. The range of many pathogens is limited by climatic requirements for over cold or over hot of the pathogen or vector. Asynchrony between pathogen, vector and host may be an effect of climate change (Cools and Fraaije, 2008).

Chancellor and Kubiriba (2006) concluded that whilst the geographical distribution of some plant hosts and disease pathogens will alter as a result of future changes in climate and, especially in Africa, this effect is likely to be strongest in areas of significant water stress. However, they emphasized that the absence of reliable epidemiological information 'makes predictions hazardous'. It is apparent that for sweet corn pests, warmer temperatures translate to increased insecticide applications to produce a marketable crop. Additionally, some classes of pesticides (pyrethroids and spinosad) have been shown to be less effective in controlling insects at higher temperatures (Musser and Shelton, 2005).

PREDICTED IMPACT OF CLIMATE CHANGE ON AGRICULTURE YIELD

Many investigators studied the impact of climate changes on agriculture production. In this concern, Eid *et al*., (2006) in an Egyptian study compared crop production under current climate conditions with those projected for 2050, and forecast a decrease in national production of many crops, ranging from –11% for rice to –28% for soybeans. El-Marsafawy (2006) studied the potential impact of climate change on the yield and ET crop of sunflower oil productivity in the main agricultural regions of Egypt. OILCROP-SUN model, embedded in the Decision Support system for Agro- technology Transfer (DSSAT3.5) was used for the crop simulations with current and possible future management practices. Equilibrium doubled CO_2 climate change scenarios were derived from the CCCM and GFD3 general circulation models (GCMs).

These scenarios predict consistent increases in air temperature, small increases in solar radiation and precipitation changes that will happened in the future. Simulation of sunflower productivity was carried out for 30 years (for Middle and Upper Egypt) and 26 years (for Delta) under the normal weather conditions and climate change conditions. The response of sunflower crop production to different sowing dates, irrigation water amounts and skipping one irrigation at different growth stages under climate change conditions were studied. The results revealed that the two climate change scenarios considered resulted in simulated decrease in sunflower yield at the three sites. The change percent of seed yield in Delta, Middle and Upper Egypt reached about -21, -27 and -38% under climate change conditions compared to their production under current conditions, respectively. At the same time, water consumptive use will be increased about 5 and 12% in Delta and Middle Egypt respectively, while in Upper Egypt, it will be decreased about 0.5% as a result of high reduction in yield under climate change conditions compared to their current water consumption.

On the other hand, results of adaptation options indicate that sunflower crop have to be sown between the 1st of May and 10th of May in Delta and Middle Egypt and between the 1st of June and 10th of June in Upper Egypt to reduce unfavorable effects of climate change on sunflower production under climate future. Reducing irrigation water amounts by 10% could be recommended as a way to conserve irrigation water without clear reduction in seed yield. Vegetative growth stage is most sensitive stage to water stress for sunflower plants. At the same time, omitting irrigation at the late seed growth could be practiced. Carter (2007) predicted that, climate change will lead to the intensification of agriculture in northern Europe and other boreal and numeral zones. For example, it will lead to shifts in the northern limits of areas thermally suitable for the cultivation of soya bean and grain maize by several hundred kilometers, and lengthen the northern European growing season by 3-12 weeks by 2085, with a stronger effect at the end than at the start of the growing season leading to substantial increases in biomass production. Thus these regions are predicted to gain many benefits from climate change, as the areas suitable for crop production will expand and new crops can be introduced to production. Easterling *et al.*, (2007) have created a synthesis of 69 model-based results that demonstrates the relative impact of temperature and carbon fertilization on changes in cereal yield. Although a wide range of variability in yield changes across the studies is found, some trends can be observed. In mid- to high latitudes, increases in temperature produce increases in yields, but with diminishing effect when temperature changes are greater than 3 degrees. Yet stronger yield-depressing effects are found in tropical and sub-tropical regions for all crops, which reflect a lower growing temperature threshold capacity in these areas.

Cline (2007) detected that, the higher temperature will increases the process of evapotranspiration and decreases soil moisture availability. Because global warming is likely to increase rainfall, the net impact of higher temperature on water availability is a race between higher evapotranspiration and higher precipitation. As the precipitation is not regular, the race will be won by higher evapotranspiration. Rainfed agriculture, mostly practiced by the poor, is likely to get affected adversely by the climate change. He added, enhanced photosynthesis can increase the yield of C_3 crops such as wheat, rice and soybean, but not of the C_4 crops such as sugarcane and maize. Lobell *et al.*, (2008) based on statistical crop models, stated that, wheat and rice in southeast Asia and maize in southern Africa were most likely to be negatively impacted by climate change in the absence of adaptation strategies.

However, the most extreme predictions for negative outcomes of climate change identified millet, groundnut, and rapeseed (*Brassica napus*) in southern Asia, sorghum (*Sorghum bicolor*) in Sahel, and maize in southern Africa as priorities for adaptation. Iglesias (2009) found that, agricultural production, including access to food, in many African countries and regions is projected to be severely compromised by climate variability and change. The area suitable for agriculture, the length of growing seasons and yield potential, particularly along the margins of semi-arid and arid areas, are expected to decrease. In some countries, yields from rain-fed agriculture could be reduced by up to 50% by 2020. Data in table 6.2 shows some of the predicted impact of climate changes on field crops globally.

Zhai and Zhuang (2009) used comparable general equilibrium (CGE) model in order to examine the impact of climate change on agriculture sector of China in 2080. Their results showed that 1.3% decline of agricultural share in GDP. The CGE simulation results showed that in 2080 agricultural output would become slow which ultimately leads to output losses except wheat which showed enhancement in output because of increase in global wheat demand.

Table 6.2: Predicted Impacts of Climate Change on Field Crops Globally

Climate and Related Physical Factors	Expected Direction of Change	Potential Impacts
Atmospheric CO2	Increase	1. Increased biomass production and increasedpotential efficiency of physiological water usein crops and weeds. 2. Modified hydrologic balance of soils due to C/N ratio modification. 3. Changed weed ecology with potential for increased weed competition with crops.
Atmospheric O3	Increase	Crop yield decrease.
Sea level	Increase	Sea level intrusion in coastal agricultural areasCausing salinization to the soil and underground water supply.
Extreme events	Poorly known, but significant increased temporal and spatial variability expected increased frequency of floods and droughts	1. Crop failure. 2. Yield decrease. 3. Competition for water.
Precipitationintensity	Intensifiedhydrological cycle, but with regionalvariations	1. Changed patterns of erosion and accretion. 2. Changed storm impacts. 3. Changed occurrence of storm flooding andstorm damage. 4. Increased water logging. 5. Increased pest damage.
Temperature	Increase	1. Modifications in crop suitability and Productivity. 2. Changes in weeds, crop pests and diseases. 3. Changes in water requirements. 4. Changes in crop quality.
Heat stress	Increases in heatwaves	Damage to grain formation, increase in some Pests.

Source: Iglesias (2009)

The simulation results also showed that as compared to world average agricultural production the agricultural productivity in China would decline less. Brussel (2009) stated that rising atmospheric CO_2 concentration, higher temperatures, changes in annual and seasonal precipitation patterns and in the frequency of extreme events will affect the volume, quality, quantity, stability of food production and the natural environment in which agriculture takes place.

Climatic variations will have consequences for the availability of water resources, frequency of pest and diseases, and soil quality, leading to significant changes in the conditions for agriculture and livestock production. In extreme cases, accordingly, the degradation of agricultural ecosystems could mean desertification, resulting in a total loss of the productive capacity of the land in question. Sinha *et al*., (2009) stated that plants grown at elevated CO_2 have changed morphology, anatomy, chemical composition and gene expression profiles, in addition to increased biomass and yield, the stimulation of photosynthesis at elevated CO_2 levels lead to increased production and accumulation of carbohydrates in plant organs, generally leading to reduced protein in grain as well as increased starch concentration in the grain of Triticum species. Kang *et al*., (2009) predicted that Africa will be one of the sectors most vulnerable to climate change and variability, because a significant proportion of the African economy is dependent on agriculture, most of Africa's water (85%) is used for agriculture, farming techniques are relatively primitive, the majority of the continent is already hot and dry, spatial and temporal changes in precipitation and temperature patterns will shift agro-ecological zones and thus have major impacts on the viability of both dryland and irrigated farming.

Hatfield (2010) stated that, although crop yield is frequently limited under agriculture conditions by carbon gain, the optimum temperature for photosynthesis, vegetative growth, and reproductive development is nearly always higher than the seasonal temperature optimum for yield. Thus, while any inhibition of photosynthesis caused by high-temperature excursions in the future should be expected to result in reduced yield, the temperature dependence of other physiological processes clearly will also play an important and in some cases more important role. The reproductive stage of development is determinant of yield in crops cultivated for seeds or fruits. In annual crops, higher temperatures can drive shorter life cycles, resulting in less seasonal photosynthesis, shorter reproductive phase, and thus lower yield.

Vegetative development is accelerated in cereals with increasing temperature, but it is the dramatically shorter grain-filling period with rising temperature that portends major consequences for yield. Even assuming no differences in daily photosynthesis, yield of cereals decreases in proportion to the shortening of the grain-filling period as temperature increases. For example, temperatures as low as 25°C can reduce the grain-filling period in wheat, after which a 1°C temperature rise shortens the reproductive phase by 6%, shortens the grain-filling duration by 5%, and reduces grain yield and harvest index proportionally. Mereu (2010) explored separately the indirect CO_2 effect (related to changed weather conditions) and the direct CO_2 effect (known as a fertilization effect), for three future periods. In general, the results show that the indirect effect of CO_2 concentration is negative. Considering the four experimental sites and the high GCM-based scenarios, crop yield will decrease by 2-6% for 2025, and by 10-18% for 2075, due in particular to the higher temperatures and more frequent drought projected. On the other hand, considering both direct and indirect effects of CO_2 concentration, the wheat yield will increase by 5-7% for 2025 and by 16-21% for 2075. This means that the positive fertilization effect of increased CO_2 concentration could be sufficient to level out the negative impact of indirect effects.

Khalil *et al.*, (2010) studied the effect of climate change on the yield of three wheat varieties (Sids1, Sakha 93 and Giza 168) and consumptive use was studied by implementing two-year field experiment in Giza, Egypt using CropSyst model with two climate change scenarios. These scenarios were A_2 (temperature increase by 3.1°C and CO_2 concentration is 834 ppm) and B_2 (temperature increase by 2.2°C and CO_2 concentration is 601 ppm) developed by Hadley Center for Climate Prediction and Research. CropSyst model was validated using the collected data of wheat yield and consumptive use. The scenarios were used to run the CropSyst model and to predict the expected yield in the year of 2038. Two early sowing dates were proposed as adaptation options, i.e. 1st of November and 21st of October to reduce the harm effect of climate change on wheat yield and a new irrigation schedule was used. The results indicated that CropSyst predictions for yield and consumptive use were highly accurate. Furthermore, A_2 scenario predicted greater reduction in wheat yield, compared with B_2 scenario in the year of 2038.

Thomson *et al.*, (2010) stated that, rising temperatures will allow both insects and pathogens to expand their ranges to regions where they were once not found. In addition, warmer winter temperatures allow more insects to survive over the winter, whereas colder winters once controlled their populations. Furthermore, changes in climate have the potential to disrupt the natural enemies of some crop pests (beneficial insects), ultimately producing greater overall crop vulnerability. Predicted impacts of climate change on agriculture production are shown in figure 6.7.

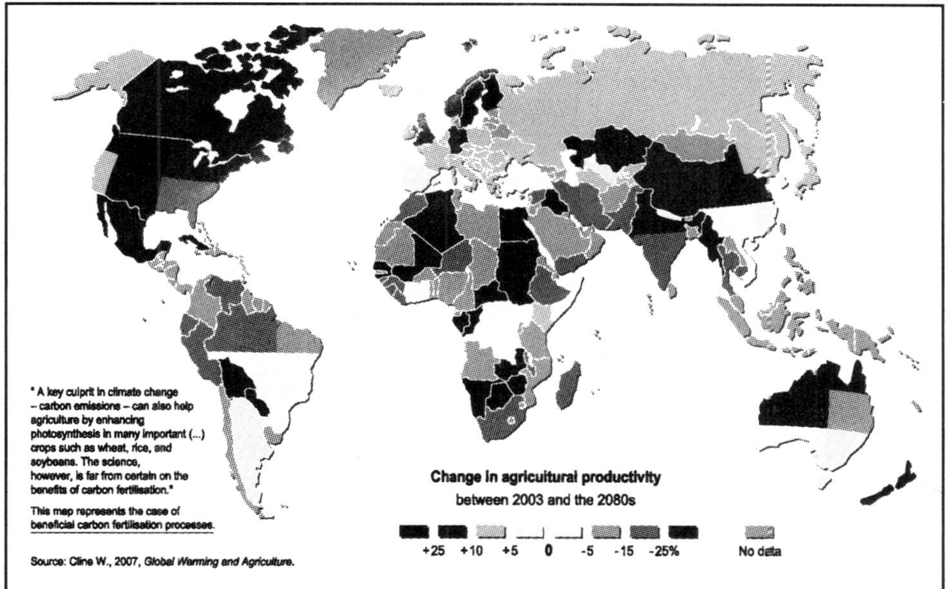

Fig. 6.7: Predicted Impact of Climate Change on Agriculture Production

IMPACT OF CLIMATE CHANGES ON EGYPT

Egypt is located in the north-eastern corner of the African continent with an area about one million square kilometers. It is considered a developing country burdened by the scarcity of natural resources associated with extreme population growth (over 85 million people in total). The inhabited area of the country constitutes only 5% of the total area of the country which is confined to the narrow strip of the Nile valley and Delta. Its only source of water -the River Nile- provides more than 95% of all water available to the country. The source of this water comes from rainfall on Ethiopian hills (86%) and equatorial lakes (14%) (Eid, *et al.*, 2006). Egypt considered one of the top five countries expected to be mostly impacted with climate changes (El-Raey, 2009).

Moreover, climate change will probably affect water resources requiring reduction in irrigation water and that might pose another problem for agricultural production (Eid, *et al.*, 2006). Climate change poses significant risks through sea level rise on the coastal zone, which is already subsiding at approximately 3-5mm/year, with country averaged mean temperature increases of 1.4°C and 2.5°C projected by 2050 and 2100 (Dasgupta, *et al.*, 2009). Sea level rise will adversely impact prime agricultural land in the Nile delta through inundation and salinization. Egypt's climate is expected to get drier and warmer thus pressures on agriculture will affect crops productivity and also their water use efficiency (Abou-Hadid, 2006). In summary, expected climatic change, population increase, urbanization and industrial development as well as irrigation intensification constantly increase water demand and can intensify the vulnerability of agriculture in Egypt (Eid *et al.*, 2006).

Also, the increase of temperature and frequency of extreme events expected to affect crop yield as well as causing changes in the agricultural distribution of crops. Furthermore, it will negatively affect marginal land and force farmers to abandon them increasing desertification and unemployment associated with loss of income consequently political unrest (El-Raey, 2009). Adaptation to climate change in Egypt is a major issue from the perspectives of food production, rural population stabilization, and distribution of water resources. Egypt is taking several actions in cooperation with global communities to protect the risked areas by serious research work and setting new environmental regulations (Fahmy, 2007). It has been stated that the Egyptian government had been working for the past decades on adaptation and mitigation strategies to reduce the negative impact of climate changes on crop production, sea erosion and shore protection, as well as improving irrigation efficiency and agriculture drainage-water reuse (Bates, 2008).

REFERENCES

Abou-Hadid, A.F. (2006): Assessment of Impacts, Adaptation and Vulnerability to Climate Change in North Africa: Food Production and Water Resources. Assessments of Impacts and Adaptations to Climate Change, Washington, DC.

Attri, S.D. and Rathore, L.S. (2003): Simulation of Impact of Projected Climate Change on Wheat in India. Int. J. Climatol., 23: 693-705.

Bates, B.C., Z.W. Kundzewicz, S. Wu, and J.P. Palutiko (2008): Climate Change and Water. Technical Paper of the Intergovernmental Panel on Climate Change, IPCC Secretariat, Geneva, 210 pp.

Blum, A. (2009): Effective Use of Water (EUW) and not Water-use Efficiency (WUE) is the Target of Crop Yield Improvement Under Drought Stress. Field Crops Research, 112: 119-123.

Branca, G., and N. McCarthy (2011): Climate-smart Agriculture: A Synthesis of Empirical Evidence of Food Security and Mitigation Benefits from Improved Cropland Management. Working Paper. Rome, FAO.

Brussel, S.E. (2009): Adapting to Climate Changes: The Challenge for European Agriculture and Rural Areas. Commission of the European Communities. Commission Working Staff Working Document Accompanying the White Paper No. 147.

Burke, M.B., Lobell D.B. and Guarino, L. (2009): Global Environ. Change, 19: 317-325.

Campbell, B. and W. Mann (2011): Addressing Agriculture in Climate Change Negotiations: A Scoping Report, Meridian Institute.

Carter, T.R. (2007): Changes in the Thermal Growing Season in Nordic Countries during the Past Century and Prospects for the Future. Agricultural Food Science in Finland, 7: 161-179.

Cayan, D.R., Maurer, E.P., Dettinger, M.D., Tyree, M. and Hayhoe, K. (2008): Climate Change Scenarios for the California Region. Climatic Change, 87: 21-42.

Chancellor, T. and Kubiriba, J. (2006): The Effects of Climate Change on Infectious Diseases of Plants. Foresight: Infectious Diseases: Preparing for the Future.

Clements, R., J. Haggar, A. Quezada, and J. Torres (2011): Technologies for Climate Change Adaptation – Agriculture Sector. X. Zhu (Ed.). UNEP Risø Centre, Roskilde, 2011.

Cline, W.R. (2007): Global Warming and Agriculture March 2008, Volume 45, Number 1, http://www.imf.org/external/pubs/ft/fandd/2008/03/cline.htm.

Cools, H.J. and Fraaije, B.A. (2008): Mechanisms of Resistance to Azole Fungicides in *Mycosphaerella graminicola*. Pest Management Science, 64: 681-684.

Cowie, J. (2007): Climate Change: Biological and Human Aspects. 487 pp, Cambridge University Press.

Dasgupta, S., B. Laplante, S. Murray, and D. Wheeler (2009): Sea-Level Rise and Storm Surges Policy Research Working Paper 4901, Washington: The World Bank- Development Research Group-Environment and Energy Team.

Deal, R.B. and Henikoff, S. (2011): Histone Variants and Modifications in Plant Gene Regulation. Current Opinion in Plant Biology, 14, 116-122.

Devereux, S. and Edwards, J., (2004): Climate Change and Food Security. IDS Bulletin, 35 (3) 22-30.

Easterling, W.E., P.K. Aggarwal, P. Batima, K.M. Brander, L. Erda, S.M. Howden, A. Kirilenko, J. Morton, J.F. Soussana, J. Schmidhuber and F.N. Tubiello (2007): Food, Fibre and Forest Products. Climate Change 2007: Impacts, Adaptation and Vulnerability. Contribution of Working Group II to the Fourth Assessment Report of the Intergovernmental Panel on Climate Change, M.L. Parry, O.F. Canziani, J.P. Palutikof, P.J. van der Linden and C.E. Hanson, Eds., Cambridge University Press, Cambridge, UK, 273-313.

Eid, H.M., El-Marsafawy, S.M. and Ouda, S.A. (2006): Assessing the Impacts of Climate Change on Agriculture in Egypt: A Ricardian Approach. Centre for Environmental Economics and Policy in Africa (CEEPA) Discussion Paper No. 16, Special Series on Climate Change and Agriculture in Africa, University of Pretoria, Pretoria, 1-33.

El-Marsafawy S.M. (2006): Impact of Climate Change on Sunflower Crop Production in Egypt. Proceeding of The 2nd International Conf. on Water Resources & Arid Environment, Saudia Arabia.

El-Raey, M. (2009): The Cost of Coastal Vulnerability to Climate Change, Conference on Climate Change and Coastal Cities, Beaches and the Delta, Cairo, Egypt.

Fahmy, A., (2007): Climate Change in Nile Delta, http://gc21.inwent.org/ibt/alumni /ibt/ docs /writoec-ahmed-kalaf-fahmy.pdf (accessed July 19, 2009).

Falloon, P.D. and R.A. Betts (2009): Climate Impacts on European Agriculture and Water Management in the Context of Adaptation and Mitigation - The Importance of an Integrated Approach." Science of the Total Environment doi:10.1016/j. scitotenv.2009.05.02.

Gornall, J., Betts, R., Burke, E., Clark, R., Camp, J., Willett, K. and Wiltshire, A. (2010): Implications of Climate Change for Agricultural Productivity in the Early Twenty-first Century. Phil. Trans. R. Soc. B., 365: 2973-2989.

Hatfield, J.L. (2010): Climate Impacts on Agriculture in the United States: The Value of Past Observations. Chapter 10. In D. Hillel and C. Rosenzwieg (eds.) Handbook of Climate Change and Agroecosystems: Impact, Adaptation and Mitigation. Imperial College Press, London UK.

Hogy, P., Wieser, H., Kohler, P., Schwadorf, K., Breuer, J., Erbs, M., Weber, S and Fangmeier A. (2009): Does Elevated Atmospheric CO_2 Allow for Sufficient Wheat Grain Quality in the Future?. Journal of Applied Botany and Food Quality, 82, 114-121.

Holst, R., Yu, X., and Grun, C. (2010): Climate Change, Risk and Grain Production in China. 2010 AAEA, CAES, WAEA Joint Annual Meeting (p. 29). Colorado: Agriculture and Applied Economics Association.

Iglesias, A., Cancelliere, A., Cubillo, F., Garrote, L., Wilhite, D.A. (2009): Coping with Drought Risk in Agriculture and Water Supply Systems: Drought Management and Policy Development in the Mediterranean. Springer, Netherlands.

IPCC, (2007): Climate Change: The Physical Science Basis, Contribution from Working Group I to the Fourth Assessment Report, Policy Maker Summary. Intergovernmental Panel on Climate Change. Cambridge University Press, Cambridge, UK.

Kang, Y., Khan, S. and Ma, X. (2009): Climate Change Impacts on Crop Yield, Crop Water Productivity and Food Security – A Review. Progress in Natural Science, 19: 1665-1674.

Khalil, F.H. Farag, Gamal S. El Afandi and Samiha, A. Ouda (2010): Vulnerability and Adaptation of Wheat to Climate Changes in Middle Egypt. Thirteenth International Water Technology Conference, IWTC 13 2009, Hurghada, Egypt.

Leakey, A.D., Ainsworth, E.A., Bernacchi, C.J., Rogers, A., Long, S.P. and Ort, D. R. (2009): Elevated CO2 Effects on Plant Carbon, Nitrogen, and Water Relations: Six Important Lessons from FACE. Journal of Experimental Botany, 60: 2859-2876.

Lobell, D.B., Burke, M.B., Tebaldi, C., Mastrandrea, M.D., Falcon, W.P. and Naylor, R.L. (2008): Prioritizing Climate Change Adaptation Needs for Food Security in 2030. Science, 319: 607-610.

Medellín, J., J.J. Harou, M.A. Olivares, K. Madani, J.R. Lund, R.E. Howitt, S.K. Tanaka, M.W. Jenkins, and T. Zhu (2008): Adaptability and Adaptations of California's Water Supply System to Dry Climate Warming. Climatic Change, 87: 75-90.

Mereu, V. (2010): Climate Change Impact on Durum Wheat in Sardinia. Ph.D., Thesis. Fac. Agric. Sardinia, Italy.

Musser, F.P and A.M. Shelton. (2005): The Influence of Post-exposure Temperature on the Toxicity of Insecticides to *Ostrinia nubilalis* (Lepidoptera:Crambidae). Pest Manag Sci., 61: 508-510.

Nabi, G. and Mullins, C.E. (2008): Soil Temperature Dependent Growth of Cotton Seedlings Before Emergence. Pedosphere, 18(1): 54-59.

Ngigi, S. (2009): Climate Change Adaptation Strategies: Water Resources Management Options for Smallholder Farming Systems in Sub-Saharan Africa. Nairobi/New York: The MDG Centre, East & Southern Africa/The Earth Institute at Columbia University.

Patil, R.H., Leagdsmand, M., Olesen, J.E. and Porter, J.R. (2010): Growth and Yield Response of Winter Wheat to Soil Warming and Rainfall Patterns. J. Agric. Sci., 148: 553-566.

Patterson, D.T., J.K. Westbrook, R.J. Joyce, P.D. Lingren, and J. Rogasik. (1999): Weeds, Insects, and Disease. Climatic Change, 43: 711-27.

Peltonen S.P., Jauhiainen, L., Hakala, K., Ojanen, H. (2009): Climate Change and Prolongation of Growing Season: Changes in Regional Potential for Field Crop Production in Finland. Agric Food Sci, 18: 171.

Pfeffer, W.T., J.T. Harper and S.O. Neel (2008): Kinematic Constraints on Glacier Contributions to 21st Century Sea-Level Rise. Science, 321 (5894): 1340-1343.

Rahmstorf, S. (2007) Recent Climate Observations Compared to Projections. Science, 316: 709.

Rosenzweig, C., Iglesias, A., Yang, X.B., Epstein, P.R. and Chivian, E. (2002): Climate Change and Extreme Weather Events: Implications for Food Production, Plant Diseases and Pests. Global Change and Human Health, 2(2): 90-104.

Sadava, D., Heller, H.C., Orians, G.H., Purves, W.K. and Hillis, D.M. (2008): Life: the Science of Biology. 8th Edition, Sinauer Associates, Sunderland, MA. 1338 pp.

Sharad, K.J. (2012): Sustainable Water Management in India Considering Likely Climate and Other Changes. Current Science, 102. (2): 177-188.

Sinha, P.G., Kapoor, R., Uprety, D.C. and Bhatnagar, A.K. (2009): Impact of Elevated CO_2 Concentration on Ultrastructure of Pericarp and Composition of Grain in Three Triticum Species of Different Ploidy Levels. Environ. Exptl. Bot., 66: 451-456.

Tadross, M.A., W.J. Gutowski, B.C. Hewitson and C.J. Jack, (2005), Simulations of Interannual Change and the Diurnal Cycle of Southern African Regional Climate, Theor. Appl. Climatol., 25: 151-159.

Taub, D.R., Miller, B. and Allen, H. (2008): Effects of Elevated CO_2 on the Protein Concentration of Food Crops: A Meta-analysis. Global Change Biology., 14(3): 565-575.

Thomson, L.J., S. Macfadyen and A.A. Hoffmann (2010): Predicting the Effects of Climate Change on Natural Enemies of Agricultural Pests. Biological Control, 52 (3): 296-306.

Trenberth, K.E. (2011): Changes in Precipitation with Climate Change. Climate Research, 47: 123-138.

Tubiello, F., Soussana, J.F., Howden, S.M. and Easterling, W. (2007): Crop and Pasture Response to Climate Change. PNAS, 104: 19686-19690.

Varshney, R.K., Bansal, K.C., Aggarwal, P.K., Datta, S.K. and Craufurd, P.Q. (2011): Agricultural Biotechnology for Crop Improvement in a Variable Climate: Hope or Hype?. Trends in Plant Science, 16: 363-371.

Zhai, F. and Zhuang, J. (2009): Agriculture Impact of Climate Change: A General Equilibrium Analysis with Special Reference to Southeast Asia. ADBI Working Paper 131. Asian Development Bank Institute.

Pages: 126-145

SOIL CHARACTERISTICS AND AGRO-ECOLOGY

Edited by: Dr. Avnish Chauhan; Dr. Pawan Kumar 'Bharti'

ISBN: 978-93-5056-758-6

Edition: 2015

Published by: Discovery Publishing House Pvt. Ltd., New Delhi (India)

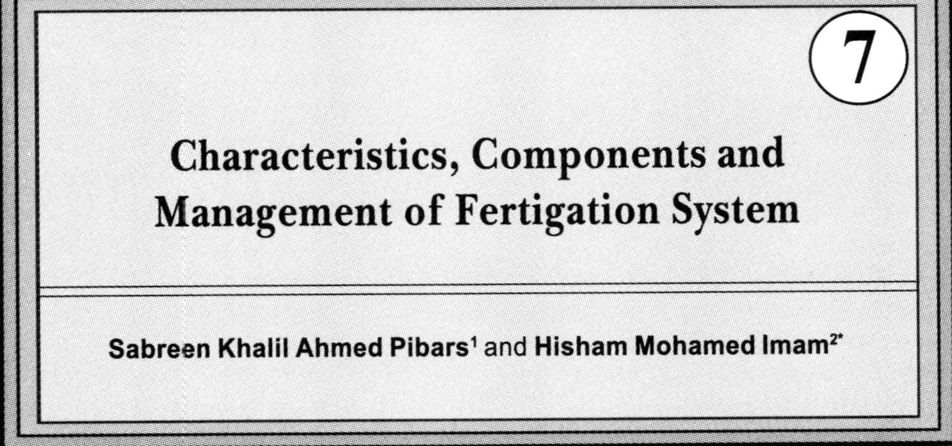

7 Characteristics, Components and Management of Fertigation System

Sabreen Khalil Ahmed Pibars[1] and Hisham Mohamed Imam[2*]

ABBREVIATIONS

ADC	Analog-to-digital converter
APP	Ammonium polyphosphates
DAP	Diammonium phosphate
EC	Electrical conductivity
ha	Hectare
kg ha^{-1}	Kilogram per hectare
MAP	Monoammonium phosphate
PIC16F87XA	Pin Enhanced Flash Microcontrollers
UAN	Urea ammonium nitrate
UP	Urea-phosphate solutions

1 National Research Centre, Agricultural Division, Water Relations and Field Irrigation Department, 33 El-Tahrir St., Dokki, Giza, 12311 Cairo, Egypt.

2 Agricultural Engineering Research Institute, Field Irrigation and Drainage Researches Department, Nadi El-Said St., Dokki, Giza, 12311 Cairo, Egypt.

INTRODUCTION

According to the population projections of the World Bank, the world's population will increase from 6 billion people in 1999 to 7 billion people in 2020. Countries in Africa or South Asia have the highest growth rates or a high absolute increase in the number of people. Consequently, the world demand on food will increase by the global population growing. World food production can be increased by: (a) intensifying food crop production on land already under cultivation and (b) expanding the planted to food crops, e.g. through more continuous use of the very large area of poor soils which are now usually employed only for "shifting cultivation". The success of both methods will depend on judicious use of fertilizers (FAO 1981; 2000).

Fertigation is application of plant nutrients through irrigation water. It is a modern agro-technique provides an excellent opportunity to maximize yield and minimize environmental pollution (Hagin et al., 2002) by increasing fertilizer use efficiency, minimizing fertilizer application and increasing return on the fertilizer invested. It can improve fertilizer timing and reduce non-beneficial losses in deep percolation and surface runoff. Although this is possible with other methods of irrigation, it is a common and easily achieved practice with micro-irrigation systems. Being applied with irrigation, the fertilizer is easy to apply, with little extra labour and no extra machinery. Provided the hydraulic design of irrigation system is adequate, the fertilizer is applied uniformly to each plant, targeted at the root zone. Fertilizer can be applied at frequent intervals and at any required concentration, to suit plant requirements (Wichelns, 2007; Kafkafi and Tarchitzky, 2011).

The factors that govern the fertigation are soil types, crops, methods of irrigation used, water quality, types of fertilizers available, economic feasibility, equipment etc. Water and nutrient are the main factors of production in irrigated agriculture and the major inputs contributing to higher productivity. In intensive agriculture, both fertilizer and irrigation management have contributed immensely in increasing the yield and quality of crops. The method of fertilizer and irrigation application affects the efficiency of these inputs in arid and semi-arid regions (Biswas, 2010).

Various types of injection equipment are used to deliver fertilizer concentrate into the irrigation mainline. The most common used injectors are pressure differential tank, venturi suction device, and positive displacement (diaphragm or piston) injection pump. Both pressure differential tank and venturi are driven by pressure differentiation, where the positive displacement is driven electrically or hydraulically. The latter is the most expensive one, but gives greatest control over fertilizer application and therefore more accurate and flexible management. Other factors in the choice of system include suitability to automation, effect on pressure in the mainline, resistance to corrosion, maintenance requirements, and whether fertilizer is to be injected in proportion to water flow through the main on a continuous basis, or in separate, defined doses (so that injection rate is independent of irrigation rate) (Southorn, 1997).

Gains in net income due to fertigation can help justify the initial investment and the variable costs of operating and maintaining micro irrigation systems. Those gains are more likely to be achieved on high-valued crops, such as fruits as vegetables (Wichelns, 2007). Fares and Abbas, (2009) reported that savings about 29-78% in application costs may result due to the improved efficiency of fertilizer application, low fertilizer leaching, precise nutrient application, and right-amount and right-time fertilizer application. Although no significant increases in crop yield have been reported (Alva et al. 2005), uptake of major plant nutrients, i.e., nitrogen, phosphorous, and potassium, is higher with fertigation than with conventional methods (Papadopoulos 1988).

The article will review the management Techniques of fetigation to maximize both water and fertilizer use efficiency under suitable irrigation methods. This targeted improving crop yield productivity with an economical costs and taking into consideration human and environmental protection aspects are the main target of the article.

FERTIGATION

Definitions

Fertigation is the application of water soluble solid fertilizer or liquid fertilizers through drip irrigation water (Biswas, 2010). The use of fertigation is gaining popularity because of its efficiencies in nutrient management, time and labour and potentially a greater control over crop performance (Treeby et al. 2011). It is an efficient and economical mean of applying inputs necessary for crop, turf, nursery, greenhouse, and landscape management among others (The Irrigation Association 2000).

Advantages

Fertigation offers a numerous benefits by applying though different irrigation methods (Evans and Waller, 2007; Biswas, 2010). These include:

- Fertilizer application is synchronized with plant need which variesrom plant to plant in drip fertigation, the amount and form of nutrient supply is regulated as per the need of the critical stages of plant growth.
- Optimization of nutrient balance in soils by supplying the nutrients directly to the effective root zones as per the requirement.
- Reduction in labour and energy cost by making use of water distribution systems for nutrient application.
- Timely application of small but precise amounts of fertilizers directly to the roots zone. This improves fertilizer use efficiency and reduces nutrient leaching below the root zone.

- Ensures a uniform flow of water and nutrients.
- Improves availability of nutrients and their uptake by crop.
- Safety application method, as it eliminates the danger affecting roots due to higher dose.
- Lower energy requirements for applying agrochemicals.
- Minimal percolation of water transporting chemicals and minerals below the root zone.
- Improves productivity through better control of the root environment relative to water and nutrient availability throughout the growing season.
- Reduces soil compaction due to much lower vehicular traffic.
- Reduces foliar crop damage.
- Improves and timely application of micronutrients (e.g., chelated iron, manganese, zinc and other micronutrients) fertilizers.
- Reduced wind drift of agrochemicals
- Improves incorporation of agrochemicals into the soil matrix.
- Reduces application cost.
- Decreases worker exposure to agrochemicals hazards.

Disadvantages

There are also disadvantages to fertigation which include (Evans and Waller, 2007):

- High management requirements. Careful management and supervision is required for accurate and safe applications, calibration, handling, maintenance and use of safety equipment.
- Uniformity of fertigation will depend upon a well-designed and operated maintained irrigation system.
- High initial equipment costs. Injectors, safety equipment, emergency showers, and containment areas are needed, but are usually less costly than for ground application equipment. Restricted storage and containment facilities for large volumes of dilute liquids may be required. Portability of injection equipment is usually limited unless mounted on trailers.
- Complexity of chemical interactions. Various fertilizers may have to be injected at separated points to limit reactions with fertilizers and/or biocides that are applied simultaneously.
- Chemical corrosion may reduce the life of irrigation system components.
- Environmental risk of system mismanagement or improper design. The possibility of water source contamination is increased if appropriate equipment is not correctly installed, operated, and maintained.

- Irrigation/fertigation scheduling difficulties. Timing, amount, and label requirements for fertigation may influence irrigation scheduling and depth of water applications.
- Fertilizers might be required when irrigations are not necessary; this increases the potential for leaching.
- Placement problems. Limited wetted area could limit access to nutrients in the dry soil volumes resulting in temporal crop nutrient stresses. Excessive applications of some nutrients may induce micronutrient deficiencies that are difficult to correct.
- Enhanced biological clogging hazards. Bacterial growth may be enhanced in the irrigation system components by nutrients addition.
- Disposal of back flush and rinse water. Back flush water from filter cleaning activities as well as rinse water from cleaning injection equipment may require special disposal measures due to the presence of various fertilizers.

SUITABILITY OF FERTILIZERS FOR FERTIGATION

Tayel, (2010) generalized the following considerations of the used fertilizers used in fertigaion:

- High solubility in irrigation water at normal temperature.
- Available in local market with suitable price.
- Contains the needed nutrients for plant in available compounds.
- Reaction may not occur between fertilizers each other or/and metal parts in the irrigation system which result in precipitates.
- Low level of vaporized loss of some forms of nitrogen fertilizers.
- Movement of fertilizer through soil profile has no restrictions comparing with water movement.
- Safe in field use.
- Improve both the quantity and quality of planted crop.
- Supplied from trusted commercial sources.

FERTIGATION SYSTEM COMPONENTS

Chemical injection into irrigation systems (Fig. 7.1) requires three basic components (Evans and Waller, 2007):

(a) Chemical supply tank;

(b) Injection system; and

(c) Safety and anti-pollution devices to prevent any potential contamination of the water source.

Fertilizer Tank

Fertilizer tank is usually made of polyethylene or fiberglass.

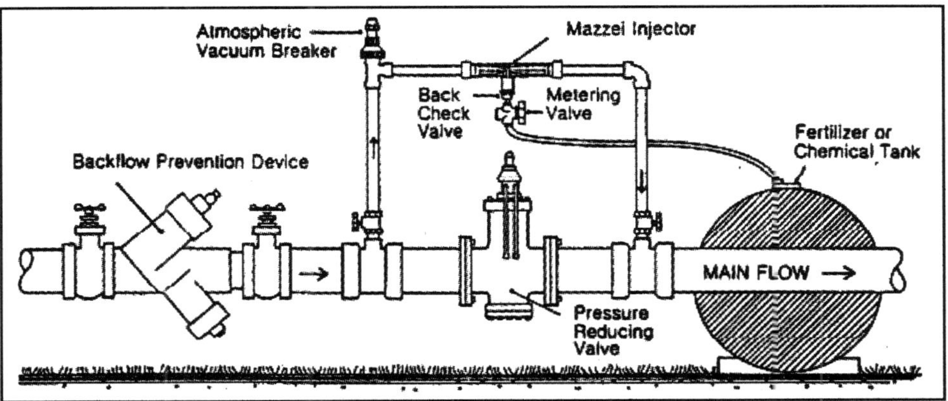

Fig. 7.1: Fertigation System Components Connected to the Irrigation System Main Line

Appropriate size chemical tanks equipped for agitation and a calibration tube are important to successful chemigation (The Irrigation Association 2000). Tank size is an important consideration for a fertigation system. Tank size should be large enough to contain the chemicals sufficient for at least one fertigation operation. To avoid overflow and to accommodate dead storage, it is always recommended to have a 10% extra tank volume. The size of the tank can be doubled, tripled, or increased to any size depending upon the number of fertigation planned between tank refilling (Fares and Abbas, 2009). As metal tanks may corrode plastic containers are preferred for the stock solution (Papadopoulos, 2001). A sensor can be placed within the fertilizer tank. The sensor shuts the injection system off after the required volume of chemical is injected. It is a good practice to place a solenoid valve on the fertilizer injection tank discharge line. The solenoid valve (normally closed) should be interlocked with the irrigation pump so that the chemical tank is isolated from the irrigation pipeline in case of malfunction The solenoid valve can also be connected to pressure switches and flow sensors to provide extra protection (Evans and Waller, 2007).

Proper selection of a chemical solution tank must include consideration of the following (The Irrigation Association 2000):

- Type of irrigation system.
- Crop grown.
- Irrigation system flow rate.
- Injection rate.
- Irrigation system operating pressure.
- Determination of whether a fixed volume ratio of chemical to water is needed.
- Duration of operation.
- Expansion requirements.

Injection Devices

There are many types of injectors available, all with their own advantages and disadvantages. Some types of injection systems are not recommended due to the safety hazards that are inherent with those systems. According to the Irrigation Association, (2000) the choice of method and equipment will depend on the following:

- Type of chemical to be injected.
- Safety consideration.
- Source of power.
- Portability versus permanent installation.

Pressure Differential Tank

This system utilizes an air tight pressure metal tank with anti-acid internal wall protection in which a pressure differential is created by a throttle valve that diverts part of the irrigation water into the tank. This is the only fertigation system that enables the use of both solid and liquid fertilizers. The entire fertilizer amount in the tank is delivered to the irrigation area. The concentration at the water emitter end is kept constant as long as a solid fertilizer is present in the tank and solubility of the fertilizer is quickly achieved. Once the solid fraction is completely dissolved the fertilizer concentration is reduced at an exponential rate. In practice, when four tank volumes have passed through it, only a negligible amount of fertilizer is left in the tank. This equipment was used in the early stages of fertigation development. A limited area can be irrigated at a time according to the tank volume. The use of solid fertilizers must be handled with care (Kafkafi and Tarchitzky, 2011).

Advantages (Imas, 1999):

- Very simple to operate, the stock solution does have not to be pre-mixed.
- Easy to install and requires very little maintenance.
- Easy to change fertilizers.
- Ideal for dry formulations.
- No electricity or fuel is needed.

Disadvantages:

- Concentration of solution decreases as fertilizer dissolves.
- Accuracy of application is limited.
- Requires pressure loss in main irrigation line or a booster pump.
- Proportional fertigation is not possible.
- Limited capacity.
- Not adapted for automation.

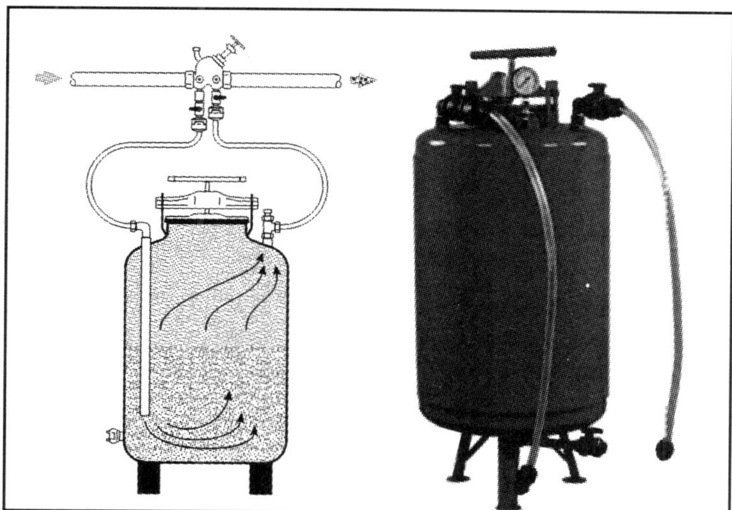

Fig. 7.2: Pressure Differential Tank

Venturi Suction Device

This is a unit that makes use of the Venturi suction principle by using the pressure induced by the flowing water to suck the fertilizer solution from the fertilizer tank into the irrigation line. A conical constriction in the pipe induces an increase in the water flow velocity and a pressure decrease to an extremely low value which causes fertilizer suction (through the filter screens) from the supply tank through a tube into the irrigation system. A valve can be adjusted to control the difference between the water velocities across the valves (Kafkafi and Tarchitzky, 2011).

Advantages (Imas, 1999):

- Very simple to operate, no moving parts.
- Easy to install and to maintain.
- Suitable for very low injection rates.
- Injection can be controlled with a metering valve.
- Suitable for both Proportional and quantitative fertilization.

Disadvantages:

- Requires pressure loss in main irrigation line or a booster pump.
- Quantitative fertigation is difficult.
- Automation is difficult.

Positive Displacement Pump

Positive-displacement pumps are able to raise the pressure of the liquid fertilizer from a stock solution tank at a predetermined ratio between fertilizer solution volumes to irrigation water volume, hence achieving a proportional distribution of nutrient in the irrigation water.

Positive-displacement pumps are recommended where precise control of injection flow rate of chemicals is required. Flow rate of positive displacement pumps remain constant over a range of irrigation pipeline pressures and chemical viscosities. Positive displacement pumps can typically control injection flow rates with a range of error of ±1% to 2%.Two types of injectors are commonly used in fertigation: piston pumps and diaphragm pumps. (Evans and Waller, 2007; Kafkafi and Tarchitzky, 2011) mentioned that the most common power sources for fertigation pumps are:

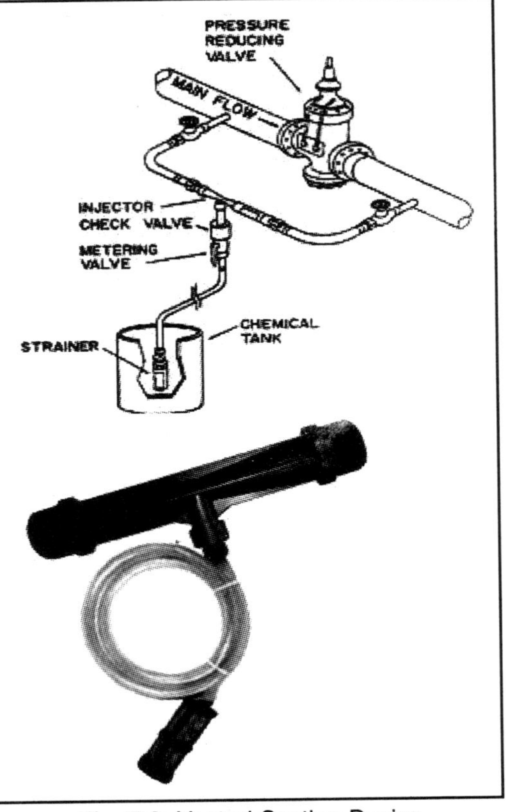

Fig. 7.3: Venturi Suction Device

- *Hydraulic energy:* The device uses the hydraulic pressure of the irrigation water to inject nutrient solution while the water used to propel it (approximately three times the volume of solution injected) is discharged. These pumps are suitable for fertigation in areas devoid from any source of energy.
- *Electric dosing pumps:* The device activates the fertilizer pump. These are common in glasshouses and in areas where electricity is available and reliable.

Advantages (Imas, 1999):

- Very accurate, for Proportional fertigation.
- No pressure loss in the line.
- Easily adapted for automation.

Disadvantages:

- Expensive.
- Complicated design, including a number of moving parts, so wear and breakdown are more likely.

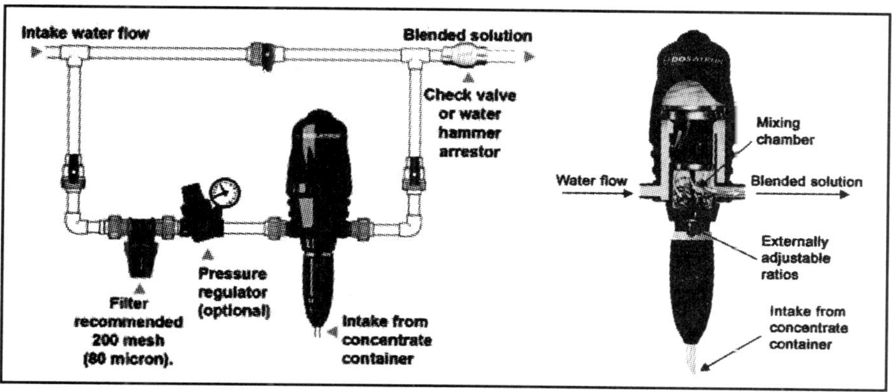

Fig. 7.4: Positive Displacement Pump

Chemicals Injection Calculations

The rate at which any chemical is to be injected into the irrigation water should be calculated carefully. It depends on the concentration of the liquid fertilizer and the desired quantity of nutrients to be applied during the irrigation. It can be computed by (Keller and Bliesner, 1990):

$$q_c = \frac{F_r A}{c' t_r T_a}$$

q_c	=	rate of injection of liquid fertilizer solution into the system,	(L/hr)
F_r	=	fertilizer application rate (quantity of nutrients to be applied) per irrigation cycle,	(kg/ha)
A	=	area irrigated in T_a,	(ha)
T_a	=	irrigation application or set time,	(hr)
c'	=	concentration of actual nutrients in the liquid fertilizer,	(kg/L)
t_r	=	ratio between fertilizing time and irrigation application time	

The fertilizer tank capacity can be calculated as follows (Ismail, 2008):

$$V = \frac{F_r A}{c'}$$

V = fertilizer tank capacity (L)

The needed amount of commercial fertilizers is:

$$F_q = c' - V$$

F_q = commercial fertilizers (kg)

Safety Components

Adequate backflow prevention is required to protect groundwater and drinking water supplies from chemical contamination. Many types of backflow prevention are available in the market. In addition, many governmental agencies in same countries specify that the location of the chemigation system must be at a minimum distance, such as 30 m, from a water well, stream, drainage way, or other water source to reduce the pollution potential.

Chemigation has three main ways of potentially polluting irrigation water sources if safety devices are not functioning correctly (Evans and Waller, 2007):

- The chemical in the supply tank and in the irrigation pipeline could flow or be siphoned back into the water source when the irrigation system shuts down because of mechanical or power failures.
- The chemigation system could continue to inject chemical into the irrigation pipeline when the irrigation system shuts down causing the chemical solution to flow back into the water source or spill onto the ground. Continued injection of concentrated chemicals into a non-flowing irrigation line can also result in toxic solutions to be applied in a small areas of the field when the irrigation system is restarted creating a potential for runoff into surface water supplies as well as crop damage.
- The chemigation system could shut down while the irrigation system continues to operate and force water back into the chemical supply tank causing it to overflow and spill concentrated chemicals onto the ground.

Backflow Prevention Device

A safety device is used to prevent water pollution or contamination by preventing flow of a mixture of water and/or chemicals in the opposite direction of that intended (ASAE, 1998).

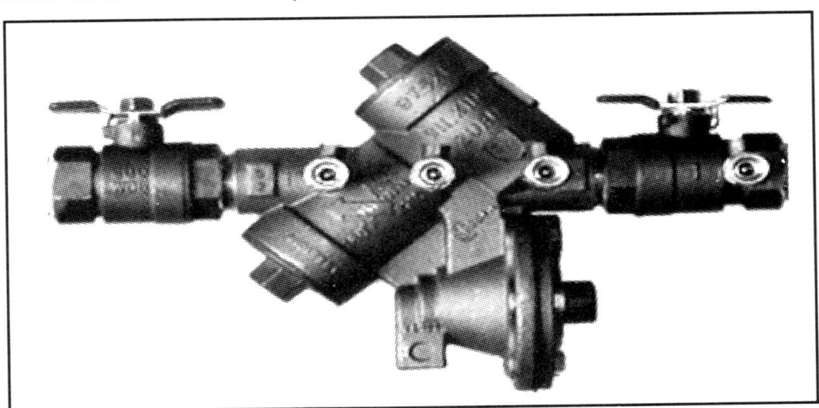

Fig. 7.5: Backflow Prevention Device

Check Valve

A device to provide positive closure which effectively prohibits the flow of material in the opposite direction of normal flow when operation of the irrigation system pumping plant or injection unit fails or is shut down (ASAE, 1998).

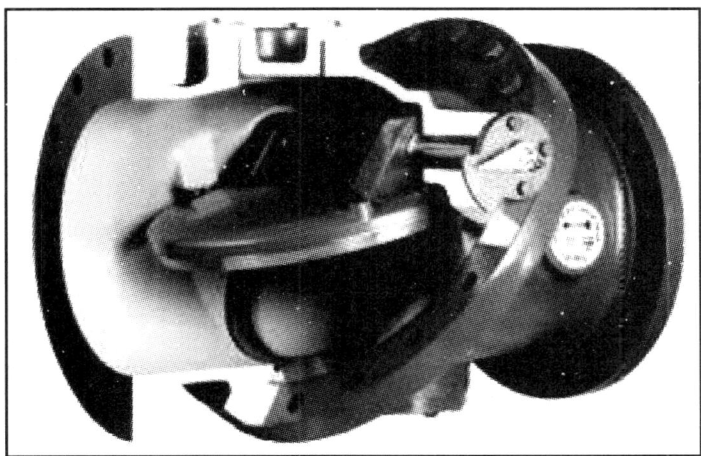

Fig. 7.6: Check Valve

Interlock Devices

Safety equipment used to insure that if the irrigation pumping plant stops, the chemical injection process will also stop. Devices may also be used to shut down the irrigation system if the injection system fails (ASAE, 1998).

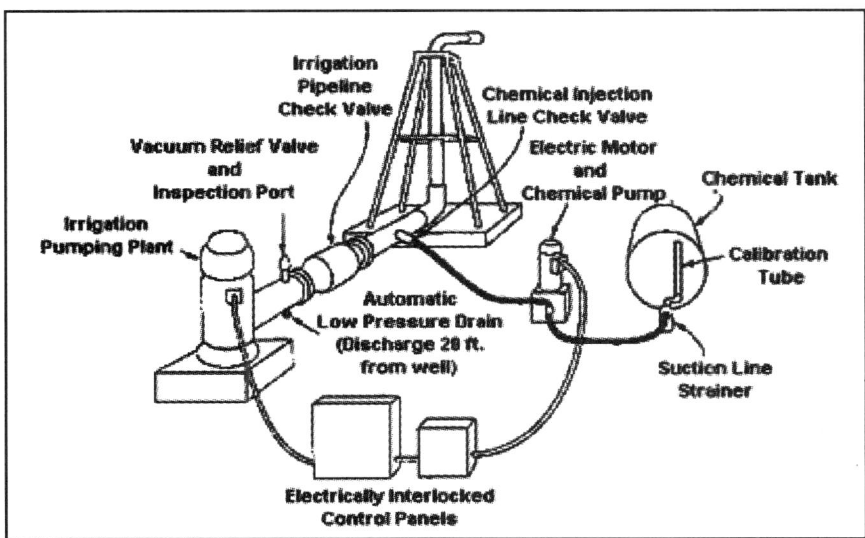

Fig. 7.7: Interlock Devices

EFFECTS OF FERTIGATION ON IRRIGATION SYSTEM COMPONENTS

Chemical Effects on Irrigation System Components

Field experience has indicated that the commonly used materials such as 28-32 percent UAN solutions, APP and UP solutions and most approved herbicides, insecticides and fungicides generally do not adversely affect system components. Recommended concentrations of fertilizer materials, although salty, will not damage galvanized surfaces, although painted surfaces are more susceptible to fertilizer corrosiveness. Caution should be used in adding solutions that they will not cause reduce water pH to 6.5 or lower, to prevent some irrigation system component damage may occur due to increasing reactivity/corrosivity of some solutions, clean out injection pumps and solution tanks with clean water (Curley et al. 1994; Kafkafi and Tarchitzky, 2011).

Clogging

Fares and Abbas (2009) had reviewed clogging caused by both alkalinity and acidity of fertilizer compounds in fertigation system. They cited that, since alkaline water forms insoluble compounds, it is not considered favorable for use in fertigation operations. Alkalinity of the water is especially crucial when P is used in fertigation, as the added P forms insoluble tri-basic calcium phosphate that can clog some irrigation equipment (Rauschkolb et al. 1976). This necessitates the continuous monitoring of pH of the P-carrying solutions flowing in the irrigation equipment (Koo 1980). Because MAP and DAP are excellent sources of P and N, these compounds are commonly used to enhance crop yield. There is a high possibility of precipitation of soluble P if MAP or DAP is mixed with irrigation water high in Ca^{++} or Mg^{++}. The precipitates formed in the irrigation equipment during fertigation can be dissolved and cleared with the use of acidic fertilizers (Bucks et al. 1979).

Although acidic fertilizers are corrosive to metallic components of the irrigation system and can potentially damage cement and asbestos pipes, they dissolve the precipitates and help to unclog the system's emitters or drippers. Periodic injection of phosphoric, nitric, sulfuric, or hydrochloric acid into the fertigation system can remove bacteria, algae, and slime trapped in the system.

Clogging is particularly crucial for drip irrigation systems because of their small orifices of the emitters (Koo 1980). Chemical solutions or low-quality, brackish water can also cause emitter clogging (Bucks et al. 1982). Very few reports on clogging of sprinklers during or after fertigation operations have been reported. Koo (1980) did not experience emitter clogging while using solution fertilizer in overhead sprinkler systems. However, Koo reported very little difference in the incidence of clogging between pre- and post-fertigation. The use of acidic fertilizers temporarily unclogs the system emitters. The irrigation and chemical injection systems should be thoroughly washed and flushed with fresh water, especially after the injection of acids into the system.

Reduction of Clogging in Fertigation Systems

- **Filter irrigation water**

  Good-quality water is crucial to reduce clogging problems in fertigation systems. If the irrigation water has visible debris and/or algae, irrigation water filters should be used to improve the quality of irrigation water and remove debris, clay particles, and algae before they enter the fertigation part of the system (Liu and McAvoy, 2012).

- **Acidify irrigation water**

  Alkaline and hard irrigation waters are difficult to manage due to its high contents of bicarbonate, Ca and Mg which easily create insoluble compounds causing clogging of the irrigation system (Patricia and Ariana, 2009). There are different acids, such as hydrochloric, sulfuric, citric, and phosphoric. Acidic fertilizers can also acidify irrigation water. For example, urea-sulfuric nitrogen fertilizers can provide acid, fertilizer, and lower water pH. Urea-sulfuric fertilizers are not compatible with many compounds. Growers should never combine urea-sulfuric fertilizers with other fertilizers or compounds when acidifying irrigation water (Liu and McAvoy, 2012).

  As a rule, never inject any chemical into micro irrigation systems that could raise the pH of the water without pre-acidification to counteract the effect. However, irrigation water pH generally should not be lower than 6.5 because of potential for system corrosion and excessive soil acidification (Evans and Waller, 2007).

- **Chlorinate irrigation water**

  To effectively prevent bacterial growth in irrigation water, chlorine may be injected continuously at low levels. Either liquid or gas chlorine can be used. Sodium hypochlorite (NaOCl) solution (household bleach) is also readily available. At a concentration of 5 ppm or lower, active chlorine, and not chloride, can effectively kill bacteria in irrigation water. After chlorine application, the free chlorine concentration should be measured at the hose ends toward the completion of an irrigation set. For irrigation water with high bacteria populations, a continuous application may be needed and 0.5-1.0 ppm free available chlorine should persist at the ends of lines. For irrigation water with relatively low bacterial populations, intermittent application of chlorine may be used. For occasional application, a concentration of approximately 5 ppm should be measured at the ends of lines. Regarding the bacterial count in the irrigation water, surface water has the potential to have greater bacterial population than deep well water (Liu and McAvoy, 2012).

- **Ensure that injected nutrients are compatible**

  A recommended method used to pre-test for chemical precipitation is to appropriately mix the chemical or mixture of chemicals in a transparent glass jar or other clear, inert container of irrigation water at slightly higher concentrations than field application. The jar is shaken and observed for 24 h or more to see whether precipitation has occurred. The presence of precipitates mandates that the mixture must be modified to avoid clogging problems. If cloudiness occurs it is highly likely that the injected mixture will also cause some clogging and that remedial measures are needed. These "jar tests" should be conducted at the same pH, temperature, and other similar conditions that the chemicals will be applied. Safety glasses and protective clothing should always be worn when conducting jar tests (Evans and Waller, 2007).

MODERN TECHNIQUES OF FERTIGTION MANAGEMENT

Fertigation System Design Software

Irrigation combined with fertigation has produced unquestionable results for the last few decades. It is arather complicated process as many factors must be controlled in order to produce good and environmentally safe fertigation practices. The efficiency and uniformity of irrigation, as well as the balance of the nutritive solution used to irrigate are highly ruled by the complex and diverse information (weather, soil,water, and crop data)(Barradas and Dolezal, 2012).For optimum plant performance under fertigation, all fertilization-irrigation-input factors must be balanced so that none impose a significant limit. Implementing a fertigation programme the actual water and nutrient requirements of the crops, together with a uniform distribution of both water and nutrients, are very important parameters.

Many software were devloped to design a fertigation system. Inputs and outputs of ideal software for fertigation system design can be summarized as follows(Papadopoulos et al. 2003; Patel and Rajput, 2004):

Table 7.1: Inputs and Outputs of Fertigation System Design Software

Inputs	Outputs
• Soil type	• Irrigation water requirement.
• Nutrient and water requirements of the crop.	• Irrigation System capacity.
• Irrigated area in one application.	• The maximum possible fertigation duration.
• Fertilizer application rate.	• Capacity of fertilizer tanks.
• Fertilizer requirement (kg/ha).	• The fertilizer injection rate.
• Solubility of fertilizer.	• Discharge through the fertilizer injector.
• Frequency of irrigation.	• Requirement of Nitrogen, Potassium and Phosphorous nutrients of the crop.
• Concentration of the liquid fertilizer.	• Nutrient concentration in irrigation water.
• Desired quantity of nutrients to be applied during the irrigation.	
• Ratio of fertilizer application time to the duration of irrigation.	

Automation of Fertigation System

Continuous cultivation within efficient management of fertilizers inputs has affected the consumed nutrients, environmental concerns and decrease in yields-qualitative and quantitative (Kaur and Kumar, 2013).Controllers are available which allow complete automation and monitoring of the chemigation operation. For instance, several are capable of initiating injections, monitoring their activity, and deactivating injections according to external sensors such as flow and pressure switches, EC and pH monitors, and weather data (Curley et al. 1994).

Benefits of Fertigation Automation

The use of electronics in fertigation/chemigation process brings many benefits due to its accuracy, powerful calculation software and automation. Iacomi et al. (2014) summarized these benefits as follows:

- Optimize water/nutrients/pesticides inputs and protects natural resources (water, soil and soil nutrients)
- Use the correct rates of nutrients and water for plants, being essential not only for the improvement of irrigation system but also for reducing inputs costs and increasing crop yield.
- The proportion of fertilizer & water proportion is set as per software.
- Reduce the cost especially for those who are involved in agriculture.
- There are no skills required.
- The system set as automated and it will reduce the human error.

Components of Fertigation Automatic System

Kaur and Kumar, (2013) developed nutrients composition control system that can automatically monitor EC and pH level of fertigation solution with respect to the parameters of soil. The system measure these parameters (pH and EC)with the help of electrical sensor and maintained their level using required amount of fertilizers. The fertilizer quantity is limited according to the crop requirement. General description of system components is (as shown in fig. 7.8):

- **Keypad:** Keypad is a part of Human Machine Interface which is used to enter or select the pH and EC values.
- **Microcontroller:** The system is based on PIC16F877A programmable controller used to measure and maintained the pH and EC according to the required values entered through keypad. The PIC controller has inbuilt ADC to measure the analog signal received from pH and EC sensor.
- **Relay:** Relay switch is electrically operated and used to operate the solenoid flow valve. The current flowing through the coil of the relay creates a magnetic field which attracts a lever and changes the switch contacts.

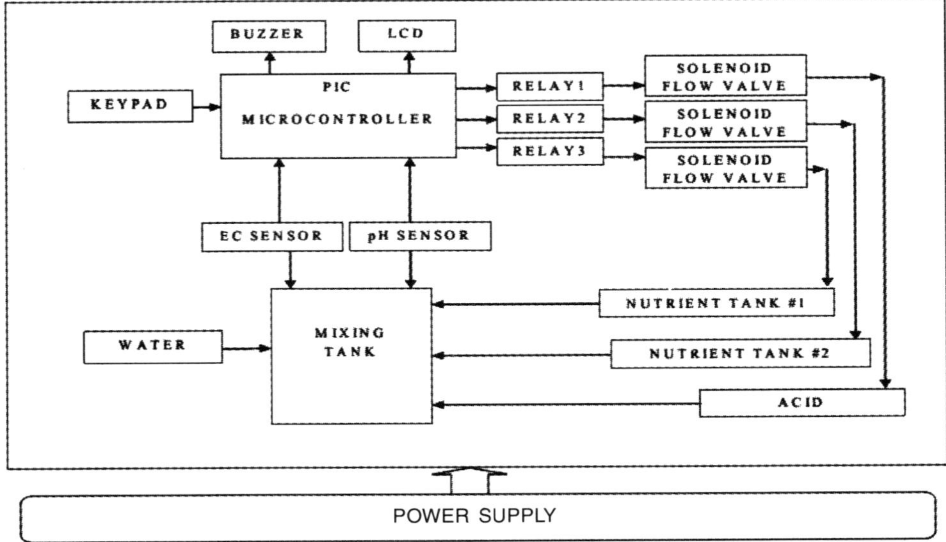

Fig. 7.8: Components of Automatic Fertigation System

- **Relay Driver:** For relay's interfacing with microcontrollers or other low current digital ICs, a power or current amplifier circuit is required known as relay driver circuits. Diodes and opt couplers are used to operate relay using micro controller.
- **Solenoid valve:** A solenoid valve is an electromechanically operated valve which is most frequently used to control fluids flow. The irrigation tasks are to shut off, release, dose, distribute or mix liquid form solutions.
- **Mixing Tank:** A mixing tank contains the fertilizer solution mixed with water dropped through solenoid valves from other fertilizers tanks.
- **Nutrient Tanks:** Fertilizer tanks contain the different types of fertilizer to make solution acidic or alkaline.
- **Buzzer:** A buzzer is an audio signal producing output device. In this system buzzer is used for the indication of completed process.
- **Liquid Crystal Display (LCD):** The LCD is used to display the computing results. The main features of Hitachi 44780 LCD are: 16 X 2 displays used for alphanumeric characters & based on ASCII codes.

Salih et al. (2012) developed a project to provide low cost solution for precise control of fertilizer mixing and irrigation to local farmers. The developed systems was powered totally by solar power system and were tested on its effectiveness to control the nutrient mixing process and injecting nutrient solutions according to plants growth rate and in the same time monitor all keys parameter in fertigation process.

They found that, by being fully operated with solar energy the system can be installed at rural and remote locations to achieve reductions in costs and produce better yield for rock melon or other crops cultivated using fertigation systems.

SUMMARY

The world demand on food is increasing by the global population growing. World food production can be increased by intensifying food crop production on land already under cultivation and expanding the planted to food crops. The success of both methods will depend on judicious use of fertilizers.

Fertigation is application of plant nutrients through irrigation water. It is a modern agro-technique provides an excellent opportunity to maximize yield and minimize environmental pollution by increasing fertilizer use efficiency, minimizing fertilizer application and increasing return on the fertilizer invested.

Basic components of fertigation system are chemical supply tank, injection system (pressure differential tank, venturi suction device and positive displacement injection pump); and, safety and anti-pollution devices to prevent any potential contamination of the water source.

The irrigation system could be affected due to unsuitable management of fertigation system. Use of fertilizers changes the injected solution pH. Some irrigation system components may be damaged due to increase of reactivity/corrosivity by lowering of solution pH to 6.5 or lower. Clogging of lines and emitters may become a problem if not managed appropriately. Since fertigation is a combination of irrigation and fertilization, clogging problems can be traced back to either the water supply or injected fertilizers.

Modern technologies provide powerful tools for both designing and managing fertigation systems. Many computer programmes had developed to facilitate the design of a fertigation system. Controllers are available which allow complete automation and monitoring of the chemigation operation. For instance, several are capable of initiating injections, monitoring their activity, and deactivating injections according to external sensors such as flow and pressure switches, EC and pH monitors, and weather data.

REFERENCES

Alva, A.K., Paramasivam, S.A., Fares, J.A., Delgado, D. Mattos, Jr., and. Sajwan, K. (2005): Nitrogen and Irrigation Management Practices to Improve Nitrogen Uptake Efficiency and Minimize Leaching Losses.]. *Crop Improvement* 15: 369-420.

ASAE. (1998): Standards (44th Ed.) The American Society of Agricultural Engineers (ASAE). Miami. USA. pp. 357-362.

Yosef, B., and Sagiv, B. (1982): Response of Tomatoes to N and Water Applied via a Trickle Irrigation System. I. Nitrogen. Agron J. 74: 633-639.

Barradas, J., Moreira, M., and Dolezal, S. Matula.(2012): A Decision Support System-Fertigation Simulator (DSS-FS) for Design and Optimization of Sprinkler and Drip Irrigation Systems. Computers and Electronics in Agriculture 86 (2012) pp. 111-119.

Baskar, B.S. (2010): Effect of Planting Techniques and Fertigation on Growth, Yield and Quality of Banana (Musa sp). Indian Agr J Agron. 2002; 48: 235-237.

Biswas, B.C. (2010): Fertigation in High Technical Agriculture. Fertiliser Marketing News, 41 (10): 4-8.

Bucks, D.A., Nakayama, F.S. and Gilbert, R.G. (1979): Trickle Irrigation, Water Quality and Preventive Maintenance. Agricultural Water Management 2: 149-162.

Bucks, D.A., Nakayama, F.S. and Warrick, A.W. (1982): Principle Practices and Potentialities of Trickle Irrigation. In: Advance in Irrigation, Academic Press, San Diego, Calif. pp. 219-298.

Curley, S., Hecht, R. and Richard, G. (1994): Fertigation/Chemigation Midwest Laboratories, Inc., Omaha.

Dalvi, V.B., Tiwari, K.N. and Phirke, M.N. (1999): Response Surface Analysis of Tomato Production Under Micro Irrigation. J Agr Water Management. 41: 11-19.

El-Gindy, A.M. (1988): Modern Chemigation Techniques for Vegetable Crops Under Egyptian Conditions. Misr. J. Agr. Eng., 5 (1): 99-111.

Evans, R.G., and Waller, P.M. (2007): Application of Chemical Materials. Elsevier Publications. pp. 285-327.

FAO. (2000): Fertilizers and Their Use. Food and Agriculture Organization of the United Nations International Fertilizer Industry Association. FAO.

FAO. (1981): Crop Production Levels and Fertilizer Use, FAO, Fertilizer and Plant Nutrition Bulletin, 2, FAO, Rome, p. 41.

Fares, A., and Abbas, F. (2009): Irrigation Systems and Nutrient Sources for Irrigation. University of Hawai at Mānoa, College of Tropical Agriculture and Human Resources, Publication SCM-25. http://www.ctahr. hawaii.edu/oc/freepubs/pdf/SCM-25.pdf.

Hagin, J., Sneh, M., and Lowengart, A. (2002): Fertilization Through Irrigation. IPI Research Topics No. 23, International Potash Institute, Basel.

Iacomi C., Rosca I., Madjar R., Iacomi B., Popescu V., Varzaru G. and Sfetcu C. (2014): Automation and Computer-based Technology for Small Vegetable Farm Holders. Scientific Papers. Series A. Agronomy, Vol. LVII, 2014.

Imas, P. (1999): Recent Techniques in Fertigation of Horticultural Crops in Israel. Workshop on Recent Trends in Nutrition Management in Horticultural Crops, 11-12 February, Dapoli, Maharashtra, India.

Intrigiliolo, F., Coniglione, L., and Germana, C.(1994): Effect of Fertigation on Some Physiological Parameters in Orange Trees. 7th International Citrus Congress, Italy 8-13 March pp. 584-589.

Ismail, S.M. (2008): Planning and Design of Irrigation Systems, Bostan El-Maarefa Press, pp. 373-375.

Kafkafi, U., and Tarchitzky, J. (2011): Fertigation a Tool for Efficiency Fertilizer and Water Management. International Fertilizer Industry Association (IFA) International Potash Institute (IPI) Paris, France, 2011.

Kaur B. and Kumar D. (2013): Development of Automated Nutrients Composition Control Fertigation System. International Journal of Computer Science, Engineering and Applications (IJCSEA). 3, (3), June.

Koo, R.C.J. (1980): Results of Citrus Fertigation Studies. Proc. State Hort. Soc. 93: 33-36.

Liu, G., and McAvoy, G.(2012): How to Reduce Clogging Problems in Fertigation. University of Florida Ifas extension 1202.

Malik, R.S. and Kumar, K.(1996): Effect of Drip Irrigation on Yield and Water Use Efficiency of Pea. J. Indian Soc. Soil Sci.; 44: 508-509.

Muralidhar, A.P. Shivashankar, H.R. and Kumargoud, V. (1999): Fertilizer and Irrigation Efficiency as Influenced by Furrow and Ferti-drip Irrigation in Capsicum-maize-sunflower Cropping Sequence. Proceedings of National Seminar on Problems and Prospects of Micro Irrigation – A Critical Appraisal, Nov. 19-20.

Papadopoulos, I. (1988): Nitrogen Fertigation of Trickle Irrigated Potato. Fertilizer Research 6: 157-167.

Papadopoulos, A.P. (2001): Computerised Fertigation for Cucumber Production in Soil and Soilless Media. Acta Hortic., 548: 112-124.

Papadopoulos, I., Metochi C.S.,and Seraphides N. (2003): Fertigation Recipes for Selected Crops in the Mediterranean Region. Agriculture Research Institute.

Patel, N., and Rajput, T.B.S. (2002): Fertigation a Technique for Efficient Use of Granular Fertilizer Through Drip Irrigation. J. Agr. Water Management. 2002 p. 85.

Patel, N. and Rajput T.B.S. (2004). Development of Softwares for Design of Micro Irrigation and Fertigation System. 7th International Micro Irrigation Congress.

Patricia I., and Ariana R.(2009): Improving the pH of Irrigation Water with Acidic Fertilizers. The Proceedings of the International Plant Nutrition Colloquium.

Phene, C.J. and Howell, T.A. (1984): Soil Sensor Control of High Frequency Irrigation. Trans ASAE. 27 (2): 392-396.

Rauschkolb, R.S., Rolston,D.E. Miller, R.J. Carlton, A.B. and Buran, R.G. (1976): Phosphorus Fertilization with Drip Irrigation. Soil Science Society of America Journal 40: 62-78.

Salih Mohd, J.E, Adom A.H., and Shaakaf, A.Y. (2012): Solar Powered Automated Fertigation Control System for Cucumis melo l. Cultivation in Green House. APCBEE Procedia 4: 79-87.

Singh, K.D.N., Yadav, M.D., Misra, G.K.and Sahi, B.P. (1998): Influence of Modified Urea Sources on Yield and Quality of Sugarcane. Indian Sug. 1998; 39 (3): 165-172.

Southorn N. (1997): Farm Irrigation (Practical farming) [Kindle Edition] INKATA PRESS, Australia.

Tayel, M.Y. (2010): Engineering of Sprinkler Irrigation. Academy of Scientific Research and Technology. Egypt. p. 75.

The Irrigation Association. (2000): Chemigation, the Irrigation Association Publications, 6540 Arlington Boulevard, Fall Church, VA 22042 – 668, USA.

Treeby, M., Falivene, S., Phogat, V. and Skewes, M.(2011): Knowledge and Tools to Manage Fertigation Technologies in Highly Productive Citrus Orchards for Minimal Environmental Footprint. Final Report to National Programme for Sustainable Irrigation.

Veeranna, H.K, and Sujith, G.M. (2000): Effect of Fertiagtion and Irrigation Methods on Yield, Water and Fertilizer Use Efficiencies in Chilli. South Indian Hort. 49: 101-103.

Wichelns, D. (2007): In Micro Irrigation for Crop Production: Design, Operation and Management, Economic Implications of Micro Irrigation. (Elsevier, Amsterdam, the Netherlands) pp. 221-259.

Pages: 146-171

SOIL CHARACTERISTICS AND AGRO-ECOLOGY

Edited by: Dr. Avnish Chauhan; Dr. Pawan Kumar 'Bharti'

ISBN: 978-93-5056-758-6

Edition: 2015

Published by: Discovery Publishing House Pvt. Ltd., New Delhi (India)

8

Agriculture Practice to Cope with the Negative Impacts of Climate Change

Tawfik[*], M.M., Wafaa M. Haggag[**], Ezzat M. Abd El Lateef[*], B.B. Mekki[*], Camilia, Y. El-Dewiny[***] and **Gehan, Sh. Bakhoom[*]**

ABSTRACT

The world faces great challenges in the coming decades including reining in global climate change, ensuring food security for the growing population, and promoting sustainable development. Changes in the agriculture sector are essential to meeting these challenges. Agriculture provides the main source of livelihood for the poor in developing countries, and improving agricultural productivity is critical to achieving food security as well as most of the targets specified under the Millennium Development Goals. A wide variety of adaptive actions may be taken to overcome adverse effects of climate change on agriculture. A wide variety of adaptive actions may be taken to overcome adverse effects of climate change on agriculture, among them is using alternative energy sources such as (solar, water and wind energy) instead of fossil fuels to limit the increasing of carbon dioxide in the atmosphere.

* Field Crops Research Department, National Research Centre, Egypt.

** Plant Pathology Department, National Research Centre, Egypt.

** Soil & Water Use Dept. National Research Centre, Dokki, Giza Egypt.

Development of new varieties of crops adapted to heat, salinity, drought and resistance to pests and diseases, with short growing season to reduce their water requirements. Modify the techniques of irrigation, including water quantity, timing of irrigation, technology and change planting dates to suit the new climatic change conditions. Expansion in organic agriculture at the expense of mineral one, as well as cultivation of appropriate varieties in its favorable climatic region to increase their water productivity.

At the level of farms, adjustments may include the introduction of later- maturing crop varieties or species, switching cropping sequences, sowing earlier, adjusting timing of field operations, conserving soil moisture through appropriate tillage methods, and improving irrigation efficiency. A recent option is (climate smart agriculture) practice which helps to protect the framers from the adverse effects of climate changes, provide means to reduce greenhouse gases, sequester carbon in the soil, use precision agricultural systems, increase the productivity on a sustainable basis and building resilience in facing the environmental pressures to help farmers to adapt to climate change. All these objects can be accomplished through climate smart agriculture practices which enhance the content of soil organic matter and improve its capacity to retain water. Thus can strengthen the resilience of agricultural crops to face the environmental pressures, tolerate the negative impact of climate change and conserve environment, as well as improving crop production.

Key words: Climate change, Agriculture production, Adaptation.

INTRODUCTION

Regardless of what local, regional and global actions are taken and which policy instruments are adopted to slow anthropogenic emissions of greenhouse gases and thus to reduce the magnitude of climate change, cumulative past emissions have already committed the planet to a certain degree of climate change and associated impacts over the coming decades. Recent observations of increased frequency of climate extremes worldwide, as well as shifts in eco-zones, might be an indication of global warming-related changes already under way (IPCC, 2007). Effective adaptation strategies and actions should aim to secure well-being in the face of climate variability, climate change and a wide variety of difficult to predict biophysical and social contingencies. In pursuing this aim, climate adaptation should focus on support for the decision-making and capacity building processes that shape social learning, technology transfer, innovation and development pathways. Adaptation is most relevant when it influences decisions that exist irrespective of climate change, but which have longer-term consequences (Stainforth *et al.*, 2007). Moreover, out of world's total land area of 13 billion hectares (ha), only 12% is cultivated (Ruane *et al.*, 2008).

Therefore, science and technology should take a lead in spearheading increased agricultural productivity. If we want to feed the world without destroying our resources, science and technology should drive the development of modern agriculture. Genetically modified crop varieties are the most cost effective ways to sustain farming in marginal areas and restore degraded lands to production (Treasury, 2009). Efforts should be made to integrate local and conventional biotechnologies with modern biotechnology strategies within national policies and legal frameworks in order to increase resilience of local crop varieties against changes in environmental dynamics (Stringer *et al.*, 2009). Despite the availability of promising research results, many applications of biotechnology have not met their full potential to deliver practical solutions to end-users in developing countries (Ruane *et al.*, 2008; Mtui, 2009). A wide variety of adaptive actions may be taken to overcome adverse effects of climate change on agriculture. At the level of farms, adjustments may include the introduction of later-maturing crop varieties or species, switching cropping sequences, sowing earlier, adjusting timing of field operations, conserving soil moisture through appropriate tillage methods, and improving irrigation efficiency (FAO, 2010).

Activating policies aimed at adaptation to climate change to mitigate the negative impact and increase resilience in agriculture production. One of these policies is using alternative energy sources such as (solar, water and wind energy) instead of fossil fuels to limit the increasing of carbon dioxide in the atmosphere. Development of new varieties of crops adapted to heat, salinity, drought and resistance to pests and diseases, with short growing season to reduce their water requirements. Modify the techniques of irrigation, including water quantity, timing of irrigation, technology and change planting dates to suit the new climatic change conditions. Expansion in organic agriculture at the expense of mineral one, as well as cultivation of appropriate varieties in its favorable climatic region to increase their water productivity (FAO, 2010).

The effective participation in the international agreements and programmes concerned with the climate change, as well as increasing interest of climate change researches and their impact on agriculture and the environment to increase the capacity and resilience of the agricultural sector to adapt to climate changes with focusing on the most vulnerable agricultural areas. Moreover, guiding and training the farmers on farming system management that protects the environment and reduces emissions of different greenhouse gases. Increase simulation research to avoid the negative impact of climate change. Another, unconventional approach including sustainable using of marginal soil, desert, and coast land for planting non-traditional crops that can tolerate droughts and salinity, has an economic value or to produce biofuels. In addition, it will lead to reducing the carbon dioxide gas in the atmosphere (carbon sequestration) (FAO, 2010).

SUSTAINABLE CROP MANAGEMENT

Crop Diversification and Using New Varieties

The introduction of new cultivated species and improved varieties of crop is a technology aimed at enhancing plant productivity, quality, health and nutritional value and building crop resilience to diseases, pest organisms and environmental stresses such as heat, drought and salinity. Crop diversification refers to the addition of new crops or cropping systems to agricultural production on a particular farm taking into account the different returns from value-added crops with complementary marketing opportunities (Bradshaw *et al.*, 2005) The aim of crop diversification is to increase crop portfolio so that farmers are not dependent on a single crop to generate their income, mitigating effects of increasing climate variability, conservation of natural resources, decreasing insect pests, diseases and weed problems and minimizing environmental pollution. Introducing a greater range of varieties also leads to diversification of agricultural production which can increase natural biodiversity, strengthening the ability of the agro-ecosystem to respond to these stresses, reducing the risk of total crop failure and also providing producers with alternative means of generating income (Nelson, 2009).

With a diversified plot, the farmer increases his chances of dealing with the uncertainty and the changes created by climate change. This is because crops will respond to climate scenarios in different ways. Whereas the cold may affect one crop negatively, production in an alternative crop may increase. The process of farmer experimentation and the subsequent introduction of adapted and accepted varieties can potentially strengthen farmers' cropping systems by increasing yields, improving drought resilience, boosting resistance to pests and diseases and also by capturing new market opportunities (Kurukulasuriya and Mendelsohn 2006).

Biotechnology for Climate Change Adaptation in Crops

The current challenges and future perspectives of biotechnology for climate change adaptation and mitigation are highlighted. Conventional agricultural biotechnology methods such as energy-efficient farming, use of biofertilizers, tissue culture and breeding for adaptive varieties are among feasible options that could positively address the potential negative effects of climate change and thereby contributing to carbon sequestration initiatives (Mittler and Blumwald, 2010). On the other hand, the adoption of modern biotechnology through the use of genetically modified stress-tolerant, energy-efficient and high-yielding transgenic crops also stand to substantially counter the negative effects of climate change (Paszkowski and Grossniklaus, 2011).

They added that, safe application of biotechnology will greatly complement other on-going measures being taken to improve agricultural productivity and food security. Both conventional and modern agricultural biotechnologies will significantly contribute to the current and future worldwide climate change adaptation and mitigation efforts (Varshney *et al.*, 2011). Recently, we use the term (Green biotechnology) referring to the use of environmentally friendly solutions in agriculture production (Treasury, 2009). Recombinant DNA technology has significantly augmented the conventional crop improvement, and has the potential to assist plant breeders to meet the increased food demand predicted for the 21st century.

Dramatic progress has been made over the past two decades in manipulating genes from diverse and exotic sources, and inserting them into microorganisms and crops to confer resistance to pests and diseases, tolerance to herbicides, drought, soil salinity and aluminium toxicity, improve post-harvest quality, enhance nutrient uptake and nutritional quality; increase photosynthetic rate, sugar and starch production, increase effectiveness of bio control agents, improve understanding of gene action and metabolic pathways, and production of drugs and vaccines in crops (Vallad and Goodman, 2004). Biotechnology and application of advanced techniques in breeding can help agriculture further to achieve higher yields and meet needs of expanding population with limited land and water resources (Treasury, 2009).

Ecological Pest Management

Ecological Pest Management (EPM) is an approach to increasing the strengths of natural systems to reinforce the natural processes of pest regulation and improve agricultural production. Also know as Integrated Pest Management (IPM), this practice can be "defined as the use of multiple tactics in a compatible manner to maintain pest populations at levels below those causing economic injury while providing protection against hazards to humans, animals, plants and the environment (Bianchi *et al.*, 2006). IPM is thus ecologically-based pest management that makes full use of natural and cultural processes and methods, including host resistance and biological control. IPM emphasizes the growth of a healthy crop with the least possible disruption of agro-ecosystems, thereby encouraging natural pest control mechanisms.

Chemical pesticides are used only where and when these natural methods fail to keep pests below damaging levels" (Leisa, 2007). One of these tactics is trap cropping i.e. planting of a trap crop to protect the main cash crop from a certain pest or several pests. The trap crop can be from the same or different family group, than that of the main crop, as long as it is more attractive to the pest. There are two types of planting the trap crops; perimeter trap cropping and row intercropping. Perimeter trap cropping (border trap cropping) is the planting of trap crop completely surrounding the main cash crop. It prevents a pest attack that comes from all sides of the field. It works best on pests that are found near the borderline of the farm. Row intercropping is the planting of the trap crop in alternating rows within the main crop

fig 8.1. In this concern, Koch and Gray (1997) proved that, varieties of radish and yellow mustard (*Sinapis alba* L.), developed and used as trap crops, effectively control the sugar beet nematode (*Heterodera schachtii* Schmidt.

Fig. 8.1: Trap Cropping Systems

Change Planting (Sowing) Dates

A biological surrogate is the plant phenology (the timing of important developmental stages in the life cycle of a plant). Plant phenology is governed mainly by temperature and may be modified by photoperiod and vernalization. If warmer than normal temperatures occurs up to an optimal temperature for plant development, the plant would develop at a greater rate and would reach a new developmental stage on an earlier date. (If there is a temperature change that is greater than this optimal temperature, then this change is probably no longer a subtle change and surrogates are not needed.) Thus, a persistent earlier occurrence of a development stage of a plant would indicate a rise of temperature from its previous value (Hu *et al.*, 2005). In this regard, AIACC (2006) studied the impact of the expected climate change (+1.5° C increase in temperature) in Egypt, Marsa Matrouh District (Fig. 8.2).

Halophytic Plants: A Nonconvential Smart Crop for the Future

Water scarcity due to climate change has been increasing and the problem is more severe in arid and semi-arid regions and cause poverty and other related social and economic issues (Qadir *et al.*, 2006). Moreover, 43% of earth land mass is arid or semi arid and 97.5% of its water is saline (Rozema *et al.*, 2008), over 800 million hectare of the world is affected by salinity (Abideen *et al.*, 2011), 45 million out of 230 million hectare of prime irrigated agricultural land has become saline and the menace is creeping into arable lands (Munns and Tester, 2008).

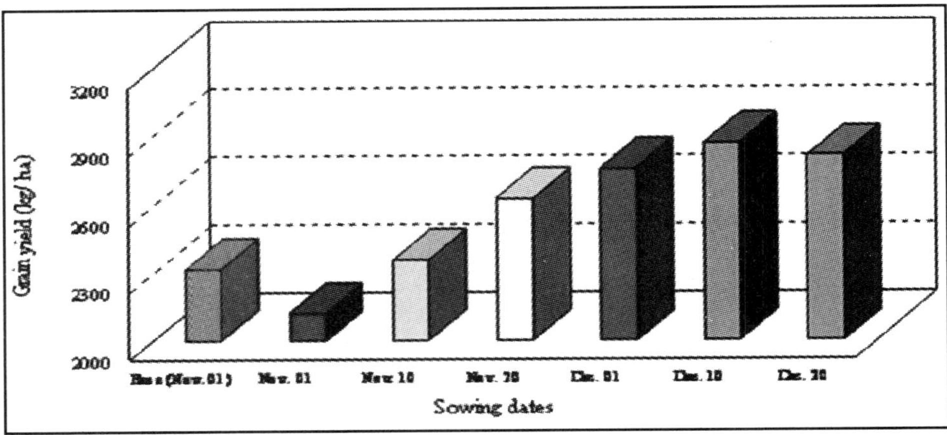

Fig. 8.2: Simulated Wheat Grain Yield (kg/ha) Under Climate Change Conditions (+1.5° C) at Different Sowing Dates at Marsa Matruh Region, Egypt

Cultivation of halophytes on these vast degraded saline lands by using huge resource of under-ground brackish water or even seawater in some cases would spare arable land and fresh water for conventional agriculture. An integrated approach therefore is imperative for the sustained development. Utilization of saline resources to mass produces halophytes of economic importance e.g. as vegetable, forage, and oilseed crops in agronomic field trials fig 8.3. Moreover, they have been used for bio-remediation of salt contaminated soils and even pharmaceutical values of their products could be one such strategy to address water issue (Wichelns and Oster, 2006). Fig. 8.4 shows some representative halophytic plants species.

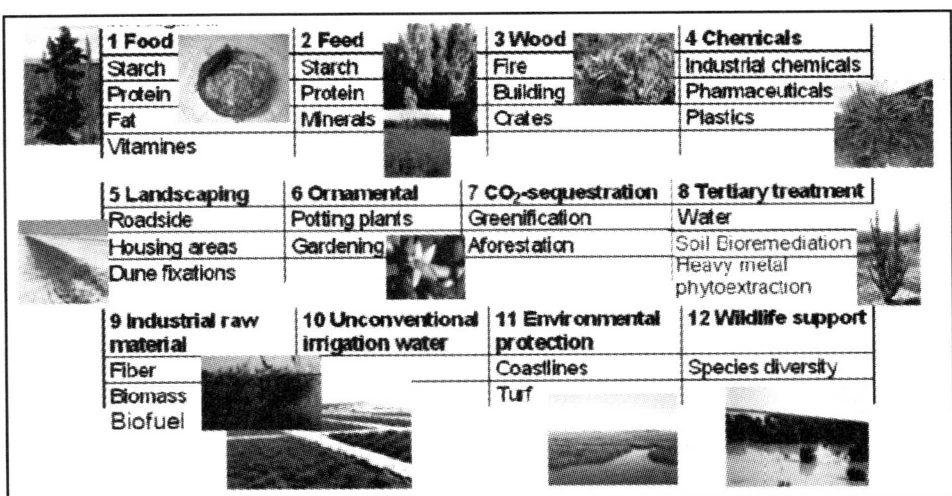

Fig. 8.3: Some Possibilities of Halophytes Utilization

Fig. 8.4: Some Halophytic Plants Species (a) Leptochloa, (b) Sporobolus, (c) Juncus, (d) Spartina, (e) Khocia and (f) Salicornia

Crop Rotation

Rotation of crops on a given piece of land can be beneficial when soils have become inhibitory to plant growth, perhaps because of the negative microbiological impacts of continuous cropping (and residue retention). Crop rotation can increase yield by up to 20% or more, via a variety of mechanisms including improved N nutrition (often by incorporating legumes within a crop rotation to fix atmospheric N) and water supply (Kirkegaard *et al.*, 2008). They added that, crop rotation maintains good soil physical condition and organic matter, Helps control weeds, some plant diseases and insect pests, reduces soil erosion and improves water quality. In this concern, Dogan *et al.*, (2008) carried out two different crop rotation systems: winter wheat and sunflower as main crops experiments.

Results were evaluated in terms of crop yielding ability, soil fertility and economic aspects. The sunflower-rapeseed-wheat, rapeseed fodder pea + sunflower-wheat and rapeseed-common vetch + sunflower-wheat were found the most suitable rotation systems because of their various advantages in the first experiment in which wheat was used as main the crop. The highest sunflower seed yields were obtained from a fodder pea + sunflower-wheat-fodder pea + sunflower crop rotation system both in the first and second three year periods in which sunflower was used as main crop under rain-fed conditions. Economic analysis based on the second three-year results of the research showed that the highest mean net returns were obtained from the rapeseed-common vetch + sunflower-wheat and a fodder pea + sunflower-wheat fodder pea + sunflower crop rotation systems under rain-fed conditions. These crop rotation systems were found the best crop rotation systems under rain-fed conditions of Southern Marmara region of Turkey. As a result, the rotation systems including common vetch and fodder peas as forage plants under rain-fed conditions gave economically the highest net profit.

More Use Intercropping

Intercropping (Fig. 8.5) which is defined as the growing of two or more crop species simultaneously in the same field during a growing season (Leisa *et al.*, 2007), it is important for the development of sustainable crops production systems. This may be due to some of the potential benefits for intercropping systems such a high productivity and profitability (Yildirim and Guvence, 2005), improvement of soil fertility through the addition of nitrogen by fixation and excretion from the component legume (Hauggaard *et al.*, 2001), efficient use of resources and improvement forage quality through the complementary effects of two or more crops grown simultaneously on the same area of land (Bingol *et al.*, 2007).

Fig. 8.5: Intercropping

Ghanbari and Lee (2003) evaluated sole crops and intercrops of wheat and field bean for whole crop forage quality characteristics of CP, NDF, ADF and Ash content. They concluded that field been intercropped with wheat led to increased forage quality compared with sole crop wheat, suggesting that wheat-bean intercrops is a relatively high quality low-input and environmentally benign forage crop considerable potential with regard to yield and quality. Contreras *et al.*, (2006) reported that forage quality in terms of NDF and ADF concentration was improved by wheat-clover intercropping compared with wheat sole crop. Javanmard *et al* (2009) used two maize hybrids (704 and 301) and four legumes (vetch, bitter vetch, berseem clover and common bean) intercrops to evaluate the effects of legumes on forage yield and quality. They found that crude protein yield, dry matter and ash content of maize forage increased by intercropping as compared with maize sole crop. Also, intercropping of legumes with maize significantly reduced NDF and ADF content, thus, increasing digestibility of the forage. Furthermore, forage quality achieved by intercropping was higher in the composition of maize with vetch, bitter vetch and common bean, where NDF and ADF content were higher in maize-berseem clover intercropping. yield, because NDF, ADF and CP of sole barley were 57.5%, 35.4% and 13% respectively and those of intercrops were 46%, 30.3% and 12% respectively.

SUSTAINABLE SOIL MANAGEMENT

Conservation Tillage

Tillage is the agricultural preparation of the soil by mechanical, animal or human-powered agitation, such as ploughing, digging, overturning, shovelling, hoeing and raking. Conservation tillage refers to a number of strategies and techniques for establishing crops in a previous crop's residues, which are purposely left on the soil surface (Fig. 8.6). This slows water movement, which reduces the amount of soil erosion. Conservation tillage is suitable for a range of crops including grains, root crops, sugar cane, cassava and vines (Frederick *et al.*,1996). They added that, conservation tillage benefits farming by minimizing erosion, increasing soil fertility and improving yield. Conservation tillage systems also benefit farmers by reducing fuel consumption and soil compaction. By reducing the number of times the farmer travels over the field, farmers make significant savings in fuel and labour. Use of conservation tillage for field-crop production has been steadily increasing over the past decade.

Fig. 8.6: Conservation Tillage

A combination of both economic and environmental reasons has caused producers to switch from intensive tillage to conservation tillage, especially on the sandy soil where the soils are inherently low in organic matter (Juergens *et al.*, 2004). The modified crops reduce the need for tillage or ploughing to allow farmers to adopt no till farming practices. In terms of climate change mitigation, this practice enhances soil quality and retails more carbon in the soil (Brookes and Barfoot, 2009). According to FAO (2010), conservation agriculture is "a concept for resource-saving agricultural crop production that strives to achieve acceptable profits together with high and sustained production levels while concurrently conserving the environment. Conservation agriculture is based on enhancing natural biological processes above and below the ground. Interventions such as mechanical soil tillage are reduced to an absolute minimum, and the use of external inputs such as agrochemicals and nutrients of mineral or organic origin are applied at an optimum level and in a way and quantity that does not interfere with, or disrupt, the biological processes." Conservation agriculture consists of different crop cultivation practices such as zero tillage, sowing of crops on permanent beds, strip tillage.

Sustainable Use of Organic Agriculture

Reduced mineral fertilizer use also means less nitrogen pollution of ground and surface waters. Artificial inorganic nitrogenous fertilizers are responsible for the formation and release of greenhouse gases (particularly N_2O) from the soil to the atmosphere when they interact with common soil bacteria (Brookes and Barfoot, 2009). Another option is the cultivation of GM crops that use nitrogen more efficiently. An example of such crops is the nitrogen-efficient GM canola which not only reduces the amount of nitrogen fertilizer that is lost into the atmosphere or leached into soil and waterways, but it also impacts positively on the economies of farmers through improved profitability (Treasury, 2009). Managing soil nitrogen to match crop needs can reduce N_2O emission and avoid adverse impacts on water quality (Johnsona *et al.*, 2007). With the introducing of green revolution technologies, the modern agriculture is getting more and more dependent upon the supply of natural inputs by using organic-fertilized farming system, this current global scenario firmly emphasizes the need to adopt eco-friendly agricultural practices for sustainable agriculture.

Organic agriculture is a holistic production management system which promotes and enhances agro-ecosystem, health, including biodiversity, biological cycles, and soil biological activity. It emphasizes the use of management practices in preference to the use of off-farm inputs, taking into account that regional conditions and locally adapted systems. This is accomplished by using, where possible, agronomic, biological, and mechanical methods, as opposed to using synthetic materials, to fulfill any specific function within the system. Organic agriculture is a system that relies on ecosystem management rather than external agricultural inputs (Samman *et al.*, 2008). Organic farming has emerged as an important priority area globally in view of the growing demand for safe and healthy food and long term sustainability and concerns on environmental pollution associated with indiscriminate use of agrochemicals. Though the use of chemical inputs in agriculture is inevitable to meet the growing demand for food in world, there are opportunities in selected crops and niche areas where organic production can be encouraged to tape the domestic export market (Karmakar *et al.*, 2007).

Another approach, is using of biofertilizers inoculation as proper management techniques for improvement the productivity and physiochemical characteristics of plants and soil (Afzal and Asghari, 2008) they added that, biofertilizer is a material containing microorganisms added to a soil to directly or indirectly make certain essential elements available to plants for their nutrition through synthesis of growth promoting substances or by enhancing the decomposition of plant residues. Various sources of biofertilizers include nitrogen fixers, phytostimulators, phosphate solubilizing bacteria, plant growth promoting rhizobacteria etc. Considerable progress has been made over the past two decades in evaluation of these technologies and development of application methods. Kaci *et al.*, (2005) added that, these microorganisms are known to deliver a number of benefits including plant nutrition, disease resistance, and tolerance to adverse soil and climatic conditions like *Azotobacters chroococcum*.

Mycorrhiza is the mutualistic symbiosis (non-pathogenic association) between soil-borne fungi with the roots of plants. Their function ranges from stress alleviation to soil bioremediation or as a biological tool for sustainable agriculture. In this concern, Ahmed *et al.*, (2011) stated that, biofertilizers application in agriculture will have greater impact on organic agriculture and also on the control of environmental pollution, soil health improvement and reduction in input use. They recommend using a mixture of chicken manure in combination with *Azotobacter chroococcum* and yeast (*candida trpoicalis*) can meet the nutrient requirement of sustainable wheat production under desert soil conditions. Moreover, Tawfik *et al.*, (2011) stated that Biofertilization with nitrogen fixing bacteria like A. chroococcum could effectively mitigate the adverse effects of saline water irrigation.

Carbon Sequestration

Soil carbon sequestration is a win-win strategy. It is the low-hanging fruit and a bridge to the future, until carbon-neutral fuel sources and a low-carbon economy take effect (IPCC, 2007). Carbon sequestration is the process through which agricultural and forestry practices remove carbon dioxide (CO_2) from the atmosphere. The term "sinks" is also used to describe agricultural and forestry lands that absorb CO_2, the most important global warming gas emitted by human activities. Agricultural and forestry practices can also release CO_2 and other greenhouse gases to the atmosphere. Sequestration activities can help prevent global climate change by enhancing carbon storage in trees and soils, preserving existing tree and soil carbon, and by reducing emissions of CO_2, methane (CH_4) and nitrous oxide (N_2O) (Powlson *et al.*, 2011).

Therefore, soil carbon sequestration is an important strategy to mitigate the increase of atmospheric CO_2 concentration. Reducing the amount of conventional tillage is one way of enhancing carbon sequestration. By leaving at least 30% of residue on the soil surface, no-till agriculture reduces loss of CO_2 from agricultural systems and may also play a role in reducing water loss through evaporation, increase soil stability and creation of cooler soil microclimate (Johnsona *et al.*, 2007). They added that, conservation practices that help prevent soil erosion, may also sequester soil carbon and enhance methane (CH_4) consumption. The modified crops reduce the need for tillage or ploughing to allow farmers to adopt no till farming practices. In terms of climate change mitigation, this practice enhances soil quality and retails more carbon in the soil (Brookes and Barfoot, 2009). Fig 8.7 shows global carbon cycle.

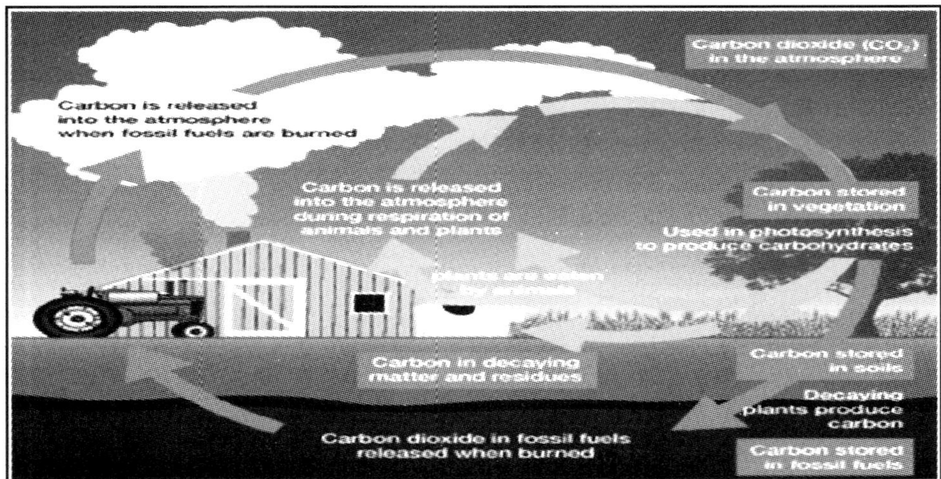

Fig. 8.7: Carbon Cycle in the Environment

Mulching

Agricultural management practices can change the characteristics of the soil surface, minimize soil evaporative losses, suppress weeds and influence the hydrothermal properties of the soil (Fig. 8.8). Zhang *et al.*, (2009) stated that straw mulching (SM) systems can conserve soil water and reduce temperature because they reduce soil disturbance and increase residue accumulation at the soil surface. Plastic mulches can be easily rolled onto fields using commercially available equipment 'on-demand', although energy costs of plastic production may be substantial. Plastic reflectivity (determined by colour) can change mean soil temperatures by up to 4 °C (Yang and Zhang, 2010). In this concern, Zhao *et al.*, (2012) investigate the effect of three mulching materials (film mulching, nylon mulching, and paper mulching) and different fertilizer (with or without fertilizer) on nitrogen accumulation in a winter wheat-fallow system. The results showed that organic fertilizer application and film mulching may be effective strategies for increasing nitrogen accumulation in wheat grains, increasing yield and improving yield wheat.

Fig. 8.8: Mulching

Rehabilitation of Salt Affected Soil

Land degradation is a major global issue because of its adverse impact on agricultural productivity and sustainability. Population pressure along with the demand for more food, fodder and fuel wood has generated a chain of interrelated economic, social and environmental issues associated with the land degradation especially in developing countries in arid and semi-arid regions (Qadir *et al.*, 2006). Restoration of productivity of saline lands, improving of ameliorative conditions, compacting desertification and rising of fertility of soils are some of the most important tasks at recent time (Ravindran *et al.*, 2007).

The methods of biological restoration of saline lands with the use of halophytes through special organ called salt gland (Fig. 8.9), successfully solve this task. Domestication of halophytes will make a promising solution for increasing fodder supply and utilization of the abandoned salt affected soils, and offers a low-cost approach to reclaiming and rehabilitating saline habitats. In this concern, Ibrahim *et al.*, (2011) stated that, establishment of salt-accumulating halophytes can sufficiently remediate the land to the point where native plants can re-establish. As well as the potential benefits for nature conservation and agriculture, an important outcome of remediation and re-vegetation is a reduction in soil erosion with accordingly reduced salt and silt discharge into water courses. Furthermore, utilization of salt tolerant plants such as *Kochia indica* for rehabilitation and reclamation of salt-affected soil could be an appropriate option for alleviating desertification problems and providing alternative good quality and economic unconventional feed materials for animals.

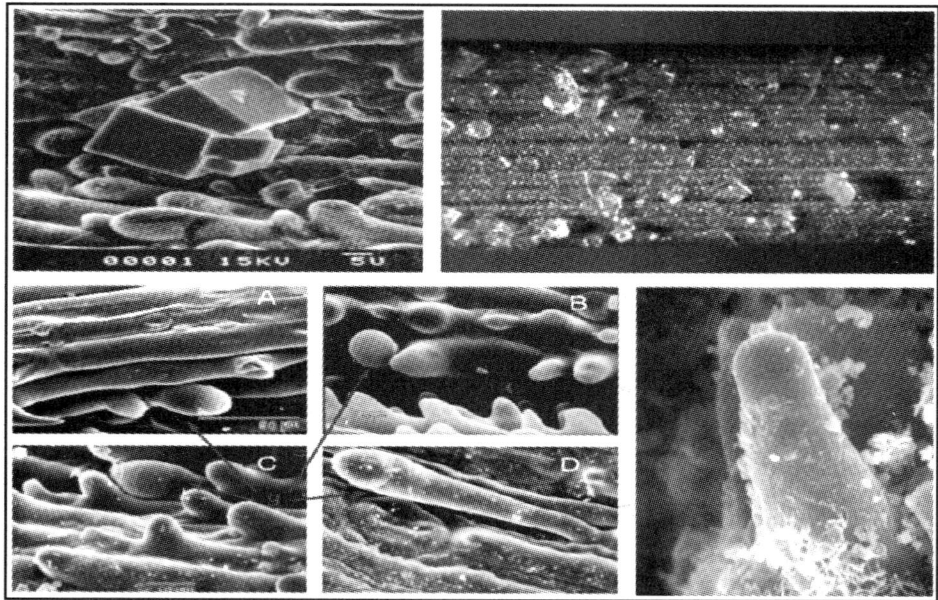

Fig. 8.9: Salt Glands

SUSTAINABLE WATER USE AND MANAGEMENT

The Intergovernmental Panel on Climate Change (IPCC, 2007) predicts that during the next decades, billions of people, particularly those in developing countries, will face changes in rainfall patterns that will contribute to severe freshwater shortages or flooding resulting in negative impacts on agricultural production. Some studies suggest that by 2025, more than a third of the world population will face absolute water scarcity (Hatfield, 2010). Enhancing water availability through adaptation technologies for sustainable water use and management is therefore a key strategy for increasing agricultural productivity and securing food security in these regions.

Many options are available for improving the efficiency of water use for field crops agriculture. Among of these options, shifting from flood irrigation to sprinkler and drip systems, Improved Irrigation Scheduling, using local climate and soil information to help farmers more precisely irrigate to meet crop water needs and applying less water to crops during drought-tolerant growth stages to save water and improve crop quality or yield (FAO, 2010).

Sprinkler Irrigation

Systems of pressurized irrigation, sprinkler or drip, can improve water efficiency and contribute substantially to improved food production. Sprinkler irrigation is a type of pressurized irrigation that consists of applying water to the soil surface using mechanical and hydraulic devices that simulate natural rainfall. These devices replenish the water consumed by crops or provide water required for softening the soil to make it workable for agricultural activities. The goal of irrigation is to supply each plant with just the right amount of water it needs. Sprinkler irrigation is method by which water is distributed from overhead by high-pressure sprinklers, sprays or guns mounted on risers or moving platforms. Table 8.1 shows the response of some field crops to sprinkler irrigation systems (AIACC, 2006).

Table 8.1: Response of Some Field Crops to Sprinkler Irrigation Systems

Crop	Water Saving %	Yield Increase %
Barley	56	16
Wheat	35	24
Maize	41	36
Groundnut	20	40
Cotton	36	49
Sorghum	32	42
Canola	25	32

Fog and Dew Harvesting

Fogs have the potential to provide an alternative source of fresh water in dry regions and can be harvested through the use of simple and low-cost collection systems. Captured water can then be used for agricultural irrigation and domestic use. Fog or dew collection is an ancient practice (Muselli *et al.*, 2009). Archaeologists have found evidence in Palestine of low circular walls that were built around plants and vines to collect moisture from condensation. In South America's Atacama Desert and in Egypt, piles of stones were arranged so that condensation could trickle down the inside walls where it was collected and then stored (Sharan, 2006).

Research suggests that fog collectors work best in locations with frequent fog periods, such as coastal areas where water can be harvested as fog moves inland driven by the wind by using the data (hourly dry and wet temperature, relative humidity, wind direction and velocity and the dew point temperature), various parameters such as the atmosphere water vapor pressure, saturated vapor pressure and the absolute humidity of the atmosphere can be estimated. However, the technology could also potentially supply water in mountainous areas if the water is present in stratocumulus clouds (Davtalab and Salamat, 2012), who prove in an investigations carried out in two regions in Iran, it was clear that the cited regions had the potential to harvest fog and moisture from the humid atmosphere for 160 - 360 days. The annual mean water harvested through this technique varies between 6.7 lit/m^2/day at Abadan station to 156.3 lit/m^2/day at Chabahar station. Fig. 8.10 shows an instrument for harvesting fogs and dew.

Fig. 8.10: Fog and Dew Harvesting

Watershed Management

A watershed is a basin-like landform (Fig. 8.11). A watershed is simply the geographic area through which water flows across the land and drains into a common body of water, whether a stream, river, lake, or ocean. Much of the water comes from rainfall and the storm water runoff. The quality and quantity of storm water is affected by all the alterations to the land-agriculture, roadways, urban development and the activities of people within a watershed. Watersheds are usually separated from other watersheds by naturally elevated areas. A watershed carries water "shed" from the land after rain falls and snow melts, drop by drop, water is channeled into soils, ground waters, creeks, and streams, making its way to larger rivers. Watershed management (IWM) is the process of managing human activities and natural resources on a watershed basis. This approach allows us to protect important water resources, while at the same time addressing critical issues such as the current and future impacts of rapid growth and climate change (Yeshey and Bhujel, 2006).

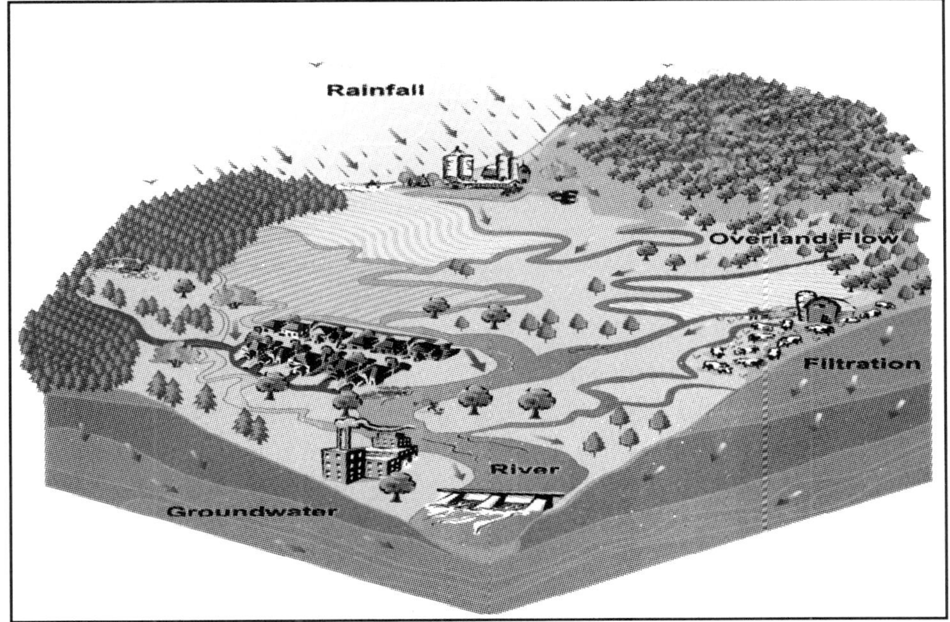

Fig. 8.11: Watershed

Breeding for High Water-use Efficiency Crops

There is a pressing need to improve the water-use efficiency of rain-fed and irrigated crop production. Breeding crop varieties with higher water-use efficiency is seen as providing part of the solution. Three key processes can be exploited in breeding for high water-use efficiency: (i) moving more of the available water through the crop rather than it being wasted as evaporation from the soil surface or drainage beyond the root zone or being left behind in the root zone at harvest; (ii) acquiring more carbon (biomass) in exchange for the water transpired by the crop, i.e. improving crop transpiration efficiency; (iii) partitioning more of the achieved biomass into the harvested product (Condon *et al.*, 2004).

Sustainable Use of Saline Water for Irrigation

Worldwide, there is insufficient fresh water to develop all potential arable land. So, the use of saline water in agriculture is a subject of vital importance especially for arid and semi-arid zones to meet the increasing food demand (ICBA, 2010). Growing agricultural crops with direct seawater irrigation has progressed within the past few years from the conceptual to the experimental phase. This has been accomplished by selecting halophytes within inherently high salinity tolerance for use as crop plants rather than by increasing the ability of traditional crop plants to tolerate seawater. Three approaches are being used by researchers in various parts of the world to develop salt tolerant crops.

In the first approach, searches have been initiated with traditional crops for salt tolerant cultivars, second approach that has been proved successfully, is the crossing of commercial species low in salt tolerance with wild salt tolerance relatives and the third approach has been to begin with wild species that have evolved high salt tolerance in their native habitats (ICBA, 2010). The fact remains that no conventional agricultural crops are yet grown with undiluted seawater, even on sand dunes (Nelson *et al.*, 2009). The seawater can be used to supplement agricultural water supplies, but only under very special conditions. Seawater irrigation would be feasible in coarse textured soils at different dilution levels, depending on the variations extent in salt tolerance of plants (ICBA, 2010).

Sustainable Use of Groundwater

The sustainability of intensive groundwater development for irrigated agriculture from the very extensive quaternary aquifer system constitutes one of the world's major water resource management issues. Unlike other natural resources or raw materials, ground water is present throughout the world. Possibilities for its abstraction vary greatly from place to place, owing to rainfall conditions and the distribution of aquifers (rocks, sand layers and so on, in whose pore spaces the groundwater sits). Generally, groundwater is renewed only during a part of each year, but can be abstracted year-round (Davis, *et al.*, 2008). Groundwater constitutes the underground part of the water cycle (Fig. 8.12). Therefore, it is closely related to atmospheric or climatic processes, to the surface water regimes of rivers and lakes, and with the springs and wetlands where groundwater naturally discharges onto the surface of the ground. All these resources are complementary, but they can be extremely varied - extending from arid areas with virtually no water to humid tropical zones with abundant surface water and rainfall (Kemper, 2004).

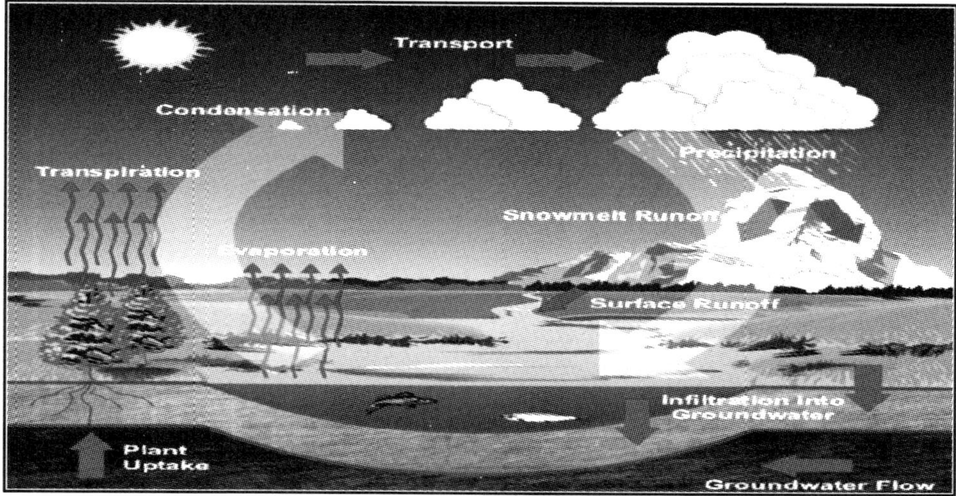

Fig. 8.12: Water Cycle

Eco-friendly System for Desalination of Seawater

The world's water consumption rate is doubling every 20 years, outpacing by two times the rate of population growth. It is projected that by the year 2025 water demand will exceed supply by 56%. The distilling of sea water is an old dream because salt-free water is in danger of running out. The seas have endless quantities of water. Water becomes salt-free by distilling it, but it requires a lot of energy. With the help of the renewable source of clean energy (e.g. solar energy) (Fig. 8.13). Desalination has become possible recently, but still desalination is expensive, at least in the sense that it requires large investments (Kalogirou, 2005).

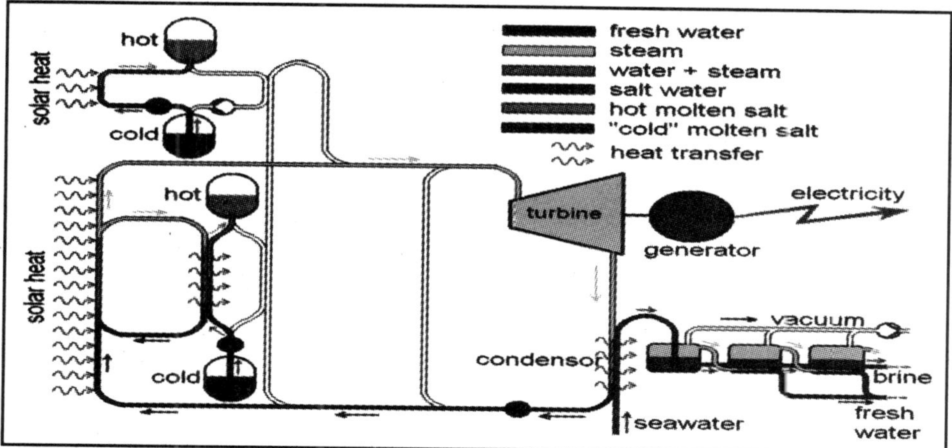

Fig. 8.13: Seawater Desalination

Water Pricing Policy

The new water pricing strategy, addresses the challenges presented by the existing and growing imbalances between the availability, supply and demand for water in the world. The policy introduces demand-side measures to manage our water resources, by encouraging all water sectors to use water more efficiently, provides a more sustainable long-term solution to the problem of water scarcity, because it takes into account the value of water in relation to its cost of provision, thereby treating it more like a commodity (Yang *et al.*, 2003).

SUSTAINABLE FARMING SYSTEMS

Farming systems are more complex than just one crop or livestock species, much of the ecological and productive resilience to climate change comes from managing a diversity of integrated production systems combining crops, mixed farming technology contributes to adaptation to climatic change because the diversification of crops and livestock allows farmers to have a greater number of options to face the uncertain weather conditions associated with the increased climate variability. Mixed farming can also give a more stable production because if one crop or variety fails, another may compensate (Bradshaw, 2005).

Agro-forestry

Agro-forestry is an integrated approach to the production of trees and of non-tree crops or animals on the same piece of land (Burnette, 2004). The crops can be grown together at the same time, in rotation or in separate plots, when products from one are used to benefit the other. Agro-forestry systems take advantage of trees for many uses, to hold the soil, to increase fertility through nitrogen fixation or through bringing minerals from deep in the soil and depositing them by leaf-fall and to provide shade, construction materials, foods and fuel. In agro-forestry systems, every part of the land is considered suitable for the cultivation of plants (Lin *et al.*, 2008).

Smart Biofuel Crops

Biofuel as bio-ethanol and bio diesel have the potential to assume an important portfolio in future energy platter. Food security concerns and risks to environment and biodiversity are parameters that necessarily need to be accessed while analyzing sustainability linkage of agriculture and biofuel. Also, conversion of wasteland to farmland with some crop options can be viewed as positive impacts. Recently we use the term (Smart Bioenergy Crops), SBC are crops that ensure food security, contribute to energy security, provide environmental sustainability, tolerate the impacts of climate change on shortage of water and high temperatures, and increase livelihood options (Koyro *et al.*, 2011). By producing non-food ligno-cellulosic biomass which, may be converted into ethanol without compromising human food production. Halophytes which produce plenty of biomass using saline resources (water and soil) may be an important alternative. *Leptochloa fusca, Kochia scoparia, sporobolus virginicus* and *Panicum turgidum* have potential as bio-ethanol crops. These perennial grasses are halophytic plants with high growth rates to produce ligno-cellulosic biomass of good quality (37% cellulose, 38% hemi-cellulose) for ethanol production (Abideen *et al.*, 2011). Another approach is using the vast desert in the world and grows some drought and heat tolerant plants (e.g) *Jatropha curcas* to get biodesel, reduce GHG emission, energy security, maintain soil fertility and reduce soil erosion (Gonsalves, 2006).

Precision Agriculture

Uses information and communication technologies (ICT) to cover the three aspects of production namely for data collection of information input through options as Global Positioning System (GPS) satellite data, grid soil sampling, yield monitoring, remote sensing, etc; for data analysis or processing through Geographic Information System (GIS) and decision technologies as process models, artificial intelligence systems, and expert systems; and for application of information by farmers. Adjustments in volume and timing of fertilizer and pesticide inputs and limited input leakage to environment are expected in precision agriculture (FAO, 2010). Precision farming has the potential to improve net farm income by: (1) identifying places in a field where additional nutrient use will increase yield, and thus farm income, by more than the added cost; and (2) identifying places where reduced input use will reduce costs while maintaining yield (IPCC, 2007). Precision farming also has the potential to reduce off-site transport of agricultural chemicals with surface runoff, subsurface drainage, and leaching (Rattan, 2011).

Climate-smart Agriculture

There are a number of variants on the concept of Climate Smart Agriculture. Climate smart agriculture (CSA) seek to sustainably, increase productivity, adapt to climate change, build resilience to shocks and variability, reduce and remove GHGs (mitigation) and enhance the achievement of national food security and development goals. The priority of CSA is to strengthen livelihoods and food security through the improved management and use of natural resources and adopting appropriate methods and technologies for the production, processing and marketing of agricultural goods (Branca and McCarthy, 2011).

Table 8.2: Climate-smart Agriculture Practices Useful in Smallholder Agricultural Production (FAO, 2010)

Crop Management	Soil and Water Management	Agroforestry
• Intercropping with legumes	• Conservation agriculture (e.g. minimum tillage)	• Boundary trees and hedgerows
• Crop rotations	• Contour planting	• Nitrogen-fixing treeson farms
• New crop varieties (e.g. droughtresistant)	• Terraces and bunds	• Multipurpose trees
• Improved storage and processing techniques	• Planting pits	• Improved fallow with fertilizer shrubs
• Greater crop diversity	• Water storage (e.g.water pans)	
	• Alternate wetting an drying (rice)	
	• Dams, pits, ridges	
	• Improved irrigation (e.g. drip)	

To maximize the benefits and minimize the tradeoffs, CSA takes into consideration the social, economic, and environmental context where it will be applied, assesses the resource and energy implications and adopts an integrated land based approach using principles for ecosystem management and sustainable land and water use (FAO, 2010). Climate-smart agriculture includes proven techniques such as mulching, intercropping, integrated pest and disease management, conservation agriculture, crop rotation, agroforestry, carbon sequestration, integrated crop-livestock management, aquaculture, improved water management at different scales, and better weather forecasting for farmers, but also innovative practices, such as early warning systems and risk management and link knowledge from diverse scientific areas (agriculture, climate change, water, energy, environment) with a view of achieving multiple benefits (Table 8.2).

REFERENCES

Abideen, Z., Raziuddin, A. and M. Ajmal Khan (2011): Halophytes: Potential Source of Ligno-cellulosic Biomass for Ethanol Production. Biomass and Bioenergy, (35): 1818-1822.

Afzal, A. and B. Asghari (2008): Rhizobium and Phosphate Solubilizing Bacteria Improve the Yield and Phosphorus Uptake in Wheat. Int. J. Agri. Biol., 10 (1): 85-88.

Ahmed, M.A., Amal, G. Ahmed, Magda, H. Mohamed and M.M. Tawfik (2011): Integrated Effect of Organic and Biofertilizers on Wheat Productivity in New Reclaimed Sandy Soil. Res. J. Agric. & Biol. Sci., 7(1): 105-114.

AIACC (2006): Assessment of Impacts, Adaptation, and Vulnerability to Climate Change in North Africa: Food Production and Water Resources. Published by the International START Secretariat 2000, Florida Avenue, NW Washington, DC 20009 USA www.start.org.

Bianchi, F.J., J.A. Booij, C.J. Tscharntke (2006): Sustainable Pest Regulation in Agricultural Landscapes: A Review on Landscape Composition, Biodiversity and Natural Pest Control. Proc. Royal Soc., 273(B): 1715-1727.

Bingol, N.T., M.A. Karsli, I.H. Yilmaz and D. Bolat (2007): The Effects of Planting Time and Combination on the Nutrient Composition and Digestible Dry Matter Yield of Four Mixtures of Vetch Varieties Intercropped with Barley. J. Veter. Anim. Sci., 31: 297-302.

Bradshaw, B., Dolan, H. and Smit, B. (2005): Farm-Level Adaptation to Climatic Variability and Change: Crop Diversification in the Canadian Prairies. Climatic Change, 67: 119–141.

Branca, G., and N. McCarthy (2011): Climate-smart Agriculture: A Synthesis of Empirical Evidence of Food Security and Mitigation Benefits from Improved Cropland Management. Working paper. Rome, FAO.

Brookes, G. and Barfoot, P. (2009): Global Impact of Biotech Crops: Income and Production Effects, 1996-2007. J. AgBio Forum, 12(2): 184-208.

Burnette, R.R. (2004): Useful Plants Commonly Integrated into Agroforest Sites in Northern Thailand. UHDP, Mae Ai, Thailand.

Condon, A.G., R.A. Richards, G.J. Rebetzke and G.D. Farquhar, (2004): Breeding for High Water-use Efficiency. J. Exp. Bot., 55 (407): 2447-2460.

Contreras-Gova, F.E., K.A. Albrecht and R.E. Muck (2006): Spring Yield and Silage Characteristics of Kura Clover, Winter Wheat and Mixtures. Agron. J., 98: 781-787.

Davis, G.B., Patterson, B.M. and Johnston, C.D. (2008): Deep Sparing of Groundwater for the Aerobic Bioremediation of Lightly Chlorinated Hydrocarbons', in Trefry, MG, (ed.), *Groundwater Quality: Securing Groundwater Quality in Urban and Industrial Environments. Proceedings of the GQ'07 Conference held in Freemantle, Western Australia, December 2007,* IAHS Publ., 324: 266-271.

Davtalab, R. and A. Salamat (2012): Water Harvesting from Fog and Air Humidity in the Warm and Coastal Regions in the South of Iran. ICID 21st International Congress on Irrigation and Drainage, 15-23 October 2011, Tehran, Iran.

Dogan, R., Goksoy, T.A., Yagdi, K. and Turan, M. Z. (2008): Comparison of the Effects of Different Crop Rotation Systems on Winter Wheat and Sunflower Under Rain-fed Conditions. African Journal of Biotechnology, 7 (22): 4076-4082.

FAO, (2010): Climate-Smart' Agriculture – Policies, Practices and Financing for Food Security, Adaptation and Mitigation. Food and Agriculture Organization of the United Nations, Rome.

Frederick, M., James, R. and P.J. Bauer (1996): Winter Wheat Responses to Surface and Deep Tillage on the Southeastern Coastal Plain. Agron. J., 88 : 829-833.

Ghanbari, B.A. and H.C. Lee (2003): Intercropped Wheat and Bean as whole Crop Forage: Effect of Harvest Time on Forage Yield and Quality. Grass and Forage Science, 58(1): 28-36.

Gonsalves, J.B. (2006). An Assessment of the Biofuels Industry in India.2nd Ed. New Delhi.

Hatfield, J.L. (2010): Climate Impacts on Agriculture in the United States: The Value of Past Observations. Chapter 10. In D. Hillel and C. Rosenzwieg (eds.) Handbook of Climate Change and Agroecosystems: Impact, Adaptation and Mitigation. Imperial College Press, London UK.

Hauggaard, H., P. Ambus and E.S. Jensen (2001): Inter-specific Competition, N Use and Interference with Weeds in Pea-barley Intercropping. Field Crops Research, 70: 101-109.

Hu, Q, Albert, W., Song, F.P. and Stephen, B. (2005): Earlier Winter Wheat Heading Dates and Warmer Spring in the U.S. Great Plains. Agricultural and Forest Meteorology, 135: 284-290.

Ibrahim, O.M., Tawfik, M.M., Elham A. Badr and Magda, H. Mohamed (2011): Biological Reclamation of Salt Affected Soils Through Revegetation of *Kochia indica*. Bull. NRC., 36 (2): 131-144.

ICBA (2010). Annual Report 2010. International Centre for Biosaline Agriculture, Dubai, United Arab Emirates, 2010.

IPCC, (2007): Climate Change: The Physical Science Basis, Contribution from Working Group I to the Fourth Assessment Report, Policy Maker Summary. Intergovernmental Panel on Climate Change. Cambridge University Press, Cambridge, UK.

Javanmard, A., A. Dabbagh, A. Nasab, A. Javanshir, M. Moghadam and H. Janmohammadi (2009): Forage Yield and Quality in Intercropping of Maize with Different Legumes as Double Cropped. Journal of Food, Agriculture and Environment, 7(1): 163-166.

Johnsona, J.M., Franzlueb, A.J., Weyersa, S.L. and Reicoskya, D.C. (2007): Agricultural Opportunities to Mitigate Greenhouse Gas Emissions. Environ. Poll., 150(1): 107-124.

Juergens, L.A., D.L. Young, W.F. Schillinger, and H.R. Hinman (2004): Economics of Alternative No-till Spring Crop Rotations in Washington's Wheat-fallow Region. Agron. J., 96: 154-158.

Kaci, Y., A. Heyraud, B. Mohamed and T. Heulin (2005): Isolation and Identification of an EPS-producing Rhizobium Strain from Arid Soil (Algeria): Characterization of its EPS and the Effect of Inoculation on Wheat Rhizosphere Soil Structure. Research in Microbiology, 156(4): 522-531.

Kalogirou, S.A. (2005): Seawater Desalination Using Renewable Energy Sources. Progress in Energy and Combustion Science, 31: 242-281.

Karmakar, S., Lague, C., Agnew, J. and Landry, H. (2007): Integrated Decision Support System (DSS) for Manure Management. A Review and Perspective Computers and Electronics in Agriculture, 57: 190-201.

Kemper, K. (2004), Groundwater – from Development to Management, Hydrogeology Journal, 12: 3-5.

Kirkegaard, J., Christen, N.O., Krupinski, J. and Layzell, D. (2008): Break Crop Benefits in Temperate Wheat Production. Field Crops Research, 107, 185-195.

Koch, D.W. and F.A. Gray. (1997): Nematode-resistant Oil Radish for *Heterodera schachtii* Control. I. Sugarbeet-malting Barley Rotations. J. Sugar Beet Res., 34: 31-43.

Koyro, H.W., M.A. Khan and H. Lieth (2011): Halophytic Crops: A Resource for the Future to Reduce the Water Crisis?, Emir. J. Food Agric., 23 (1): 001-016.

Kurukulasuriya, P and Mendelsohn, R. (2006): Crop Selection: Adapting to Climate Change in Africa. CEEPA Discussion Paper No. 26, Centre for Environmental Economics and Policy in Africa, University of Pretoria.

Leisa (2007): Ecological Pest Management, LEISA Magazine, Volume 23, Issue 4.

Li, L., Li, S.M., Sun, J.H., Zhou, L.L., Bao, X.G., Zhang, H.G. and Zhang, F.S. (2007): Diversity Enhances Agricultural Productivity via rhizosphere Phosphorus Facilitation on Phosphorus-deficient Soils. Proceedings of the National Academy of Sciences, USA 104: 11192-11196.

Lin, B.B., Perfecto, I., Vander, S. (2008): Synergies Between Agricultural Intensification and Climate Change could Create Surprising Vulnerabilities from Crops. Bio Sci., 58(9): 847-854.

Mittler, R. and Blumwald, E. (2010): Genetic Engineering for Modern Agriculture: Challenges and Perspectives. Annual Review of Plant Biology, 61: 443-462.

Munns, R., Tester, M. (2008): Mechanisms of Salinity Tolerance. Ann. Rev. Plant Biol., 59: 65-81.

Muselli, M., D. Beysens, M. Mileta and I. Milimouk (2009): Dew and Rain Water Collection in the Dalmatian Coast, Croatia, Atmospheric Research, 92: 455-463.

Mtui, G.Y. (2009): Recent Advances in Pretreatment of Lignocellulosic Wastes and Production of Value Added Products. Afric. J. Biotech., 8(8): 1398-1415.

Nelson, G.C. (2009): Agriculture and Climate Change: An Agenda for Negotiation in Copenhagen. 2020 Focus No. 16. May 2009. http://www.ifpri. Org/2020/focus/focus 16.asp.

Paszkowski, J. and Grossniklaus, U. (2011): Selected Aspects of Transgenerational Epigenetic Inheritance and Resetting in Plants. Current Opinion in Biology, 14: 195-203.

Powlson, D.S., Whitmore, A.P., Goulding, K.W. (2011): Soil Carbon Sequestration to Mitigate Climate Change: A Critical Re-examination to Identify the True and False. Eur. J. Soil Sci., 62: 42-55.

Qadir, M., Noble, A.D., Schubert, S., Thomas, R.J., Arslan, A. (2006): Sodicity-induced Land Degradation and its Sustainable Management: Problems and Prospects. Land Degradation and Development, 17: 661-676.

Rattan, L. (2011): Soil and Water Management Options for Adaptation to Climate Change. The Ohio State University Columbus, Ohio.

Ravindran, K.C., Venkatesan, K., Balakrishnan, V., Chellappan, K.P. and Balasubramanian, T. (2007): Restoration of Saline Land by Halophytes for Indian Soils. Soil biology and biochemistry, 39 (10): 2661-2664.

Rozema, J., Flowers, T.J. (2008): Crops for a Salinized World. Science., 322: 1478.

Ruane, J. Sonnino, F., Steduro, R., Deane, C. (2008): Coping with Water Scarcity in Developing Countries: What Role for Agricultural Biotechnologies? Land and Water Discussion Paper No. 7. Food and Agricultural Organization (FAO). p. 33.

Samman, S., Chow, J.W., Foster, M.J., Ahmad, Z.I., Phuyal, J.L. and Petocz, P. (2008): Fatty Acid Composition of Edible Oils Derived from Certified Organic and Conventional Agricultural Methods. Food Chemistry, 109: 670-674.

Sharan, G. (2006): Dew Harvest, Center for Environment Education, pp. 84-92.

Stainforth, D.A., Downing, T.E., Washington, R., Lopez, A. and New, M. (2007): Issues in the Interpretation of Climate Model Ensembles to Inform Decisions. Philosophical Transactions of the Royal Society, 365: 2163-2177.

Stringer, L.C., Dyer, J.C., Reed, M.S., Dougill, A.J., Twyman, C. and Mkwambisi, D. (2009): Adaptation to Climate Change, Drought and Desertification: Local Insights to Enhance Policy in Southern Africa. Environ. Sci. Policy, 12: 748-765.

Tawfik, M.M., E.M. Abd El Lateef, Amany, A Bahr and M. Hozyn (2011): Prospect of Biofertilizer Inoculation for Increasing Saline Irrigation Efficiency. Res. J. Agric. and Biol. Sci., 7(2): 182-189.

Treasury, H.M. (2009): Green Biotechnology and Climate Change. Euro Bio., p.12. Available online at http://www.docstoc.com/docs/15021072/Green-Biotechnology-and-Climate-Change.

Vallad, G.E. and Goodman, R.M. (2004): System Acquired Resistance and Induced Systemic Resistance in Conventional Agriculture. Crop Sci., 44: 1920-1934.

Varshney, R.K., Bansal, K.C., Aggarwal, P.K., Datta, S.K. and Craufurd, P.Q. (2011): Agricultural Biotechnology for Crop Improvement in a Variable Climate: Hope or Hype?. Trends in Plant Science, 16: 363-371.

Wichelns, D.and Oster, J.D. (2006): Sustainable Irrigation is Necessary and Achievable, but Direct Costs and Environmental Impacts can be Substantial. Agricultural Water Management 86: 114-127.

Yang, H., X. Zhang and A.J. Zehnder (2003): Water Scarcity, Pricing Mechanism and Institutional Reform in Northern China Irrigated Agriculture. Agricultural Water Management, 61: 143-161.

Yeshey, M. and Bhujel, A.K. (2006): Irrigation Water Sharing Equity and Traditional Systems in Lingmutey Chhu Watershed. A Series of Case Studies on Community-Based Forest and Natural Resource Management in Bhutan, 2006. MoA. Bhutan.

Yildirim, E. and I. Guvence (2005): Intercropping Based on Cauliflower: More Productivity, Profitable and Highly Sustainable. European Journal of Agronomy, 22: 11-18.

Zhao, W.F., Z. Q. Gao, M. Sun, L. Deng and Q. Li (2012): Effect of Fertilization and Mulching in Fallow Period on Nitrogen Accumulation of Dryland Wheat. Afric. J. Agric. Res., 7(12): 1849-1854.

Index

* * * * * *